ITALO CALVINO

CROSSCURRENTS

CONSTANCE MARKEY

University Press of Florida

GAINESVILLE·TALLAHASSEE·TAMPA·BOCA RATON·PENSACOLA·ORLANDO·MIAMI·JACKSONVILLE

Italo Calvino

A JOURNEY TOWARD POSTMODERNISM

04 03 02 01 00 99   6 5 4 3 2 1

LIBRARY OF CONGRESS CATALOGING-IN-PUBLICATION DATA
Markey, Constance.
Italo Calvino: a journey toward postmodernism / Constance Markey.
p.   cm. – (Crosscurrents)
Includes bibliographical references and index.
ISBN 0-8130-1722-x (alk. paper)
1. Calvino, Italo—Criticism and interpretation. 2. Postmodernism
(Literature)—Italy. I. Title. II. Series: Crosscurrents (Gainesville, Fla.)
PQ4809.A45Z786   1999
853'.914—dc21   99-42653

For copyrights and permissions regarding excerpted material, see page 153.

The University Press of Florida is the scholarly publishing agency for the
State University System of Florida, comprising Florida A & M University,
Florida Atlantic University, Florida International University, Florida State
University, University of Central Florida, University of Florida, University
of North Florida, University of South Florida, and University of West
Florida.

University Press of Florida
15 Northwest 15th Street
Gainesville, FL 32611-2079
http://www.upf.com

To my mother, Anna Schuster, and the fairy tales of my childhood.

CROSSCURRENTS

Comparative Studies in European Literature and Philosophy
Edited by S. E. Gontarski

Roland Barthes on Photography, by Nancy Shawcross (1996)

Carlos Emilio Gadda and the Modern Macaronic, by Albert Sbragia (1996)

The French New Autobiographies: Sarraute, Duras, Robbe-Grillet, by Raylene
L. Ramsay (1996)

The Ghosts of Modernity, by Jean-Michel Rabaté (1996)

Improvisations on Butor: Transformation of Writing, by Michel Butor; edited,
annotated, and with an introduction by Lois Oppenheim; translated by Elinor
S. Miller (1996)

Lévinas, Blanchot, Jabès: Figures of Estrangement, by Gary D. Mole (1997)

Samuel Beckett's Hidden Drives: Structural Uses of Depth Psychology, by
J. D. O'Hara (1997)

Pirandello and His Muse: The Plays for Marta Abba, by Daniela Bini (1998)

An Introduction to Fernando Pessoa, by Darlene J. Sadlier (1998)

The Writing of War: French and German Novels and World War II, by William
Cloonan (1999)

Italo Calvino: A Journey toward Postmodernism, by Constance Markey (1999)

CONTENTS

FOREWORD

The arc of Italo Calvino's career, from the neorealist stories of a politically committed writer in post–World War II Italy, through a period of
fantasy writing, into the French Oulipo group (the *Ouvoir de littérature
potentielle* headed by Raymond Queneau, whose work Calvino had
translated into Italian), is one of the fundamental trajectories of modernist and postmodernist literature. Constance Markey takes us on a "journey toward postmodernism" as she traces the light and dark sides of
Calvino's work and rereads much of it with a freshness that allows her to
see, for example, that Calvino's "realism" of the 1950s "actually had
little more to do with conventional realism than did the author's fantasies." Instead, even those early literary efforts were "evolutionary tales,
stories that mark just one more step in what can now be easily perceived
as the general dynamic of all of Calvino's work: its restless movement

from the tangible to the abstract, . . . from the mundane to the mythic." Realist, fabulist, postmodernist, Calvino's art is always "an authentic portrait of late twentieth-century life." Moreover, Markey's critique of the postwar European sensibility in *Italo Calvino: A Journey toward Postmodernism*, of the existential condition of "living between Buchenwald and the H bomb," makes it a companion piece to another volume in the *Crosscurrents* series, William Cloonan's *The Writing of War: French and German Novels and World War II*, as well as to the other studies of *Crosscurrents* in Italian modernism: Albert Sbragia's analysis of Carlo Emilio Gadda, *Carlos Emilio Gadda and the Modern Macaronic*, and Daniela Bini's study of Pirandello's theater for Marta Abba, *Pirandello and His Muse*.

Such insights as Markey offers, then, constitute an exemplary addition to the *Crosscurrents* series, which is designed to foreground comparative studies in European art and thought, particularly the intersections of literature and philosophy, aesthetics and culture. Without abandoning traditional comparative methodology, the series is also receptive to the latest currents in critical, comparative, and performative theory, especially that generated by the renewed intellectual energy in post-Marxist Europe. It will, as well, take full cognizance of the cultural and political realignments of what, for the better part of the twentieth century, have been two separated and isolated Europes. While Western Europe moves aggressively toward unification into the European Community, with the breakup of the twentieth century's last major, overtly colonial empire, the Soviet Union, Eastern Europe continues to divide into nationalistic and religious enclaves with the collapse of Communist hegemony. The intellectual, cultural, and literary significance of such profound restructuring, how history will finally be rewritten, is difficult to anticipate. Having had a fertile period of modernism snuffed out in an ideological coup not long after the 1917 revolution, the nations of the former Soviet Union have, for instance, been denied (or spared) the age of Freud and Jung, most modernist experiments, and postmodern fragmentation. While Western Europe continues reaching beyond modernism, Eastern Europe may be struggling to reclaim it. Whether a new art can emerge in the absence—or from the absence—of such forces as shaped modernism is one of the intriguing questions of post–Cold War aesthetics, philosophy, and critical theory.

Italo Calvino: A Journey toward Postmodernism, then, forms precisely the sort of comparative social and literary study that the *Crosscurrents* series was designed to foster. The series henceforth will continue to critique the developing, often conflicting currents of European thought through the prism of literature, philosophy, and critical theory.

S. E. Gontarski
Series Editor

PREFACE

This volume surveys the evolution of Italo Calvino's writing from the author's beginning in neorealism, or anti-Fascist fiction, to his later development as a postmodern author. It differs from other studies in several ways. First, it embraces the novice reader: teachers, students, or a general audience who seek an introduction to the writer's life and career. Next, it favors the author's work in translation, serving as a resource for the many who are now reading Calvino in English. Finally, this study emphasizes the author's international background, devoting particular attention to literary influences important to him, both past and present, both within Europe and beyond Europe.

I am grateful to all who helped me with this book. First, I would like to acknowledge DePaul University for the Competitive Research Grant which enabled me to begin the project. Next, I extend my profound gratitude to my colleagues Wiley Feinstein and Sante Matteo for their insightful reading of the manuscript. Thanks also to my student reader, Lia Markey, for her persistent questions, and to my husband, William Markey, for his steadfast patience and encouragement. Finally, and most important, I extend a posthumous *grazie* to Italo Calvino who generously listened to my thoughts on his work, first while I was a graduate student and later after I became a teacher.

CHRONOLOGY

THE LIFE OF ITALO CALVINO

1923 Born 15 October at Santiago de las Vegas near Havana, Cuba, where his parents (Mario, an agronomist, and Evelina Mameli, a botanist) work at an experimental agricultural post.

1925 His family moves home to San Remo, Italy, where the elder Calvino directs a nearby experimental floricultural station.

1927 A brother, Floriano, is born, who will later become a noted professor of geology at the University of Genoa.

1941 He briefly attends the University of Turin enrolled in the school of agronomy (agriculture).

1943 Transfers to the University of Florence, where his agricultural studies are interrupted when he is called to the draft by Mussolini's Salò government. Goes into hiding for some months.

1944 With his brother joins the Garibaldi division of the northern Italian partisans and sees months of active duty against Nazi occupation forces.

1945 Returns to his university studies at Turin, this time enrolling in the Faculty of Letters. An active member of the Communist Party, he writes politically oriented short stories and articles for Party magazines and newspapers.

1946 Takes an entry-level job at the Einaudi Publishing House in Turin. Begins a novel about the Italian Resistance.

1947 Takes his degree in letters with a thesis on Joseph Conrad. Promoted to Publicity at Einaudi. Publishes first novel, *Il sentiero dei nidi di ragno* [*The Path to the Nest of Spiders*] (now called *The Path to the Spiders' Nests*, 1998), which wins the Riccione Prize.

1949 Publishes *Ultimo viene il corvo* [The Crow Comes Last], a first collection of short stories.

1950 Promoted to an editorial position at Einaudi.

1951 Visits Russia for about two months. Father dies while he is away. Publishes *Il visconte dimezzato* [*The Cloven Viscount*].

1952 Publishes a novella, *La formica argentina* [*The Argentine Ant*].

1954 Publishes a second collection of short stories, *L'entrata in guerra* [Entering the War].

1955–56 Assumes a directorship at Einaudi (1955). Publishes *Fiabe italiane* [*Italian Folktales. Selected and Retold by Italo Calvino*]. Writes libretto for a one-act opera, *La panchina* [The Bench], with musical score by Sergio Liberovici.

1957 Quits the Communist Party. Publishes *Il barone rampante* [*The Baron in the Trees*] as well as the novella *La speculazione edilizia* [*A Plunge into Real Estate*].

1957–58 Publishes an earlier-written novel, *I giovani del Po* [Young People of the Po] in the magazine *Officina*.

1958 Publishes a novella, *La nuvola di smog* [*Smog*], and *I racconti* [Short Stories], a one-volume collection of his short stories, novellas, and early Marcovaldo tales.

1959 Becomes codirector (with friend and colleague Elio Vittorini) of the literary journal *Il menabò della letteratura*, a position he will keep until 1967. Collaborates with composer Luciano Berio on *Allez-Hop*, a musical spectacle performed at Venice. Leaves to spend six months in America under the sponsorship of a Ford Foundation Grant. Publishes *Il cavaliere inesistente* [*The Nonexistent Knight*]. *I racconti* wins the Bagutta Prize.

1960 Returns from New York. Publishes *I nostri antenati* [*Our Ancestors*], which unites in one volume his three fantasy novels: *Il visconte dimezzato*, *Il barone rampante*, and *Il cavaliere inesistente*.

1961–62 Named editorial consultant at Einaudi in 1961. Begins to write for the Milanese newspaper *Il Giorno*. In Paris meets his future wife, Esther Judith Singer, an Argentinian translator who works for UNESCO and the International Atomic Energy Agency.

1963 Publishes a novella, *La giornata d'uno scrutatore* [*The Watcher*], and *Marcovaldo, ovvero, Le stagioni in città* [*Marcovaldo, or, The seasons in the city*].

1964 Marries Esther Judith Singer in Havana. The couple moves to Rome. Republishes *Il sentiero dei nidi di ragno* [*The Path to the Nest of Spiders*] with the addition of an important preface by the author.

1965 An only child, daughter Giovanna, is born. Publishes *Le cosmicomiche* [*Cosmicomics*].

1967 Moves to Paris. Publishes *Ti con zero* [*t zero*] and *I fiori blu*, an Italian translation of Raymond Queneau's *Les fleurs bleues* [The Blue Flowers].

1968 Frequents Parisian literary circles including Tel Quel and Oulipo [*Ouvroir de littérature potentielle*], a literary circle headed by Queneau. Publishes *La memoria del mondo e altre storie cosmicomiche* [Memory of the World and Other Cosmicomic Stories], a newer edition of *Le cosmicomiche*.

1969 Publishes a group of stories, *Il castello dei destini incrociati* [*The Castle of Crossed Destinies*], which appears in the elegantly illustrated edition *Tarocchi, Il mazzo visconteo di Bergamo e New York* [*Tarots: The Visconti Pack in Bergamo and New York*].

1970 Publishes *Gli amori difficili*, which appears as "Stories of Love and Loneliness" in *Difficult Loves*. Also publishes *Orlando furioso di Ludovico Ariosto raccontato da Italo Calvino con una scelta del poema* [*Orlando Furioso* by Ludovico Ariosto, as recounted by Italo Calvino with a selection from the poem].

1971 Directs the publication of *Centopagine* [One Hundred Pages], a selection of works by classical European authors and Calvino favorites, including Stevenson, Conrad, Stendhal, and others.

1972 Wins the Feltrinelli Prize for Literature in Italy. Publishes *Le città invisibili* [*Invisible Cities*].

1973 Expands and publishes separately *Il castello dei destini incrociati* [*The Castle of Crossed Destinies*] with eight new stories.

1974 Begins writing for the Italian daily *Il Corriere della sera* (1974–79), where the first *Palomar* stories appear the following year.

1976 Visits the United States and participates in several university conferences. Also travels to Mexico and Japan. Awarded the Staatpreis at Vienna.

1978 Mother dies.

1979 Begins his collaboration with the Roman newspaper *La Repubblica*. Publishes *Se una notte d'inverno un viaggiatore*, [*If on a winter's night a traveler*].

1980 Moves back to Italy with his family and settles in Rome. Publishes *Una pietra sopra. Discorsi di letteratura e società* [*The Uses of Literature*].

1981 Edits a collection of Queneau's works. Awarded the Italian Legion d'onore.

1982 Writes the libretto for two musical works, again with Berio: *La vera storia* [The Real Story] and *Duo*, later to be the inspiration for Berio's opera *Un re in ascolto* [A King Listens]. *La vera storia* is produced at La Scala in Milan.

1983 Speaks on "*Science et métaphore chez Galilée* (Science and Metaphor in Galileo) at the Greimas seminar in Paris. Lectures at New York University. Publishes *Palomar* [*Mr. Palomar*].

1984 Travels to Argentina and later to Seville, where he is invited to attend a conference on fantasy literature with Jorge Luis Borges. Leaves Einaudi Publishing House. The opera *Un re in ascolto* [A King Listens] is performed at Salzburg. Publishes *Collezione di sabbia* [Collection of Sand] and *Cosmicomiche vecchie e nuove* [Old and New Cosmicomics].

1985 Works on the *Lezioni americane. Sei proposte per il prossimo millennio* [*Six Memos for the Next Millennium*, The Charles Eliot Norton Lectures], which he has been invited to deliver at Harvard University in the fall of 1985. Dies suddenly of a cerebral hemorrhage 19 September 1985.

The following works were published posthumously:

Sotto il sole giaguaro [*Under the Jaguar Sun*, 1986].

The Uses of Literature, 1986 (derived from *Una pietra sopra*, 1980).

Lezioni americane. Sei proposte per il prossimo millennio [*Six Memos for the Next Millennium*, The Charles Eliot Norton Lectures, 1985–86, 1988].

Sulla fiaba [On Fables, 1988].

La strada di San Giovanni [*The Road to San Giovanni*, 1990].

Perché leggere i classici [Why Read the Classics, 1991].

Romanzi e racconti [Novels and Short Stories, 1991].

I libri degli altri: Lettere 1947–1981 [Other People's Books: Letters, 1947–1981, 1993].

Prima che tu dica "Pronto" [*Numbers in the Dark and Other Stories*, 1993].

Eremita a Parigi. Pagine autobiografiche [A Hermit in Paris. Autobiographical Pages, 1994].

Saggi, 1945–1985 [Essays, 1945–1985, 1995].

INTRODUCTION

Italo Calvino was an author with an explorer's eye. Inquisitively he stood on the edge of each new written adventure surveying the unlimited horizon of his own imagination. He was also an eager scholar, who, in his enthusiasm to learn, steeped himself in world literature, philosophy, history, biology, mathematics, and even astrophysics. Enterprisingly, he tested these divergent interests in his work: writing something of everything, including science fantasy, slice-of-life, political satire, and perhaps, best of all, whimsically ironic fairy tales. A consummate storyteller, a darkly cynical philosopher, and a postmodern prankster, there was no gamble Calvino would not risk in the name of venturesome fiction. For this courage he personifies, perhaps more than any other Italian writer, the speculative drive of late twentieth-century literature.

With amazing agility, the author scurries from genre to genre, from actuality to fantasy and back again, steadfastly refusing to limit his vista to the narrows of everyday melodrama.[1] For him reality has two sides: the events at surface, which are tangible, and those beneath, fantastical and clearly at odds with the everyday. It is the tug and pull of these elements, the dynamic interplay between the commonplace and the extraordinary, between today and yesterday, that feed his contemporary curiosity. At times, Calvino rebels against history: his postmodern skepticism straining irreverently against a traditional worldview; his Sartrean philosophy cynically undermining orthodox values; his narrative experiments in semiotics and the French "new novel" colliding willfully with conventional storytelling. At other times, however, he lovingly plays with tradition: lightbulbs finding their way amusingly into knightly sagas, and Amazon feminists frolicking in fairy-tale kingdoms. A controversial composite of ancient and modern lore, an eclectic blend of melancholy and humor, shapes the challenge of Calvino's fiction.

In fact, it has been said that penetrating the learned contradiction that is Calvino demands a reader nearly as ambitious as the author himself. Particularly challenging are *The Castle of Crossed Destinies, Invisible Cities, If on a winter's night a traveler,* and *Mr. Palomar,* for these highly innovative works represent years of studied experimentation. Fortunately, there is an easier way to become acquainted with the author and that is to start at the beginning of his career with his wartime stories and novel *The Path to the Spiders' Nests.* There on the "terra firma" of his early works, and with a footing in his personal history, we can follow Calvino as he evolves from the high-minded young idealist of the *neorealismo* into the skeptical postmodern fantasist that he later became. Like his own ingenuous heroes, Palomar and Pin, we find the author all eyes, bearing witness to worlds both here and elsewhere, sifting and interrogating the countenance of the Earth as we know it and of the cosmos as we dream it.

1

---·✦·

THE AUTHOR AND HIS WORKS

EARLY YEARS

Italo Calvino was born in Cuba in 1923 to Italian parents, Evelina
Mameli Calvino, a botanist, and Mario Calvino, an agronomist. By 1925,
however, the couple, who had been living in Cuba for professional reasons, returned to Italy. Hence the young Italo, sentimentally named for
his homeland, would remember nothing of his Cuban experience.[1] The
family settled near San Remo, a horticultural center on the Italian
Riviera. There, Calvino's father directed an experimental floricultural
station and a brother, Floriano, was born in 1927. Given the low-profile
nature of their work, the Calvinos might have anticipated a quiet life,
but the calm was to be short-lived.

The family's critical stance toward Fascism was to have great impact on the young Calvino's early personal and artistic formation. Mussolini had been in power for three years when the family returned and Italy was an established Fascist state. As a socialist, Mario Calvino was clearly out of step with the regime, as was his wife Evelina, an avowed pacifist. That his parents fit awkwardly within the social framework of the times was confirmed later by Calvino, who stated that his "family was rather out of the ordinary be it in San Remo or in Italy then: scientists, lovers of nature, freethinkers. . ." whose lives were entirely devoted to the pursuit of science.[2]

The Calvinos were not religious in a traditional sense. In fact, to avoid submitting their children to the Roman Catholic instruction that was then a customary part of the public school curriculum in Italy, they sent them to a private Waldensian elementary school where compulsory catechism apparently was not an issue.[3] Later, in high school, Calvino's parents saw to it that he was exempted from any religious education whatever. As evidenced in his later fiction, the family's secularism impressed the young Calvino. Because of their unorthodox convictions, the author tells us that he grew up "tolerant toward others' opinions, particularly in the area of religion" (ER 154), and, as his fiction later reveals, scornful of those religious practices that were prejudicial, dogmatic, or hypocritical.

Given their unconventional background, Calvino and his brother, Floriano, lived somewhat apart from their peers. Calvino recalled that, because of his family's independent political and religious views, as a young student he was often perceived as something of a "rare beast," a situation that sometimes compelled him to shut himself off "in a kind of passive, silent resistance before companions and teachers" (ER 154 and 153). Several autobiographical stories from the collection *The Road to San Giovanni* [*La strada di San Giovanni*, 1990] testify to a rather lonely childhood.[4] From "A Cinema-Goer's Autobiography" ["Autobiografia di uno spettatore"], for example, one learns that the young Calvino spent days hidden away at the movies, immersing himself in another world unlike the one he lived in. This need to displace himself, to obliterate the real and extend himself into other worlds seemed to him a natural part of his personal evolution. His expressed feeling that the movies, and not home, manifested the richness and clarity necessary to life not only confirms the author's strong desire to escape his less-than-fulfilling childhood, but also hints of his blossoming literary career (37).

There were other reasons for stealing away from the house. In the same story, Calvino describes his home life as rather repressive. His austere mother, he says, did her best to keep him away from activities that, to her thinking, did not have significant objectives or were not properly educational (39–41). From the book's title story, "Road," we further learn that Calvino's relationship with his father (a man some fifty years older than young Italo) was similarly constrained. The author portrays the elder Calvino as taciturn and indifferent to the world outside of his scientific sphere. Talking to him was not always easy for the son, who neither shared his father's interest in science nor fully enjoyed the compulsory botanical surveys that he and the older man took on the road to San Giovanni (*Road* 3–34).

Calvino did, however, share the family political views. In a later interview, he remarked with bitterness that one of his first childhood memories was the brutal beating of an elderly socialist by Mussolini's musclemen or *squadristi* (ER 149–50). Other of the author's pre-Partisan recollections of Fascism appear in *L'entrata in guerra* [Entering the War, 1954], a volume of three autobiographically inspired short stories based on the sixteen-year-old Calvino's compulsory experience as a member of the *balilla*, or Fascist Youth. The title story reveals in retrospect the author's early political noncompliance as well as his strong identity with Italy's oppressed populace. It also introduces the reader to what would later be the author's signature fictional character: the eyewitness, on the surface a child or childlike reporter, but underneath a wary and sagacious skeptic.[5]

The story focuses on the narrator's anguished memory of Mussolini's declaration of war on the Allies in June 1940. With despair, the young onlooker sees the first wave of Italian peasants evacuated from the northern front and commiserates with the physical and emotional upheaval that they experience at this cruel displacement. The casual observation by a Fascist official that this journey is only a lark for the refugees because the war would soon be over does nothing to reassure the dubious boy. Instead, the official's remarks only underscore for the narrator the folly of the Italian political position. A final ironic aside is added when Mussolini himself makes a flamboyant whirlwind stop at the scene. A hint of Calvino's partisanship emerges in the cynical contrast the author draws between the tanned, exhilarated dictator and the already world-weary young narrator (5–22).

By the time he was of university age, Calvino, a closet writer, was aware of his literary vocation. Lacking the courage of his convictions, however, he kept these aspirations secret, even from friends. Instead, in 1941 he reluctantly followed family tradition and enrolled in the Faculty of Agricultural Studies, first at the University of Turin, and later at the University of Florence. His studies in Florence, however, were rudely interrupted when he was called up to serve in the Italian army under Mussolini's Salò government. By this time (1943), having been influenced by leftist friends, Calvino was a clandestine Communist opposed to fighting for the Fascist cause. With their parents' support, young Italo and Floriano resisted the draft and went briefly into hiding. Soon after, they joined the Italian Resistance where, as freedom fighters or *garibaldini*, they saw active combat against the detested Nazi army occupying Italy.

The Calvino family held fast to its anti-Fascist principles and was not intimidated, even when the elder Calvinos were held for a time under house arrest by the Germans and when Mario Calvino was threatened with death. Later, Calvino would describe his mother in particular as an "example of tenacity and courage during a Resistance [movement] understood [by her] as natural justice and family rectitude" (ER 163). He also recalled his final year as a Partisan and what it was like to live dangerously, always on the run and in peril for his life (CR LXVIII). In the future, he would look back fondly on the anti-Fascist community in which he had grown up, recognizing that the citizens he knew then had been his "defense against the world around him, a world then dominated by corruption and madness" (ER 158–59).

When the war ended in 1945 and Italy had been liberated, Calvino resumed his normal life, but with a new maturity. He returned to his interrupted university studies, but, significantly, not to his original vocation in agronomy. Although his scientific background would always serve him well in his writing, he had now resolved to play what he called the "black sheep," the only one in a family populated by scientists, to take a degree in letters.[6] In 1947 he would graduate with a thesis on Joseph Conrad, a modernist author for whom he felt a spiritual affinity, fostered perhaps by Calvino's grim wartime experiences and by a suspicion he may have subsequently shared with Conrad of a darkly unpredictable universe.[7]

He maintained his ties with the Communist Party that had championed the Resistance and, with social reform in mind, began to work for the Communist paper *L'Unità*, first as a journalist and later as an editor.

A novice short story, "Angoscia," brought him to the attention of well-known novelist Cesare Pavese, who saw it published in *Aretusa* in 1945. Calvino also began writing for the leftist magazine *Il Politecnico*, where more of his early works were published under the auspices of another famous author, Elio Vittorini. Later, a disillusioned Calvino would downplay his political allegiance to Communism forged during these years. Rather, he insisted that his loyalties then had not been based on ideology as much as on the feeling that "at that moment what counted [in the new Italy] was action; and the communists were the most active and organized force" (CR LXVII).

The early years of the author's career brought the same artistic and financial struggles endured by many young writers. For a time, Calvino lived meagerly in a frigid attic in Turin, waiting for money orders from home. Refining his literary skills was not effortless either. Calvino was always the first to say that writing did not come easily to him, and that when he first started to write, he was actually a self-taught man "of few letters." In an article, a friend recalls the youthful Calvino complaining that he found writing to be "the most squalid and ascetic of occupations." Even in later years, the author continued to write in longhand, frequently lamenting his work as a sweaty task (CR LXIX).[8]

To support his early literary efforts, he sought work at the Einaudi Publishing House in Turin, a logical step, as in Italy it is quite customary for budding writers to seek a livelihood in publishing. Moreover, because Einaudi had been an important wartime hub for anti-Fascist propaganda, it was quite natural that Calvino was drawn there. Although he perhaps did not realize it at the time, Calvino's relationship with Einaudi would prove enduring and fruitful, artistically and financially. First hired there in 1946 for such tasks as selling books on commission, he was soon promoted to publicity in 1947. A conscientious worker, he moved up through the ranks quickly, learning the publishing trade from the ground up. By 1950 he was promoted to staff editor, and by 1955 he was already a youthful director. In 1961 he was named editorial consultant, a distinguished role he would keep until 1984 when his relationship with the publishing house ended.

At Einaudi, numbered among Calvino's literary colleagues were some of Italy's most prominent writers of the day. In addition to Pavese and Vittorini, the novice author was exposed to the stimulating companionship of such established authors as Natalia Ginzburg, Carlo Levi, and Alberto Moravia. Furthermore, with editors Giulio Einaudi and Daniele

Ponchiroli, he established enduring, personal friendships that would last a lifetime. Not surprisingly, it was Einaudi, the center of his artistic life, that subsequently published most of the author's major works.

NEOREALISM: RESISTANCE STORIES

Like numerous fellow writers at the time, young Calvino took part in *neorealismo*, or "new realism," a left-wing Italian literary movement that celebrated the wartime Partisan struggle as well as the plight of the common man at war's end. Calvino's earliest Resistance stories, borrowed from personal experience, were published in one volume for the first time in *Ultimo viene il corvo* [The Crow Comes Last, 1949]. In English these tales appear in several different editions, including *Adam, One Afternoon and Other Stories*, 1957, and the much later *Difficult Loves*, 1984.[9] Left to lengthier discussion in the next chapter are some of the best tales, "Going to Headquarters," "Fear on the Footpath," "One of the Three is Still Alive," as well as the title story. All of these are Partisan narratives, ironically coupling playful adventure with a strong sense of war's arbitrary cruelty.

Besides the earlier Conrad, popular American writers, especially from the thirties and forties, also influenced Calvino's initial works, most specifically his use of spare, everyday dialogue and his portrayal of the stalwart Everyman caught up in personal tragedy and triumphs. Calvino and colleagues like Pavese perceived American literature as "bound to the doings of men" and devoted to "creating a new poetic language from the vernacular."[10] Good role models for the two authors were William Saroyan, William Faulkner, Ernest Hemingway, and even the earlier Mark Twain, who drew their heroes in an unaffected way, using colloquial language. Such unpretentious styling, less common in Italian letters, was to be adopted by Italian neorealists.[11]

At his mentor Cesare Pavese's suggestion, Calvino undertook a first novel, *The Path to the Spiders' Nests* [*Il sentiero dei nidi di ragno*, 1947]. Like all neorealistic works, *Path* focuses largely on the Partisan movement and, in this case, on one small band's clandestine activities in the northern Italian hills. Unlike the typical Partisan novel, however, it also delves into one youth's difficulties in comprehending the rights and wrongs of a war where brothers and countrymen were inexplicably called upon to fight each other. It is one of Calvino's more personal works because in the central figure, a naive waif called Pin, the author identified something of himself. In fact, it was through the eyes of this baffled young witness that Calvino admittedly vented his own still-recent and conflicted memories of the Resistance (*Path* 24–25).[12]

The novel's small hero reflected the author's skepticism of the sharply defined black-and-white morality so often portrayed in neorealism. Even unintentionally, Pin came off less a Partisan idealist than a doubting Thomas. For example, as recently observed by Lucia Re, the name Pin itself more likely points to Carlo Collodi's ambiguous fairy-tale figure Pinocchio rather than to any Pollyanna hero.[13] Comparisons between Pin and Mark Twain's classic misanthropic figure Huck Finn should not be overlooked either, especially because Calvino later acknowledged Twain as an influence. Indeed, the overall affinity between Calvino and Twain's misfit characters, principally their shared isolation and mistrust of society, are traits to be addressed in the subsequent chapter, as such sentiments constitute controlling motives in all of the author's future work.[14]

At the time of the novel's writing, however, most contemporary critics, many of them Communists, ignored Calvino's discreet negativity. They also minimized his fondness for fantasy, even when this Calvinian penchant was clearly evidenced in other of the author's fanciful stories, such as "Adam, One Afternoon," and "The Enchanted Garden." Both of these stories take place in bucolic settings, possess youthful protagonists, and are suffused by the warm glow of childish make-believe. Eventually, the author's choice of a fantasy ambience as a fictional alternative to the popular neorealism stirred controversy among critics who puzzled over the dual direction of his work. At the time, however, only his friend Pavese would take more than a casual interest in Calvino's whimsical otherworlds, and Pavese's view was decidedly approving. He openly admired Calvino's new daring direction, his impish childlike characters.[15]

The Path to the Spiders' Nests would effectively be Calvino's only neorealistic novel. The fact that it subsequently won the important Riccione Prize for literature did not insure the author's future in the genre. A second novel, *Il bianco veliero* [The White Sailing Ship, 1949], was never published, probably on friend Vittorini's advice. A third, *I giovani del Po*, [Young People of the Po], written in 1951, nearly met the same fate. Although it appeared in a serial edition in *Officina* (1957–58), Calvino never published it under separate cover. Several critics, including Beno Weiss, suggest that Calvino recognized the book's failure and that its shortcomings rested with the author's ignorance of its working-class subject matter.[16] Although Calvino's own candid admission of his limited acquaintance with simple people tends to corroborate Weiss's observations (ER 155), it is equally likely that, for his purposes, Calvino had already rejected neorealism. Later, he said that he had refused to republish certain early neorealistic stories simply because they were "out of style" or too "regional," but his future works reveal that Calvino's disenchantment with neorealism went deeper.[17]

POSTWAR TRANSITIONS: THE FIFTIES

The immediate postwar period in Italy was a time of immense vitality as a once-again united citizenry threw its energy into what was to be a swift economic recovery. By the 1948 elections capitalism was in the wind. Much to the surprise and chagrin of the Italian Communist Party, champion of the Resistance, the left wing was painfully defeated by the traditionalist Christian Democrat Party. Memories of the hated German occupation and the difficult days during and after the war were fading from the minds of the busy Italian population. The freshness of the pain had passed and with it enthusiasm for left-wing causes. Scarcely looking back, a once largely agrarian Italy now moved rapidly toward industrialization as farmers migrated to the city in a race for jobs, cars, and consumer goods. The so-called Big Boom exploded and Italy flourished.

From his essays and short stories during this time, we see that Calvino looked askance at the growing new materialism and at the lost sense of community it engendered.[18] Yet, like his compatriots, he too was changing. Although he still professed himself a socially committed writer, the nature of that commitment had subtly begun to alter course for reasons both artistic and political. In the political arena, writers were being asked by the Communist Party to regiment their art, and Calvino, given his artistic calling and his memory of Fascist censorship, could not condone this. According to the author, the conflict within Communist political culture had in fact already started by war's end. Since that time, under Party pressure, "the danger that the new [neorealistic] literature would be required to fulfil a celebratory and didactic function was in the air" (Path 16–17). Ironically, castigation by leftist critics replaced Fascist censorship, and Calvino would not be excluded.

More significantly, Cold-War politics in Eastern Europe had begun to sour Calvino and fellow intellectuals. According to the author, the diary of his visit to Soviet Russia published in 1952 in L'Unità is occasionally less than sincere because, in accordance with Communist Party dictates, he had felt constrained to present only the more idyllic aspects of Soviet life (ER 224). Disappointment with aggressive Stalinist policy and with the hypocritical direction of the Italian Communist Party also stirred within him and soon would be directly addressed by the author in political articles in *Contemporaneo,* March-June 1956.

But the final blow to Calvino's Communist allegiance probably came with the brutal Soviet takeover of Hungary in 1956. In an interview years after the incident, Calvino acknowledged that the news of the Hungarian invasion, which spelled the end of personal freedom in that country, also ended once and for all his Communist Party affiliation (ER 231–32). His letter of resignation from the Party followed in *L'Unità* (7 August 1957). In it, the author conceded his indebtedness to the Party for having played an essential role in his "cultural and literary formation," and expressed his ardent hope that in the future the Party would move away from its dogmatic authoritarianism toward a stance "more directly democratic" in which all classes of society would be able to participate actively.[19] From this moment on, the author's politics took on an Italian flavor, in that (not unlike other Italian writers, including the great political poet Dante), he declared himself a party unto himself. Indeed, by the end of his life, the author fairly bristled at the mention of politics.

Calvino's fiction of the fifties testifies amply to his faltering trust in political solutions and to the resultant new direction of his art. Long before many of his literary contemporaries, Calvino recognized that both the form and the idealistic expectations of neorealism had dead-ended. As observed in late neorealistic films and literature, efforts to sustain the glow of Partisan fervor were becoming forced and melodramatic. According to the writer, the tension that neorealism had once created was gone, the story lines having grown stale and predictable. It was time to save what was important to him as an author, not the form of neorealism perhaps, but rather the important things, "the energy, the spirit."[20]

That spirit for Calvino was no longer found in mundane happenings nor in political platitudes. As a literary mode, those inspirations had failed him. "Certainly, I belong to the last generation that believed in a design for literature which could be integrated into a design for society. And both these designs went up in smoke," the author later admitted ruefully (ER 208–9). In fact, since the war, his hopes for humanity's progress had ebbed as he became aware of precisely how complex world problems really were. If there were solutions to the postwar world disorder Calvino saw around him, they were not to be found in fabricated morality or in banal realism. Driven by curiosity, both artistic and philosophical, the author deliberately moved on.

As his works of this decade reveal, Calvino began to put aside daily events like politics to explore abstract issues, namely the metaphysical. Practical answers he now replaced with philosophical questions: persistent existential inquiries that explored man's place on this earth and interrogated the very reason for his being. "What is the role of the individual man in history? And what sense does history have?" (ER 168), the disenchanted Calvino would eventually ask himself. Other of his questions would explore the relationship of man to the Other, or what Ferretti terms the "*integrazione uomo-mondo* " (the integration of man in his world).[21]

Exploring these issues became a lifelong crusade for Calvino and, as he acknowledged in an interview, frequently required him to "change gears" in order say something that he had not succeeded in saying in a previous work.[22] Moving from realism toward areas newer and decidedly more experimental also meant play for the gamester author who always delighted in catching his readers and critics off guard with each of his innovations. Especially disconcerting in Calvino's fifties fiction were its several, and seemingly incompatible, directions. Alternating now from the author's pen were ironic fairy tales and eccentric, modernist short stories that explored the gloomy inner workings of postwar man. Traditionalist critics were hard-pressed to define the new Calvino and were reluctant to surrender the old one. Baffled, they hung their hats on the neorealistic author, seeking in Calvino's later works a hidden grain of the old political truth. Only years later would Calvino's eclectic blend of realism, modernism, and fantasy come to be understood as the ingredients to contemporary postmodernism, the author's final fictional resting place.

MODERNIST INTERROGATIONS

Of all Calvino's digressions from neorealism, the least conspicuous at the time was his drift toward a more subjective, modernist literature. Postwar short stories, many now found in *Difficult Loves*, were hastily dubbed realism, though today some are recognized as modernist in both form and narrative style. For example, even when these narratives focus on the daily life of the average man, they do not emphasize objective reality, much less dwell on social issues. Story lines are ambiguous and facts precarious. Events are capriciously traced through stream-of-consciousness, modernist introspection laced with gloomy doubts and ruminative speculations. Stories no longer end—they trail off, shrouded in equivocation and relying heavily for their interpretation on the confused and dismal observations of the sole protagonist.

The all-important Calvinian witness also is much changed, having grown older (like the author) but not wiser since *Path*. Because the central figure in this body of stories is no longer a child, his childlike disorientation in the face of circumstance dramatizes less neorealistic confidence than Cold War uncertainty and human inadequacy. A paranoid, unreliable reporter of events, the protagonist frequently alienates himself from fellow characters and from the reader, who may or may not sympathize with him. This regression in Calvino's "hero" marks a cynical rejection of certain of the author's earlier models and allies him more firmly instead with Conrad and Samuel Beckett, both of whom portray man as diminished.

Diverse short stories, as well as the author's novellas, merit subsequent close study. *A Plunge into Real Estate* [*La speculazione edilizia*, 1957] focuses on the perils of capitalism for the would-be entrepreneur. *Smog* [*La nuvola di smog*, 1958] recounts an eccentric Beckettian observer's cynical meditations on man the self-destructive polluter, straining to keep one step ahead of his own toxic wastes. Another novella with Beckettian undercurrents is *The Watcher* [*La giornata d'uno scrutatore*], a more complex story begun in 1955 but not published till 1963. This last tale focuses on the existential angst of a Communist named Amerigo Ormea who, while monitoring the voting in a mental institution, is seized by the futility of both his political and personal life. Short stories from *Difficult Loves* similarly testify to the dehumanizing effects of modern society, to the isolation of man from his fellows, and to his retreat to the consolation of private fantasies, all essentially modernist themes in Calvino's fiction.[23]

Anonymity now frequently became a key attribute in Calvino's main character, with one exception—Marcovaldo. This endearing Chaplinesque character from the story series *Marcovaldo, or, The seasons in the city* [*Marcovaldo, ovvero, Le stagioni in città*, 1963] is, like Pin in *Path*, both sympathetic and identifiable. We know him to be a gentle, amiable, but impoverished blue-collar worker whose fantasy life exceeds the small, cramped realm of his city apartment.[24] Sustained as he is by hopes and dreams, Marcovaldo has in the past been conceived by some critics as a "Noble Savage," a survivor, who in the face of adversity, will not knuckle under to despair. To other critics, however, despite his likability, Marcovaldo's existential predicament seems no less dreary than that of his fellows in *Difficult Loves*.[25] To them, he appears a decidedly more controversial and contemporary figure than he is credited with being. For this reason, the naive witness, Marcovaldo, and what he and his alienated small world actually mean to Calvino warrant separate and attentive inquiry in a subsequent chapter.

The Argentine Ant [*La formica argentina*, 1952], an early Calvino novella, also deserves particular consideration. Its menacing depiction of one of God's smallest, most innocuous creatures skirts the supernatural and marks a more daring step into contemporaneity than many of Calvino's other works of the same vintage. Its melange of the comic and strange, of the possible and the impossible, clearly recalls similar elements in such postmodern authors as Kurt Vonnegut, Jorge Luis Borges, and Gabriel García Márquez, not to mention Franz Kafka, a recognized postmodern precursor. *Argentine Ant*, its early publication notwithstanding, draws Calvino closer to his postmodern contemporaries and foretells of his step into the sixties.[26]

THE TRILOGY: FANTASY QUESTS

Although some of Calvino's postwar fifties stories mentioned above were wrongly construed as realism, the same misapprehension did not apply to other fifties works: namely, the disarming and innovative fantasy trilogy. The first novel of the threesome, a magical black comedy called *The Cloven Viscount* [*Il visconte dimezzato*, 1951], abandoned any semblance of daily Italian life for the world of the fabulous. This seemingly dramatic change in the author not only astounded critics, but eventually caused them consternation. Fantasy (until Calvino) had never been a particularly popular genre in Italy. Now one of Italy's most promising socio-realistic novelists had suddenly chosen to make it his métier. Had Calvino decided that reality was burdensome? Had he sought temporary escape in the fabulous, asked an early critic, Emilio Cecchi. Or had he merely chosen fantasy as an alternate vehicle to express a new (albeit tangled) mandate for modern living, as J. R. Woodhouse and others would insist?[27]

It was difficult to assess this bizarre turn in the author, especially when

Viscount soon proved to be more than an isolated aberration. Two more sinister fairy tales followed: *The Baron in the Trees* [*Il barone rampante*, 1957] and *The Nonexistent Knight* [*Il cavaliere inesistente*, 1959]. To- gether, the three novels comprised a curious trio of darkly amusing picaresque fables, later republished under the satiric title *Our Ancestors* [*I nostri antenati*, 1960].[28] Despite the divergence from his original path, however, the author preserved his central figure, the childlike witness, but once again, this figure underwent strange metamorphoses.

The first fable, *Viscount*, concerns an ingenuous Calvino rube, Vis- count Medardo, who sets out to become a hero in the seventeenth-cen- tury Austro-Turkish Wars. Unfortunately, on the first day in battle, a fatal error in judgment on his part finds him neatly shorn in two by cannon-fire. With humorous fairy-tale plausibility, however, both halves of Medardo miraculously survive. One half returns from war an idealis- tic and saintly do-gooder spreading charity and saccharin cheer; the other slinks back morosely, consumed by malign thoughts and bent on mali- cious misdeeds. To some readers, *Viscount* implied a moralistic Jekyll and Hyde story, a dialogue on good and evil designed to enlighten man and spur him on toward a new integrity (Pescio Bottino 25). But this rather conventional exegesis of the work did not satisfy everyone, least of all Calvino.

The author's second full-length fantasy, *The Baron in the Trees*, focuses on the life of Baron Cosimo Piovasco di Rondò. A spirited son of the Enlightenment, Cosimo, at the tender age of twelve, rebelliously vows to live his life in the trees, where he will combine treetop humanitarianism with the solitary independence of a Robinson Crusoe. A perennial favor- ite with both adult and child readers, *Baron*, for all its fun, should be read just as cautiously as *Viscount* because it actually raises more questions than it resolves. Through the ongoing dialogue between the characters, Cosimo's life evolves as a sobering philosophical study of existential freedom. Alone and lonely, Cosimo wrestles with the contrary Sartrean dilemma of choosing between duty to self and duty to community and ends his life ambiguously as a solitary, alienated figure. Here, as in *Vis- count*, Calvino plays with a theme that would be central to all his work: life conceived as a series of binary, and necessarily incompatible, choices.

The last of the fairy-tale trilogy, *The Nonexistent Knight*, has for its unlikely narrator a cloistered nun, Sister Theodora, whose virginal worldview should reveal her to be utterly guileless. However, like most of the author's storytellers, she is not to be trusted, because in Calvino there is often a difference between what the narrator says and what the author means. This truism is especially evident here, where the self-conscious narrator delights in addressing the reader directly, prevaricating and playfully stringing him along with teasing innuendo and sarcastic asides. A trickster figure, this particular storyteller foreshadows Calvino's later self-reflexive postmodern mode, where Sister Theodora will appear in other novels under other names and guises.

The novel's plot concerns Agilulf, a medieval gallant serving in the court of King Charlemagne. In every way Agilulf proves a peerless example of chivalry, his perfection unmarred save for one incredible circumstance: he possesses no body; instead, he exists as a vacant suit of armor. Agilulf is both literally and figuratively a mechanical man, a vacuous shell incapable of humor, warmth, or physical contact with his fellows. In a written afterthought, Calvino later adds his own less than flattering opinion of Agilulf and the other characters in the trilogy. Here he compares them to defective contemporary man, "*dimidiato, mutilato, incompleto*," or "cloven, mutilated, and incomplete."[29]

In separate chapters on the trilogy and on other later Calvino works, more will be said of the author's dark reflections on humanity's inherent frailty and on the ambivalent nature of all life choices. For now, however, it suffices to observe that, of the three novels mentioned, *Knight* was clearly the author's most avant-garde work to date. Via its haphazard blend of fanciful nostalgia and modern social commentary, its self-conscious verbal thrusts at the pretensions of authors and their writing, its playful disregard for genre barriers, *Knight* heralds Calvino's escalating drive toward postmodernity.

Because of his own popular success with fairy tales, the author became the logical choice to prepare Einaudi's *Italian Folktales: Selected and Retold by Italo Calvino* [*Fiabe italiane*, 1956], a bestseller both in Italy and abroad, which introduced Calvino to an enthusiastic international audience. To complete the task properly, the author had steeped himself in Vladímir Propp's pioneer research on the universal patterns that occur in fables. Despite the enormity of the work involved, Calvino's natural reserve later inclined him to quietly divorce himself from *Folktales*, pointing out that, although he had some small hand in the writing, his real contribution to the book was merely that of editor: choosing the stories and transposing them from dialect into standard Italian ("Fabulist" 77).[30]

But not all critics concur with Calvino's modest assessment of his contribution to *Folktales*. After a thorough study of the work, Mark Beckwith indicates that, in the two hundred tales that he transposed, Calvino frequently made changes that could only be regarded as substantive. It is observed, for instance, that the author consistently reduced religious references, sanitized vulgar humor, tempered moments of violent retribution, shortened stories, and in the end, finally took liberties with the story plots.[31] Writer or editor of *Folktales*, whichever the reality of Calvino's role, it is clear that the author's study of Propp's theories, coupled with his own experience writing the fantasy trilogy, had gone a long way toward sharpening his taste for the braver literary otherworlds he would invent in the sixties.

THE POSTMODERN MOVE: THE SIXTIES AND BEYOND

By 1960 Calvino was approaching the high point of his career and was beginning to reap the rewards of literary success. In Italy, he had just won the noteworthy Bagutta Prize for his collection of tales, *I racconti* [Short Stories]. With Elio Vittorini he had just founded the prestigious *Menabò della letteratura* (1959), a short-lived periodical that he and his colleague had hoped would solicit literary discourse treating problems of actual life, and that did, in reality, become the vehicle for several of the author's more important essays.[32] He would stay with the esteemed literary journal as codirector until 1967 when it folded after the death of Vittorini.

Now more than ever, the author was drawn to new horizons, both geographic and literary. Requests to write for newspapers and theater were frequent, but being a deliberate man, Calvino was selective. A lifelong lover of music and theater, he had already collaborated on two musical productions, *La panchina* [The Bench, 1956] and *Allez-hop*, 1959, and would later take on theatrical ventures including libretti for the opera.[33] Over the years he wrote for several Italian newspapers, including *Il Giorno, Il Corriere della sera*, and finally *La Repubblica.* He had already visited and chronicled Russia in the fifties, but now his travels began in earnest. With the assistance of a Ford Foundation Grant, he spent six months (from 1959 to 1960) in the United States, touring widely and lecturing at colleges and universities. His yet-untranslated reminiscences of this American journey provide the reader with an uncommon glimpse of the personal man, the possessor of an ironic sense of humor, as well as a rare gift for acute observations.[34]

Though he traveled the United States over, most of Calvino's stay in America was, by his own choice, spent in New York, "maybe the only place in America where one feels at the center and not the periphery" (ER 100). In New York he met a wide variety of stimulating people: literary figures, journalists, artists, publishers, actors, and even beatniks. Years later he spoke of the city's vitality with a kind of warmth rarely expressed by the public Calvino, calling it the city he most felt was his. Upon his first return from America in 1960, he spoke affectionately of his love for the place, wondering facetiously whether or not one day he should not add the words "New Yorker" to his tombstone (CR LXXVI). He returned there more than once, but much as he loved New York, he would never call it home.

Besides his sojourn in America, there were now other lengthy stays abroad, especially in Paris, the city that would indeed soon be home. There in 1962 he met his future wife, Esther Judith Singer, an Argentinian translator who worked for several international organizations, including UNESCO and the International Atomic Energy Agency. There he was also exposed to an intellectual climate different from that in Italy. Inevitably these enthusiastic explorations of foreign lands and of the new French methods in literature catapulted Calvino beyond the confines of his homeland. All his major works of the next decades revealed his curiosity about the international literary scene, particularly in France. He became interested in experiments in narrative technique and in scholarly research in both story structure and linguistics. These innovations called for drastic changes in the status quo of fiction, dissecting the standard novel and dismembering those trite works that the author later labeled "best sellers . . . written in bad faith" ("Fabulist" 82).

Authors and critics such as Alain Robbe-Grillet and Roland Barthes, in their respective work with the *nouveau roman* (new novel) and "writing degree zero," advocated a fresh literary aesthetic: a fiction that did not spoon-feed readers on omniscient narration and verisimilitude, but furnished only observable phenomena that the creative reader was free to interpret as he would. Besides Propp, Robbe-Grillet, and Barthes, Calvino was also interested in Ferdinand de Saussure, whose science of semiology, or language signs, had a great impact on Calvino's sixties works. In France he became involved in Tel Quel, a group of writers Calvino described as focused on the "ontology of language," that is to say, on its metaphysical and otherworld ingredients.[35]

Soon he would also participate in Oulipo or *Ouvroir de littérature potentielle* (the Workshop for Potential Literature), Raymond Queneau's radical Parisian literary society that applied the principles of mathematics and science toward the generation of a playful "potential" literature. Still later, the author was influenced by Jacques Derrida's poststructuralist movement and its skeptical critique of language as the bearer of ultimate truth. All of these fresh literary endeavors Calvino saw as a means to enliven fiction, to escape the monotony of traditional historical narrative, and thereby elude (at least on paper) the natural limitations of the human world. Little by little, via these eclectic postmodern inquiries, the social writer Calvino inevitably gave way to the restless intellectual within.

More skeptical of the fashionable new trends in novel-writing than Calvino, however, were Italian critics, endowed with a certain caution of the new continental literary trends. The old-fashioned "committed" novel that Robbe-Grillet had recently dismissed as "backward" and an "embarrassment" had, after all, served as a powerful vehicle of popular expression in Italy's neorealism and had precipitated a golden period in postwar Italian literature and film.[36] Furthermore, the traditional novel's emphasis on people, situations, and *moralità* eminently suited the body of Italian literature still known today for its strong emotional and political sensibilities.

Calvino's experiments with speculative literature and his abandonment of conventional narrative was therefore bound to dismay some reviewers who neither welcomed nor understood the author's new direction and were quick to say so. Even Renato Barilli, an admirer of the new French fiction, was not entirely comfortable with Calvino's seeming inconsistency: his "mixed and hesitant narrative vein," his "halfway positioning of his stories," or more simply stated—the author's unorthodox blend of realism and fantasy, a phenomenon today more rightly associated with postmodernism.[37] Charges of artifice and empty intellectualism would be leveled at some of Calvino's later novels. Well-intentioned Italian critics urged the author to get back on the "right" track, to retreat to a more conventional style, and to return to novels with a solid political message.[38] Such a narrow critical perception of the author was only indicative of Calvino's separate place in Italian literature.

Time would reveal that, in the search for coherence in Calvino, too much critical attention in those days was focused on the author's role as social commentator and on the polemics of his writing: namely, his erratic shifts in genre. Overlooked in the critical discourse was something more pertinent to any discussion of Calvino today: namely, the consistency—if not in the shape of his work—then in the melancholy, philosophical direction of his thinking. This dark direction, contends Gian Carlo Ferretti, is already hinted at in early Calvino where "a deep-seated mistrust in the powers of reason and in the prospects for progress," is already observed (158). Ferretti's observations are in fact corroborated by the author himself who, in the introduction to his important collection of essays *Una pietra sopra. Discorsi di letteratura e società* [*The Uses of Literature: Essays*, 1980], acknowledges that as a youth he idealistically envisioned a literature that would be helpful in building a new world. However, now, with society in a state of disintegration he could not conceive of a world "more opposite" than that of his early, naive expectations (*Pietra* vii).

Disenchanted with life's discrepancies and with humanity's ineffectualness in the face of the unknown and unpredictable, the Calvino of the sixties readily acknowledged a postwar, postmodern sense of loss and a feeling of displacement from society. He began to separate himself from events around him, admitting that he no longer felt the same "push to be in the middle of things personally." Gone were his youthful idealism and high hopes for the future. Not without sarcasm he commented that he felt he had already been young a very long time and that now was the moment to begin old age in "the hope that by getting a head start he might prolong it."[39]

Although his hopes for a new social order were, by this time, at an end, Calvino's quest for new fiction was only starting. He sought the order missing in life elsewhere—in literature; he chose, in his own words, the "vocation of library mouse" (Camon 190). From the safe haven of books, he continued his inquiry into the hows and whys of man's being, not just in this world, but in others too. Perhaps *"altrove"* (elsewhere, in otherworlds), says Ferretti, Calvino might yet achieve the "integration of man in his world" (95). Armed with his maturing philosophical convictions and with sights set on fresh literary goals, Calvino was about to make his next years the most rewarding, both artistically and personally.

In 1964 he visited Cuba and there, near his birthplace, he married Esther (Chichita) Singer. Upon their return to Italy the couple settled for a time in Rome where, in 1965, their only child, daughter Giovanna, was born. Soon afterward, in 1967, however, the family moved to Paris. When asked later by Ferdinando Camon why he was living in Paris and not in Italy, the author responded that for him Paris was a haven of tranquil anonymity. It meant "family life," in "a place . . . where everyone minds their own affairs" (193). Although he did not say so openly, it has been speculated that, at the time, the author's move was partly motivated by the fact that in Paris he had found both the literary climate and the critical reception more supportive than in Italy.

Artistically, this was Calvino's most intensely productive period. Besides the major works to be addressed here, he completed a large number of smaller projects as well. One was *I fiori blu* (1967), the author's Italian translation of Queneau's *Les Fleurs Bleues* [The Blue Flowers], a novel that probably impacted the style of Calvino's later *Invisible Cities*. Another was *Orlando furioso di Ludovico Ariosto raccontato da Italo Calvino, con una scelta del poema* [*Orlando Furioso* by Ludovico Ariosto, as recounted by Italo Calvino, with a selection from the poem, 1970], a book of excerpts from the epic poet's masterpiece inspired by Calvino's 1968 radio reading of the work. For Einaudi, he also directed *Centopagine* [One Hundred Pages, 1971], a selection of readings from many Calvino favorites, including Stendhal, Robert Louis Stevenson, and, of course, Conrad.

Within a brief time span (1965–73) he also produced four remarkable novels representing new worlds mastered by Italy's foremost literary explorer. Widely translated, these would bring him much acclaim, not only in Europe, but in America as well. All his new novels, and even some works neglected in the past, would now be translated. American writers such as Gore Vidal, John Barth, and John Updike praised the author and made it their responsibility to inform the American public about him. For this recognition and for their critical admiration, Calvino remained forever grateful.

The first of Calvino's major and explicitly postmodern works was *Cosmicomics* [*Le cosmicomiche*, 1965], published on the eve of his move to Paris.[40] One of his most original and engaging writings, it is a delightful science fantasy that at once reveals the author's subversive literary skills: his prankish semiotic wordgames, paradoxical otherworlds, disconcerting merger of past and present, and Queneauian blend of science and silliness. As is Calvino's custom in all his later works, *Cosmicomics* is not a fully integrated novel. Instead, like many postmodern pieces, it is a loosely arranged group of story fragments. In this instance we encounter a sequence of dramatized scientific theories wherein the everyday blends with the magic of intergalactic events and evolutional theories. Plot is replaced by postmodernism's favorite tool: parody. Character, too, is economically reduced to one, Calvino's ever-present eyewitness and this time cordial reporter, Qfwfq. This talking equation, however, is less a person than a phenomenon: a cross between a scientific theorem and a wacky, heavenly prophet who comments familiarly on a wide range of newsworthy galactical happenings. A uniquely innovative and entertaining work in tune with today's literature, Calvino's otherworld visit, *Cosmicomics*, could arguably be called his masterpiece.[41]

In this same highly productive period, other ingenious works followed swiftly. Another collection of loosely united stories, *t zero* [*Ti con zero*, 1967], begins as a sequel to *Cosmicomics* [42] but then two-thirds through the book changes direction. The final group of stories in *t zero*, named for the book title, is decidedly less amusing and more polemical than *Cosmicomics*. Here Calvino tries (or at least pretends) to exclude the writer, describing his role in the novel as that of a "writing machine," or a mere recorder of phenomenological data observable at the fiction's surface.[43] Built on the ideas of Barthes and Robbe-Grillet, these tales emulate the flat, "colourless" narrative style they espoused.[44] Elements of both Robbe-Grillet and postmodernist Borges are much in evidence in *t zero*'s final pages, especially in "The Night Driver" ["Il guidatore notturno"] and "The Count of Monte Cristo" ["Il conte di Montecristo"], stories notable for their riddling and Borges-like labyrinthical meanderings. Inevitably, such contorted itineraries dominated Calvino's later fiction, mirroring the author's lost faith in well-made agendas, not only those of literature, but of mankind as well.

Calvino's next two novels, *The Castle of Crossed Destinies* [*Il castello dei destini incrociati*, 1969 and 1973] and *Invisible Cities* [*Le città invisibili*, 1972], express best the antithetical position of postmodernism. Invariably, they illustrate both the delights and anxieties associated with its literature and juxtapose the best of the new against the best of the old in storytelling.[45] Old in both novels are their historical settings and their traditional frames, which readily illustrate Propp's structuralist theory of the universality of story patterns. Like the medieval *Decameron* and *Canterbury Tales*, both works recount tales within a tale and open with a cornice that unites all the different stories. In both works the outer story has undoubtedly been chosen for its vast appeal, or for what Calvino saw as its "primitive tradition," the "pre-fabricated components," that offer the reader a reassuring sense of wholeness or integrity.[46]

New and original here, however, is the author's deliberate and subversive deconstruction of these traditional frames. For example, the individual, and sometimes violent, tales in *Castle* are ambiguously told by way of tarot card readings. The tales in *Invisible Cities,* although decidedly more harmonious, are not more whole, but exist as mere fragments of poetic prose. Both works are experiments in storytelling, games that share the semiotician's skepticism of words as fixed values and the author's own postmodern obsession with doubling or paired opposites. Both are works that shift the responsibility for making meaning from writer to reader, once again underscoring the author's disdain for the traditional well-made novel with its smug assumption of reality.

The resultant untidiness in the texts, the "craving for disorder" and contradiction, according to Calvino, only documents the efforts of modern literature "to arrive outside the boundaries of language" and to play with the unlimited combinations of narrative ("Process" 97). Just as important thematically, however, is the fact that both works reflect Calvino's philosophic rejection of the artist as seer and thus subtly underscore once more the author's postmodern misgivings regarding the creative significance of man on Earth. Such antihumanist sentiments, especially as grimly expressed in *Castle,* document the author's worst fears: a universe chaotic and incomprehensible and the human role in it as pointless or unintelligible. Fortunately, *Castle,* Calvino's gloomiest work, would not be his last. Other novels, including the transitional *Invisible Cities,* adopted a more compromising attitude and exhibit in Calvino, a latent postmodernism that would be both more indulgent of humanity and more forgiving.

LAST YEARS: FINAL JOURNEYS

The last decade of Calvino's life (1975–85), in many ways, can be viewed as the author's final reckoning with both his art and with himself. Perhaps the single most telling personal event in this time span was his return to Italy in 1980. Despite his affection for the Paris literary scene, a part of him had, in a sense, always stayed behind in the homeland he loved well, even if with occasional ambivalence. During his thirteen-year absence he had continued to commute to Turin for work and to spend long summers with his family at their seaside home in Tuscany. Furthermore, in 1972 Calvino won the Antonio Feltrinelli Prize, one of Italy's most coveted literary awards, and perhaps the one Calvino valued above the others he had received.[47] Clearly, the rumored breach with Italian critics, such as it might have been, had proven neither lengthy nor irremediable.

This same decade included some final travels: a trip to the Orient and, of course, journeys to the Americas, including South America and Mexico. At least two more pilgrimages were made to the United States: one for a seminar at Johns Hopkins in 1976, and one to teach briefly at Columbia, and then act as James Lecturer at New York University in 1983. These last appearances in America must have been important to Calvino for they required him to put aside his natural shyness. A private person (particularly in later years), the author was not given to public speaking, especially in English, a language with which he was never fully comfortable. In fact, even in Italian, Calvino was not at ease before audiences, once remarking with his usual dry wit that he always felt "a certain disgust . . . for the spoken word," above all, when spoken by him (Camon 183).

More tributes came his way. In Italy, he achieved merited recognition when he was awarded the prestigious Legion d'onore in 1981. Then in 1985 he thought himself privileged to be invited to deliver Harvard University's distinguished Charles Eliot Norton Lectures scheduled for that fall. Of the six papers he was to give, however, Calvino would write only five. These would be published posthumously under the title *Six Memos for the Next Millennium* [*Lezioni americane. Sei proposte per il prossimo millennio*, 1988] and would focus on the spiritual qualities of literature that were most precious to the author. The lectures themselves never took place. Calvino died suddenly of a stroke in September 1985, just a month before his sixty-second birthday.[48]

Although his last decade of life may have been less productive than the previous one, Calvino worked scrupulously up to the end. Almost as if he had intuited his demise, in *Pietra*, he gathered together all his essays since 1955. Later, in *Collezione di sabbia* [Collection of Sand, 1984], Calvino, himself the eyewitness par excellence, put together various news pieces based on his own eclectic travel observations. Some Calvino works would be published after the author's death. These include the already-cited *Road to San Giovanni, Numbers in the Dark and Other Stories* [*Prima che tu dica "Pronto,"* 1993], an interesting, random collection of tales, and *Under the Jaguar Sun* [*Sotto il sole giaguaro*, 1986], an intriguing, unfinished fiction.[49]

Two final major works were also completed and published during the author's last years. These are *If on a winter's night a traveler* [*Se una notte d'inverno un viaggiatore*, 1979], an encyclopedic fiction, and *Mr. Palomar* [*Palomar*, 1983], Calvino's intimate epitaph.[50] In these works we see that Calvino, the reluctant orator, has, as ever, reserved his best conversation for his novels. More than the author's other works, these two reveal the empathetic side to Calvino's postmodernism. Candidly, they expose the personal author and disclose his final accord with life and literature. For example, the outrageously playful *Winter's night*, a postmodern spoof of fictional genres and their authors, also has its serious side. In it, the author addresses the reader and sums up his own final literary credo, giving his views on the far-reaching role of literature in human lives. He sees this role as decidedly more substantive than daily events, political or otherwise. Literature and its nuances are inexhaustible, extending back in time to oral tradition and surviving, unlike mortals, into the indefinable future.

More evocative is *Mr. Palomar*, Calvino's thinly disguised, late-life autobiography. Through the sensitive gaze of the central figure, named ironically for the California telescope, the novel unflinchingly scans the protagonist's empty future. With uncanny accuracy, it also anticipates the author's dying, just as surely as his earlier fairy tales had anticipated his living and discovering the magic lands of cloven viscounts and invisible cities. The central figure, Mr. Palomar, is just another of life's observers, but unlike some earlier Calvino characters, he gamely accepts what fate has in store for him. Older and reconciled to life's arbitrary circumstances, he leaves existential issues necessarily unsettled. Instead, he good-naturedly embraces life for what it is: a series of bittersweet and bewildering events. Not without sadness he contemplates his passing, and then with astonishing equanimity, he predicts a tomorrow without him—and the author.

If Mr. Palomar personifies Calvino, as many critics conjecture, then his character summarizes the course of the author's evolution, both in life and literature. In youth, like his boy character Pin, Calvino began his literary pilgrimage as a Partisan adventurer, idealistically seeking the means to build a better world out of the travesty of war. Seeing these dreams ravaged by postwar disillusionment and political dissension, he pushed his obstinate quest for Truth forward into the future. If final answers could not be found in practical actions, he would seek them elsewhere, perhaps amid the moody philosophical speculations of modernist characters, such as Amerigo the pollwatcher, or in otherworlds like *Cosmicomics*, where the either-or of everyday anxiety is bypassed for eternity.

Coming to the end of his existence, the author had made a last decisive turn, this time toward a more harmonious postmodern itinerary. Like Palomar, he came face to face with the only certainties he felt man will ever know: namely, the stubbornness of being and the inevitability of death. Graciously, he braved the enigma of living, and with the quiet dignity of the mature postmodern author, he stoically embarked for a final Otherworld and a last adventure larger than life.

2

FIRST STEPS IN NEOREALISM

The end of World War II brought Italy not only hardship but blessings. As author Italo Calvino explains, it was like starting over "from scratch" (*Path* 7). Incredibly, a victory of sorts had been wrested from the rubble of the Italian defeat and the country had won a fresh beginning. Liberated from more than twenty years of Fascist suppression, Italy was a nation finally free, both of the world war and the civil war that had beset and split its citizenry for five agonizing years. With renewed hope and a sense of unanimity, Italians began the task of peace. But before the job of postwar reconstruction could properly begin, the past had to be laid to rest.

Each Italian, including Calvino, had his personal war experience to relive, his own moment in history to recount. As the author describes it, there emerged a kind of "choral" autobiography:

we were face to face, on equal terms, bursting with stories to tell;
everyone had experienced their own drama, had lived a chaotic, ex-
citing, adventurous existence; we took the words from each other's
mouths. The rebirth of freedom of speech manifested itself first and
foremost in a craving to tell stories. (Path 8)

From this unique world of stories was born *neorealismo,* or "new realism," a creative era in contemporary Italian literature (and film), and a
moment in time that marks the beginning of Calvino's literary career.
Faithful to its appellation, neorealism would be a literature that focused
on actuality, particularly the harsh wartime and postwar realities of Italian life. Its goals, however, would not be diversional, but rather a means
to ventilate recent pain and to examine what needed to be done in order
to create a better future. In the end, neorealism proved itself to be a
literary period as artistically stimulating as it was controversial.

Even the very term "neorealism" remains problematic. For example,
there are critics today, such as Frank Rosengarten and Ferretti, who, like
Calvino contemporaries Vittorini and Pavese then, dispute the very
meaning of neorealism, not to mention its historical context (perhaps
encompassing 1945–62). They suggest, not without a measure of truth,
that neorealism should not be considered a literary movement at all, as
it was never more than a loosely assembled group of very diverse Italian
writers with a "hybrid" of ideas.[1] Even Calvino himself, who has perhaps
the final word on this matter and whose definition seems practical, pre-
ferred to describe neorealism as "not a [literary] school but an epoch and
a climate" ("Currents" 4).

But no matter what the definition or the debates that surround the
what and when of neorealism, critics are unanimous, and often as spirited as neorealistic writers, when speaking of the movement's mood. It
was a time when authors and filmmakers "attempted to deal directly and
honestly with the problems of war-ravaged Italy," and with the factors
precipitating Italy's downfall (Rosengarten 212). It was a time to express
"disgust for the moral emptiness" of Fascism and reaffirm human solidarity (Weiss 10). Clearly what neorealism lacked in definition, it more
than made up for in zeal, or what Calvino had so succinctly called the
"craving" to narrate.

Those who have not experienced neorealism's fervor through such
popular novels as Vittorini's *Men and Not Men* [*Uomini e no,* 1945] or
Ignazio Silone's precocious *Bread and Wine* [*Pane e vino,* 1937] have

perhaps seen it come alive on the screen in such emotional film classics as Vittorio De Sica's *The Bicycle Thief* [*Ladri di biciclette,* 1948] or Roberto Rossellini's *Rome, Open City* [*Roma, città aperta,* 1945].[2] Through these films and novels much can be learned of the grim truth of a divided wartime Italy and of the plight of the ordinary Italian caught up in the tragedy of war and the pain of postwar recovery. In fact, it is the humble working-class person who is often the protagonist of the new realism, and who, in *Open City,* for example, acts as a force for social change and an exemplum of the uncorrupted life to which postwar Italians aspired.

In both the literature and films it was a period of small heroes and high hopes. To correct the error of Fascism necessitated a return to basic values, to the essentials of right and wrong. To accomplish this, neorealistic writers, many of them Communists like Calvino, deliberately focused on the lives of simple folk and on the facts of their reality, however bleak or banal. Through grim chronicles of war, poverty, and suffering, they dramatized the disadvantaged, Partisan or peasant, whose elemental courage defined the meaning of honor. The result was a popular literature, designed for the people and written in an everyday language they would understand.

As has been related, American naturalist writers of the time often served as neorealism's models. Hemingway was singled out for his blunt, unsentimental prose. Faulkner was admired for his use of local characters and vernacular speech. Melville, Saroyan, and others were valued for their unaffected regionalism, their love of nature, or their devotion to society's little people.[3] To Italian writers like Vittorini and Calvino, these authors represented that American "reserve of natural vitality, an ideal battlefield for the contest between new stylistic inventions and academic traditions, between passions of weariness and fury and the weight of inveterate hypocrisies and morals" ("Currents" 5).

Calvino, then and later, was a man and a writer for his times. Neorealism suited him initially because, for other authors and himself, "the Resistance had been the formative experience" (*Path* 21). Nonetheless, like other writers in neorealism's eclectic circle, he had his own private agenda. His first works, including short stories and the novel *The Path to the Spiders' Nests,* were chiefly written in the neorealistic vein. Yet, even these initial stories reveal that, unlike some other Resistance chroniclers, Calvino had left the Partisan movement with mixed feelings. His Partisan background and his own love of epic adventure shaped the emplotment of many of his early tales, but did not always inspire them with an uplifting message. Later, the author's graver reflections would signal the demise of his season in neorealism.

Early on there were signs that Calvino was a writer at cross-purposes, though at the time he himself may not have realized it. Witness, for example, his eclectic tastes in literature, American or other. Here we see that his sensibilities are decidedly contradictory and vacillate between positive and negative poles. For example, in his later essay "Romanzo," he recalls his early admiration for nineteenth-century writers like Rudyard Kipling and Robert Louis Stevenson. For Calvino, their youthful heroes embodied a new dawn for mankind and evoked the "possibility of transforming every experience into a victory" (*Pietra* 30). At the opposite end of the spectrum, however, he was also drawn to authors whose heroes had far fewer noble illusions. The darker Hemingway hero was not without appeal even though the author skeptically saw him as a man who, for better or sometimes worse, "identifies himself through his actions" (*Pietra* 32). In Conrad (the subject of Calvino's university thesis) the author perceived yet another shadowy, but alluring, protagonist: a man caught between "two visions of chaos," his own inner uncertainty and his perception of an incomprehensible universe (*Pietra* 28).

Other diverse authors whose names, surprisingly, can be linked to early Calvino, include the already-mentioned Italian writer Carlo Collodi, author of the ambivalent fairy tale *Pinocchio*,[4] as well as Mark Twain, the cynical American creator of proletarian adventure yarns. Twain's misanthropic spokesperson Huck Finn, as well as his playful digressions in fantasy, particularly establish him as Calvino's early literary kin. It was Mark Twain's subversive *Adventures of Huckleberry Finn* that Calvino called "America's most authentic poem" (*Pietra* 31), and later Calvino would acknowledge Twain as his American role model.[5]

Calvino's youthful short stories date back to the end of the war when the author had barely left his life in the Resistance and the events of the Partisan struggle were still vivid in his mind. At that time he had just resumed his studies and was again a student at the University of Turin in the Faculty of Letters. Many of these early stories were printed in Communist publications like *Il Politecnico* or *L'Unità*. Some, written from 1945 to 1949, would eventually comprise his first short story collection, *Ultimo viene il corvo* [The Crow Comes Last, 1949]. Very much later, a selection of these narratives would be republished in English, in *Difficult Loves* (1984), the volume that is cited here.

It is worth digressing briefly to observe that *Difficult Loves* is not exclusively devoted to Calvino's neorealistic tales. Rather, it is an assortment of Calvino's writing from both the forties and fifties, loosely arranged into four separate sections: "Riviera Stories," "Wartime Stories," "Postwar Stories," and "Stories of Love and Loneliness." The last group, "Stories of Love and Loneliness," has no place in the present discussion because it belongs to the later Calvino and will be considered at length in the next chapter. "Riviera Stories" is also less relevant to conventional neorealism. Atypically, these tales do not dwell on war or politics but conjure up allusions to Calvino's childhood and to the Ligurian setting where he grew up. Furthermore, they rely heavily on make-believe and fanciful worlds which baffled early critics, who deemed them escapist.

One significant ingredient of neorealism *is* readily observed in "Riviera Stories," however, and that is the *fanciullo,* or "child." The child would be a dominant image in neorealistic literature (and films), as well as in early Calvino. To neorealism, the child symbolized all that was innocent and unsullied by war and thus heralded a brighter future to come. In the strongest tales from "Riviera Stories"—"Adam, One Afternoon," "The Enchanted Garden," "A Ship Loaded With Crabs," and "Big Fish, Little Fish"—all the protagonists are ingenuous youngsters, like those found in other of Calvino's early works, including his novel, *Path.*[6] With their mischievous, make-believe games, these wily urchins not only provide a glimpse of Calvino's brand of neorealism, but also an early sighting of his prototype character: a naive misfit who loquaciously spins Huck Finn yarns for the reader's amusement or who, like the misanthropic Pin in *Path,* suspiciously withdraws to a world of private fantasies.

Touching neorealism more closely, at least for their historical context, are Calvino's "Postwar Stories" that focus on the misery suffered by the populace during Italy's economic recovery. The best of these are two bittersweet tales: "Desire in November" ["Desiderio in novembre," 1946] and "Theft in a Pastry Shop" ["Furto in una pasticceria," 1946]. With deft wit "Theft" narrates a break-in at a bakery by three inept thieves who escape the police not as richer men, but happier for having stuffed themselves on sweets after long years of chronic hunger.[7] "Desire," on the other hand, describes the desperate postwar scramble for shelter, heat, and clothing and recounts one homeless man's amusing quest for some much-needed trousers. Broad humor relieves the melancholy of these two tales, foretelling of Calvino's taste for physical comedy. Later there will be bawdy laughter exploiting man's elemental functions, including eating and sex. Early suggestions here of ribald humor anticipate some of the funnier scenes in *Marcovaldo*, the fantasy trilogy, as well as the much later *If on a winter's night a traveler.*

Calvino's most powerful tales of this period are without doubt those called "Wartime Stories." These tales best reflect his own recollections of the Partisan movement and embrace what must cautiously be called the "classic" elements of neorealism. Some readily reveal Calvino's emerging doubts about the Partisan cause, while others still resound with a youthful enthusiasm that belies Calvino's ambivalence. Anthems of praise for the enemies of Fascism, these tales pay respect to the unsung warriors of a just and united anti-Fascist movement. The events are few, concentrating on the misfortunes of war and fundamental moral exigencies. Evil incarnate is the Fascist or Nazi enemy, while good is embodied in the mild but noble warriors who form a solid front in the anti-Fascist cause and who often sacrifice themselves for the common good.

Such a prototype tale is Calvino's "Hunger at Bévera" ["La fame a Bévera," 1946], which concerns the trials of a group of peasants in the Bévera valley who are caught in the cross fire between the Nazis and Allies during the stalled liberation of northern Italy (1944–45). Having come to the end of their food, the starving populace asks for volunteers who would risk the hazardous daily trip to nearby Ventimiglia for provisions. To their surprise, an impoverished old man named Bisma, who owns little more than a skinny old mule, volunteers for the job. With amazing cool he goes for food, confronts heavy shelling by the Nazis, feeds the citizenry, and eventually dies in a daring showdown with Mussolini's hated Black Brigade. Bisma is a hero of the least likely kind, an ordinary man who, by sacrificing himself for the group, portrays the highest ideals of Partisanship and personifies the ultimate neorealistic hero (*Difficult Loves* 79–86).

Another engrossing tale is "Fear on the Footpath" ["Paura sul sentiero," 1946], which recounts some anxious moments in the life of courageous young Binda, a courier for the Partisan First Battalion. It is his task, modest yet essential, to carry news on foot from one sequestered guerrilla band to another. He is good at his work, not only because he knows every stone and bush in the forest, but because he walks faster than anyone in the Partisan brigade. Binda's job, the story tells us, is lonely and difficult. Along the path, he faces a myriad of fears, some real like the German enemy, some as imaginary as the fairy-tale bogeymen from Binda's all-too-recent childhood. Despite his night terrors, he arrives in the next camp and finds himself safe at last among friends. "Comrades, of course; who could ever have thought they'd be anything else?" proclaims the story's final lines with a show of bravado and Partisan pride (78). Melodramatic as this ending is, the story succeeds, not simply because of its adventurous spirit, but because of its hero's unwavering faith in the Cause and in his confederates (*Difficult Loves* 71–78).

Not all of Calvino's "Wartime Stories" are as confident as the two above, however. Some, in fact, are uncommonly cynical for a young writer and they underscore the author's growing reservations about the Partisan movement, and neorealism. Counter to neorealism's optimistic coding, for example, is "Mine Field" ["Campo di mine," 1946], a tale in which a young man is fated for instant death when he resolves to cross a field of flowers known to be planted with mines (*Difficult Loves* 122–28). In "One of the Three Is Still Alive" ["Uno dei tre è ancora vivo," 1947], a nameless individual barely escapes being murdered by angry villagers who are indiscriminately seeking someone, anyone, to punish for the wartime atrocities that have been committed against them (*Difficult Loves* 102–11). True to neorealism, both stories focus on the little man and his grim wartime plight. On the other hand, both lack the warm sense of camaraderie and positive assurance associated with other neorealistic narratives, which, as Re observes, already possessed a prescribed rhetoric, one that "celebrated a heroic and necessary triumph of good over evil" (172).

Instead, whether Calvino consciously intended it or not, these last two tales, Hemingwayesque for their terse prose, stoic hero, and stark adventure, take a tentative step toward darker existential considerations, particularly the issue of man's alienation from his fellows. "Mine Field" underscores the protagonist's frightening isolation when, halfway into his trek, he reaches the point of no return. Knowing that he is completely at the mercy of circumstance, he suddenly realizes that "now there was nothing to do but continue climbing, at random, and let what would happen, happen" (126). Similarly alone is the naked and undaunted hero of "One of the Three Is Still Alive," who survives only by dint of his inordinate tenacity while fleeing enemies who ironically are his own countrymen. This last story in particular highlights what the young Calvino already perceives as the faltering boundaries between right and wrong in wartime and the inhumane traits of both victims and perpetrators.

Other stories illustrate even more concisely Calvino's paradoxical, but realistic, portrait of Partisan combat, as well as what Ferretti describes as the author's "cold acceptance of [wartime] violence and ruthlessness as inescapable necessity" (38). Take the example of "The Crow Comes Last" ["Ultimo viene il corvo," 1946], the title story from Calvino's first collection and the narrative often regarded as the masterpiece of his wartime short stories. In it, a cunning *fanciullo* joins a group of Partisans chiefly to play with their weapons. As it turns out, he is both an expert marksman and an indiscriminate shooter. Eventually, the men must relieve him of his gun because he is wasting ammunition and noisily calling attention to the guerrilla group's position. Annoyed but undaunted by his leader's reprimands, the young man subsequently rises early, steals a weapon, and departs on a shooting spree. Nothing escapes his certain aim: not frogs, not squirrels, nor even toadstools. Before long he attracts nearby enemy (German) soldiers, a situation that might unnerve even a veteran—but not the boy. Either he is too innocent to understand his predicament or too hardened to war and violent death to be intimidated.

The latter appears true for he soon engages in a cynical cat-and-mouse game with the enemy. In fact, as Olken rightly observes, he treats his new human quarry as casually as any other of his earlier targets (102). Cornering one specific German soldier, he toys with him cynically by handily picking off first his gilded uniform buttons, next his shoulder straps, and then the top of his helmet. At last, just as an ominous black crow swoops low over the scene, he delivers a stunning coup de grace, finishing off the enemy (now victim) with one well-placed bullet ironically directed at the eagle in the middle of the soldier's uniform. Again dramatized is the dubious morality of "honorable" war. Also introduced here, in the crow, is an arcane and typically Calvinian (and Conradian) allusion to destiny's dark side (*Difficult Loves* 95–101).

Perhaps a more compelling story than the last is "Going to Headquarters" ["Andato al comando," 1945], a tale that vacillates between modernist uncertainty and neorealistic lucidity, and thus in many ways foreshadows the author's transition from the forties to the fifties. As presented initially the situation and the characters are deceptively modest. The issues too at first seem simplistic, for the reader knows immediately who is supposed to be the hero and who is not, just as he would in an old-fashioned Western. The story concerns two nameless men winding their way through a forest. Even though they are countrymen, they are enemies: the armed man a Partisan, the other an unarmed Fascist informer who has been captured and is apparently being taken to guerrilla headquarters.

The events that follow are once again narrated with Hemingwayesque dispatch, swiftly and in short economical phrases, atypical of Italian prose before neorealism. The Partisan here is much like the Hemingway man about whom Calvino expressed mixed feelings.[8] He is a man of action, who sees his duty and does it without wavering or wasting time on words. Even in the first paragraph, the Partisan's grim resolve is apparent as he urges his prisoner on with the false promise that after only a short walk and a few brief questions the captive will be let go. The story's direction seems obvious, even formulaic. The day clearly belongs to the Partisan, who will see that justice is quickly served.

As the two men move ever deeper into the tangled, Dantesque wood, the reader, however, finds his sense of what is right suddenly inverted. Neorealistic convention ordains that the reader should look to the Partisan as his hero, but intuition tells him otherwise. It is after all the Fascist who is portrayed as the helpless, bewildered victim being led to slaughter, while it is the cool, uncaring, and, as is soon proven, lying Partisan whose stony silence conjures up malevolence. Furthermore, by supplying the reader with only the Fascist's tortured thoughts, and not those of the Partisan, the author contributes substantially to the story's ambivalence. Such role reversal serves as a beautiful dramatic ploy, forcing the reader to empathize with the villain.

As the distinction between hero and scoundrel blur, the reader finally and inevitably takes the informer's part, hoping confusedly for his getaway as he runs through the unending forest. But apparently this wood is not, after all, in the Dantesque model: a place where God's order holds sway and where redemption is possible. Rather, it is a modernist, Conradian jungle, straight out of *Heart of Darkness*. It is a forest of chaotic values, dark and unknown; it is a place where issues such as right and wrong fall prey both to capricious bullets and to the arbitrary laws of nature that, in the dramatic finale, reveal the spy's corpse covered with ants. This seems an apt resolution to a micro-drama that is at times broodingly modernist in its hedging over the order (or rather disorder) of circumstance (*Difficult Loves* 87–94).

It is a neorealistic tale too, perhaps, but one with the same contentious Calvinian twist, the same equivocation over moral issues, that will be seen again in Calvino's first novel. The charitable sentiments frequent to other neorealistic novels and films are again missing here, as is any confident homily that might tidy up the story's loose ends and assert the rightness of the Partisan cause. The Partisan hero of these last two tales is hardly of the proper neorealistic mettle either, for he is neither honorable nor well-intentioned. Nor does he receive the homage usually paid him in standard neorealistic stories, including some by Calvino himself.

Unexpectedly—and one questions with how much authorial forethought—shadowy leitmotivs creep into these early Calvino tales. Through indirect discourse, existential and ethical riddles are placed before the reader, questions are raised about the perplexing nature of right and wrong in wartime (or any time), about what Ferretti calls the author's "tragic and mysterious sense of existence," and finally about the meaning of life—and death (159). All of these themes will reoccur in future Calvino works, from the trilogy to *The Castle of Crossed Destinies*, from *The Path to the Spiders' Nests* to *Mr. Palomar*. In each instance, just as in this brief tale, these issues will help shape the nucleus of the author's metaphysical and ontological explorations.

It was through these first stories and his essays that Calvino came to the attention of prominent Italian authors Vittorini and Pavese, both of whom would be instrumental in fostering the author's career. Through them, Calvino was introduced to the inner circle of writers at Einaudi, an editorial house known then for its left-wing political activism. Because it was Pavese in particular who had encouraged Calvino to write a novel, it is not surprising that it was also he who personally presented the finished *Path to the Spiders' Nests* to Einaudi where it was subsequently published. The book dealt with the activities of the Resistance and recounted the apparent initiation of a boy named Pin into the Movement. The novel attracted much favorable attention and was praised as a model of neorealism by critics who, in those days, forgave its occasional drift from documentary to fable and who also overlooked the central figure's overt ambivalence toward the Partisan cause.

The conception, or perhaps "misconception," that *Path* was written purely as a vehicle for social or political discourse was in those days however, perfectly plausible, given the political climate and Calvino's emerging reputation as a left-wing writer, as well as the reader's customary expectations of the novel. As George Prince points out, the novel has, until this century, traditionally been associated with moral attitudes.[9] To understand what Prince means one need look no further than writers like Charles Dickens, Jane Austen, and even Calvino's own favorites,

Kipling and Stevenson, all of whose heroes resemble Calvino's young protagonist, at least superficially. In the novels of these authors, a rite of passage, as in what today is popularly called a bildungsroman, is often dramatized. Such works explore the trials of a youth growing up, trace his apprenticeship in living, and at the end show him fittingly integrated into his society. Granted its moralizing tendency, the bildungsroman appealed to the neorealistic canon. Indeed, Re tells us, neorealistic writers strove to emulate it, and through stories of individual wartime heroism, sought, with mixed success, to elevate the message of the Resistance to a universal plane.[10]

There was no reason, therefore, to expect that young Calvino's novel would be different from conventional expectations. Quite the contrary. He was writing at a crucial moment in Italian history, a moment exacting the drastic reform of a failed political system. Besides fiction, the author had already written political pieces for Communist publications. In these essays he advocated the cause of the little man and the establishment of a new society with civil equality for all. There was in fact every indication that, coming from an author known for his social commitment, *Path* was what it appeared to be at surface: a straightforward neorealistic drama, unabashedly propagandizing the heroics of the Partisan crusade against Fascism.

At first glance the novel supports this facile assumption. The story takes place typically enough during the dramatic final years of the Italian war (1943–45) when the Resistance was active against the Nazi occupation and when the general populace was suffering most acutely from deprivation. In like manner, the protagonist, Pin, also initially appears perfect in his role as a neorealistic hero. He is a sympathetic proletarian, an abused, impoverished *fanciullo* barely surviving in a small town on the Italian Riviera. His mother has been dead since he was little more than a baby and his father has not been seen for many years, having abandoned him to the care of a callous and indifferent older sister, a prostitute called La Nera.

Due to his unusual social circumstance, and particularly because of his sister's irregular occupation, Pin finds himself understandably alone, ostracized and desperate for affection. Adults harass him and other children are not allowed to play with that bad little boy. Unsupervised, he spends his days at the local tavern, wisecracking and singing bawdy songs, in the hope of winning approval from the drunks who frequent the place. Eventually, he is persuaded to steal a weapon from the German soldier who regularly beds his sister. But instead of surrendering the weapon to the needy Partisans as he originally promised, Pin secrets it away in a magical place in the forest known only to him, a "place where the spiders make their nests" (52).

It is during this forest interlude that the story suddenly and dramatically shifts from the neorealistic model and, for a time, goes on to indulge in childish make-believe quite reminiscent of Calvino's "Riviera Stories." Toying with the gun like a film hero, Pin pulls it from its holster waving it about. Now he too can cry, "'Forward, men!' as boys do when they play at pirates. But he cannot understand what pleasure those silly fools get in saying and doing that" (52). Much as Pin does not comprehend or like the ways of people and guns, he does envy them both their power. For him the gun is a talisman, a magic charm, that could earn him a place in adult society. This fantastical bent, coupled with the protagonist's open misanthropy, was clearly out of step with neorealism, but early readings of the novel overlooked these departures.

After serving a brief time in prison for stealing the German's gun, Pin escapes only to find himself destined for greater adventure in the company of a freedom fighter named Cousin. Through him Pin finds refuge in a Partisan encampment that in some ways romantically recalls the rustic life portrayed in *Treasure Island* but, in other ways, recalls the reality of Partisan existence: the bruised, bleeding feet, the body lice, and the hunger that Calvino himself personally endured (Camon 185). At this particular juncture, if the novel were to follow its rightful neorealistic course, Pin would accept the guidance of camp elders and would learn from them the rights and wrongs of his society. With his apprenticeship or rite of passage completed, he would be transformed into a man, in this instance, a Partisan. Once grown, he would no longer feel confused or alone but would share the company of other honorable men like himself. But, as is soon amply illustrated, that scenario never comes off in the novel, the author backing away from a conventional happy ending just as he had in certain of his short stories.

Try as he might, the novice author either stubbornly "would not" or else in good faith "could not" completely commit to the affirmative neorealistic model. Given *Path*'s waffling between fantasy and actuality, its lapses into oversentimentality, coupled with its irresolute conclusion, it appears that, to the author, "could not" was a very real issue. Although it seems unlikely that, with his novel, the green young writer intentionally set out to challenge convention, it is nonetheless evident today that, despite himself, he did precisely that.[11] Once begun, it is likely that the novel defied him, saying what it *would* say instead of what it *should* say. Calvino himself was the first to admit that, in any writer, there is frequently a difference between what the author intends and what he finally reveals.[12] *Path* no doubt is ultimately the product of just such a difference.

Even the work's smaller moments testify to the author's vacillation in the face of literary convention and Resistance propaganda. Bits of neo-realistic rhetoric are dutifully introduced into the novel, but are not always fully convincing. Efforts like these stand out from the pages, largely because their histrionics conflict with Calvino's usually economical and unaffected prose:

> The dreams of the partisans are short and rare, dreams born of nights of hunger, linked to food which is always scarce and always to be divided among so many; dreams about chewing bits of bread and putting them away in drawers. Stray dogs must have dreams like that, about gnawing bones and burying them. (109)

Melodrama here suggests a youthful author, straining conscientiously to adhere to contemporary literary and political custom. Another romantic moment suffices to illustrate the supreme effort made by the inexperienced author to write a bona fide neorealistic novel and to persuade the reader (and perhaps himself) of his unqualified partisanship:

> Pin has always wanted to set eyes on partisans. Now he is standing open-mouthed in the middle of the clearing in front of the hut, and no sooner has he begun staring at one of them than another two or three arrive, all looking different and all hung with weapons and machine-gun belts. (95)

Given the emotional tenor of the times, some critics reveled in the above sentimentality and went on to apply their own impassioned view of neorealism both to the novel and to its hapless hero. Rosengarten, for one, idealistically conceived that *Path* communicated "the idea that the Italian Resistance movement marked the birth of an era in which even the most degraded people of Italy were able at last to find a reason for being that transcended the brute struggle for survival, in which love and trust could overcome hatred and deceit" (225). Germana Pescio Bottino, impressed by the naive perspective of Calvino's central figure, was emphatic about Pin's optimistic role. In his character she identified a statement on the joys of nature and also saw a romantic warmth akin to Dickens's Pip in *Great Expectations*. Through Pip/Pin's childish eyes the world's vices were not only disclosed, but more importantly, his dreams revealed that faith in the world could be miraculously reborn (8–13).

Giuseppe Bonura also saw Pin, and subsequent youthful Calvino characters, as serving a "pedagogic function" within neorealism. Pin's naive worldview was interpreted as corrective, a symbolic affirmation of traditional morality. According to Bonura, it was through Pin and other youthful characters that Calvino, the author-tutor, led the reader along the path of life, paternally guiding him through encounters with a harsh reality and instructing him along the way on right and wrong.[13] Teacher, picaresque adventurer, and antihero, Pin meant many things, even to his own creator (see *Path* 17). Possessed of a deceptive, childish appeal, Pin retains meaning for today's reader, and is still perceived as serving an essential neorealistic role in Calvino, though perhaps not the positive one that early critics once saw.

Less prejudiced by the impassioned political temper of that time and favored by historical hindsight, today's critic sees the novel differently. Armed with a knowledge of Calvino's subsequent works, he or she is more reluctant to make conventional assumptions either about Calvino's unique brand of neorealism or about the role of his maverick character Pin within it. Today, in fact, Pin is more often regarded with the same cautious eye reserved for later Calvino characters. In the present view, his suspicious nature easily cancels the facile childish wisdom critics once attributed to him.[14] Even Calvino himself was less than heartening in his own later appraisal of Pin, sadly remarking that the boy's inability to fathom the war and the unreliable world of adults around him only mirrored his (the author's) own similarly confused state at that same time (*Path* 24).

It was Calvino himself, therefore, who established Pin as his less-than-positive alter ego, the naive witness not so much to Partisan convictions, as earlier thought, but rather to the author's growing misgivings—those political, but even more tellingly, those philosophical. Before very many years, in fact, political causes would pass out of the author's life forever, but not so the existential misgivings he had culled from those experiences. Pin's guarded response to the Other would linger, casting a shadow over the author's future protagonists. At work in *Path* was a spiritual uneasiness that was bound to undermine its hopeful message, whether political or metaphysical.

Too little has been said in past criticism about Pin's existential misgivings in *Path*, his so-called *alterità*, or "sense of estrangement"; it shall be expanded upon later in this chapter (Ferretti 39–45). But before touching on Calvino's philosophy, further clarification of the novel's political stance is merited, especially in light of the recent and substantive research that has been done in this area. Thanks to Lucia Re's critical study, *Path* today has at last been recognized as the politically subversive novel it really is. Calvino's failure to write a conventional neorealistic drama was certainly symptomatic of the reservations about the Resistance that troubled the novice writer, caught as he was like Pin between boyish good will and mature conjecture. Intentionally or not, in the novel these equivocations take on the shape of a political debate, one that goes beyond the usual Partisan tributes of the day in order to explore the morality of a movement in which, according to one character in the novel, it was sometimes difficult to distinguish the Partisans from Mussolini's Black Brigade (*Path* 140).

According to Re, the novel's political dialogue begins innocently enough but soon detours. She views both the name for Calvino's central character as well as the novel's fairy-tale formula as borrowed from Carlo Collodi's well-known fable *Pinocchio*. She further contends that in his work Calvino initially follows the "inner logic" of a "familiar fairy-tale plot structure" and by so doing "seduces" the unsuspecting reader into expecting a conventional Partisan drama (Re 205–6). Having established this predictable scenario, however, the author turns the tables on the reader, and, by juxtaposing the honest observations of Pin against the false fairy tales of Resistance literature, he prods at Partisan pretensions, ironizes the pat morality of the Resistance, and finally exposes the hypocrisies evident there (Re 169–75).[15]

To corroborate her observations, Re turns logically to the novel's actual events, where several large contradictions to neorealistic convention and early Calvino criticism come readily to light. For instance, in the novel there are really few examples of the noble Partisan role models that critics like Bonura thought they saw. Pin's principal friend, Cousin, in particular, is in no way the elder statesman Pin should emulate. Instead, he is a man driven by hatred, an indifferent, lone assassin who forages for enemy quarry, meting out his own private form of justice. Worse still, as one recent critic observes, at the novel's close Cousin has just murdered

Pin's sister, and, ironically enough, with the boy's own weapon. Within the norms of conventional neorealistic values, Cousin's integrity, either personal or political, is highly suspect (Benussi 8).

Another, more major contradiction to the earlier innocent presumptions about *Path*'s political agenda is the novel's questionable ending. When, in the last lines, the boy Pin goes off with the reprobate Cousin, "and they walk on, the big man and the child, into the night, amid the fireflies, holding each other by the hand" (185), Calvino has sabotaged the conventional happy ending (Re 310–12). He has thwarted the affirmative movement of the hero's rite of passage and actually jeopardized Pin's chances for a wholesome adult life. In making this untoward break with neorealistic rhetoric, the author (again, according to Re) has nonetheless ultimately accomplished a significant literary (and political) coup. Not only has he created in *Path* a new approach to the bildungsroman, one "far more flexible and 'dialogical'"(24), but he has also shaped a political image of the Resistance, that, while substantially less idealistic, is ultimately more valid (Re 257–60).

But this is not all that Calvino has wrought in the novel. Even without questioning Calvino's political motives, his first book raises doubts, not just about the Italian Resistance, but about the author's worldview as well. By undoing the hero's formative journey in the novel and particularly by tampering with the novel's conclusion, the author, whether he meant to or not, has held up to scrutiny not only Partisan politics but the behavior of mankind at large.[16] Something deeper than political misgivings had, after all, drawn the young writer to authors such as Conrad, Hemingway, and maverick storyteller Twain. None of these authors had shared Calvino's political experiences. Yet, whatever the diversity among them, they did share a strong sense of life's ironies, a mistrust of the herd mentality, and a certain existential uneasiness before the Other—the crucial issue now to be addressed.

From the existential point of view, Calvino's *Path*, in fact, often has more in common with Mark Twain's satirical *Huckleberry Finn* than with Collodi's *Pinocchio*. Although it is difficult to speculate about what the young Calvino thought then of Twain, the kinship uniting the two authors' protagonists and the social, moral, and narrative dilemmas the authors shared in writing their works is astonishing. In fact, comparing the two novels proves instructive, for it casts a different light on *Path*, one that focuses less on politics and more on the hazards faced by any writer (whether the youthful Calvino or the seasoned Twain) when he is eventually forced to choose between society's hypocrisies and the well-being of his prized protagonist.

Significant are the analogies to be drawn in the way Twain and Calvino carve their youthful heroes. Both Pin and Huck are primitives: crude and pathetic misfits who speak an inferior parlance and live on the ragged edge of society; both are orphans who have been mistreated and abandoned even by their closest family. Educated in misanthropy even before their stories open, they have consequently already learned that the Other is trouble, and have come to expect the worst from the counterfeit adults around them. This trait in the two characters bespeaks not of the enlightened and enlightening viewpoint of childhood that one sees in much literature, including neorealism, but instead postulates both central figures' existential alienation.[17] Indeed, given Pin's isolation in the novel, his conflict with what the author describes as the offensive world of humans, is it any wonder that Pin (like Huck) often seeks comfort in make-believe?

Fantasy, it has been said, is the simplest existential solution to the "I-thou" dilemma, or quandary of what to do about the unknowable Other.[18] In fact, philosopher Paul Tillich contends that fantasy constitutes the individual's major line of defense against threats from outer events, for it "shrinks" both the world and its society down to manageable size.[19] Both Pin and Huck intuitively share this fear of the Other as well as the remedy, freeing themselves when expedient from troublesome externals simply by fleeing to childish reverie. Huckleberry's escape takes the form of a romantic Mississippi raft trip that he thinks will make him feel less "cramped up and smothery" and more "free and easy."[20] Pin's fantasy focuses on the pistol and the power it will afford him. In dreams Pin finds a respite from the pain inflicted from without and, better still, enjoys a beguiling (and non-neorealistic) moment of self-validation in his own private dominion:

> So Pin decides that he will keep the pistol himself and not give it to anyone or tell anyone that he has it. He'll just hint that he possesses a terrible power, and everyone will obey him. Whoever owns a real pistol must be able to play wonderful games, games which no other boy has ever played. (51)

But of course Pin has deluded himself, as the author points out in the very next lines. Even his private fantasy offers him no measure of protection because Pin is not the kind of boy who knows how to play games, whether those of children or adults. In other words, because he is neither fish nor fowl, neither child nor adult, Pin like Huck, is the existential odd man out. He does not fit in society, nor will he ever, for in the novel, Calvino, for motives perhaps more personal and Twainian than political, has neglected to figure his growing up. Indeed, by portraying his central figure as antisocial, by painting black the society of adults, the author has rendered adulthood anathema.

This repudiation of adulthood by both Twain and Calvino constitutes a major narrative dilemma, one that inevitably threatens the resolution of both their novels. Endowed with a jocular sense of misanthropy, both writers had no doubt originally intended to use their naive characters playfully in order to bare society's pretensions. But the literary game got out of hand for both of them, not to mention for their protagonists. Huck's and Pin's separateness from society symbolically stands for their (and for their authors') firm resistance to the Other and to his deceitful community. Together the two characters defy what Huck cynically describes as that "dismal regular and decent" society that seeks to "sivilize" him (Twain 49) and what Pin sees as those dangerous and "untrustworthy" grown-ups (Path 50). So antagonistic are their authors to the corrupting forces of adulthood that, in an ironic twist, not growing up easily becomes the only morally appropriate conclusion to both books.

But children cannot stay children, at least not in historically linear novels like these, where growing up and accommodating are necessary. Both authors doubtless realized this truism, Twain quite painfully. Midway through Huckleberry Finn Twain understood that he had in fact written himself into a corner. Leaving Huck on the raft meant violating the novel's logical sequence; taking him off the raft meant surrendering him to the very same dissolute bourgeois values that he had, in the work, so roundly vilified. According to Peter Coveney, James L. Johnson, and other critics, once aware of this impasse, Twain's anguish was so acute that he had to put the novel aside for several years. In the end the author compromised, putting Huck ashore. This unholy submission to the Other made Twain forever unhappy with Huckleberry Finn. Yet, in his day and time, compliance with social and literary convention was the only reasonable recourse, if he were to publish the novel.[21]

Like Twain, Calvino too wanted to publish his novel, though we can only speculate how thoroughly he was aware of the quandary he had placed Pin in at novel's end. Allowing Pin to grow up in the keeping of Cousin, the symbol of all Calvino mistrusted in Partisan society, was unconscionable. This the youthful writer surely sensed, for he drew back just short of writing that conclusion. We therefore never do really see Pin complete his rite of passage into the suspect Partisan community, the author's concern for his small charge having rendered a conventional finish impossible. Nonetheless, like Twain, Calvino apparently still felt tied enough to traditional fiction to earnestly desire a serene resolution to the novel.

Caught between existential angst and happy endings, like his predecessor, the contemporary Calvino bowed but (unlike Twain) did not bend to convention. Less by plan, perhaps, and more by instinct, Calvino instead abandoned his small hero to the horns of his (the author's) own personal existential dilemma: poised on the outer edge of childhood and armed for the future with nothing more than trepidations and naive fantasy. This ambiguous fairy-tale ending settled neither Calvino's political conflicts nor his suspicions of the Other. Nonetheless it may well have been the only honest ending the novice author could write in the face of his own misgivings.

The Path to the Spiders' Nests merits the attention that has been devoted to it here, not because it is Calvino's best novel, but because it is his first, and as such marks the author's awakening both as a writer and a thinker. Through the novel he had grown much, even if Pin had not. In it, as in his short stories, many of the characteristics that distinguish him, both stylistically and thematically, appear in nascent form. At a thematic level it is evident that Calvino had already begun to reassess his youthful values, both existential and political. Politically, he had probably endured more disappointment as a Partisan than he was ready to admit openly in this first work. Obviously, his experiences with the freedom fighters (and those of Pin) had opened his eyes to the frailties of factional causes and had brought him to question the integrity of those who participate in them. Even though the reader should be careful not to go as far as one critic who recently dismissed *Path*'s ideology as "perfunctory,"[22] it is safe to say that the author's enthusiasm for left-wing causes, or political matters in general, from this point in time falters. This observation is amply born out by the fact that *Path*, for all practical purposes, was the first and only neorealistic novel that Calvino truly sought to publish.

At a more personal level, the seeds of Calvino's existential skepticism had clearly already taken root in this first novel. The injustice of war and the arbitrary violence and misuse of the individual had caused him to question, not only Pin's place in the world, but his own and other men's as well. Traditional values were at stake: the meaning of right and wrong was imperiled by the selfish, enigmatic workings of the Other and his private set of rules. Otherness, therefore, was already a dominant theme in *Path* and would remain so in Calvino's future works, as the author's search for a new literary and philosophical direction widened.

Although Calvino left this novel dangling (just as he would others), in *Path* he had nonetheless found his metier as a writer; he had discovered a way to explore the world of fiction and humankind. The dialectic discourse he had inadvertently initiated in *Path* would now become a conscious and deliberate modus operandi in his fiction. Time and again, the saga of the hero and his seemingly solid virtues would be pulled out and tested against the uncertain reality faced in today's life experience.

Furthermore, in Pin, Calvino had created a perfect foil for a decidedly contemporary rite of passage. He had found a naive rube who would explore this world and others more magical, in the author's stead. In future novels it would be precisely this bumpkin, this sometimes amusing, stargazing spectator, so reminiscent of Huck, who would face the whirl of events around him and interrogate man's choices in the inscrutable realm of the Other. It would be his task to engage the world in ironic dialogue, expose conventional fallacies, explore existence, and try to make sense of things. In the author's future works, however, "making sense" continued to be a stubborn dilemma while practical answers remained elusive.

3

MODERNIST TRAVELS

Calvino's *The Path to the Spiders' Nests* had breached the limits of conventional neorealism and revealed the author's faltering commitment to the left-wing movement. It was not that Calvino had abandoned the humanitarian causes neorealism espoused; it was that his hopes for implementing them politically had been sorely tried. Postwar events in Italy only confirmed what the author had already intuited in his first novel: his altruistic concern for the common good was not shared by all, not even by everyone in his own political party. The divisiveness among Italian Communist Party members, the aggressive actions of Soviet Russia in Eastern Europe—not to mention Party determination that literature be an instrument of propaganda—had disillusioned Calvino. Such unsettling circumstances shook the author's trust in a community built upon shared values and a common understanding of reality. It was apparent now that the fabric of life, the authenticity that he sought to discover through his work, would have to be found at a more personal level, in a domain less tethered to society and more connected to the private person.

This inward crusade would lead Calvino's writing of the fifties away from the solid ground of historical realism toward more speculative terrain, where his personal inner vision and acerbic sense of dark comedy found alternate and timely havens. One of the fictional arenas Calvino explored in this new decade is exemplified by tales from *The Watcher and Other Stories*, *Marcovaldo, or, The seasons in the city*, and "Stories of Love and Loneliness" from *Difficult Loves*. Fragmented, subjective narratives wanting for external action, many of these tales could be called "armchair dramas." Modernist in inclination, they contemplate the impermanence of contemporary Truth and meditate on what James McFarlane cites as "the breaking up and the progressive disintegration of those meticulously constructed 'systems' and 'types' and 'absolutes,' that lived on from the earlier years of the century."[1] Populated by the rejects of society, "the loner, the exile, the restless and rootless," the characters in these Calvino stories live out their static existences by ruminating obsessively over petty dreams and seeking escape in self-deception (McFarlane 82).

The fantasy trilogy, a second area of Calvino's writing during this time, is, by contrast, decidedly more animated and amusing. *The Cloven Viscount*, *The Baron in the Trees*, and *The Nonexistent Knight* also forsake realism, but in a different way than the modernist stories. Instead, they recount magical chivalric gestes that are imbedded with philosophical implications. At a deeper level, dialogically they address what Calvino calls "themes of incompleteness, bias, the lack of human fullness; . . . isolation, distance, difficulties in relationships with others," as well as the "awareness of being in the world and building one's own destiny, or lack of involvement altogether."[2] From these remarks, one readily sees that the thematic dynamics of the trilogy are scarcely dissimilar from those of the modernist stories described above.

Both of Calvino's chosen means to decamp literary verisimilitude, therefore, eminently suited the author's inquiring philosophical nature. For him the shift away from neorealism was undoubtedly a natural and welcome change. The enchanted "Riviera Stories" had already hinted at the author's taste for realms more fabulous than the actual; *Path* had alluded to Calvino's modernist talent for getting under the surface of events to follow the protagonist's personal narrative. Other early Calvino stories similarly reveal the author's desire to jettison what is "out there" for a look at the world within. Stifled by what he later called the "dead waters" of traditional realism with its predilection for facile plots and bathos, Calvino was clearly an author in transition, and already on his way toward new modes of literature (Calligaris 33).

Although some critics, like the earlier-mentioned Cecchi, perceived Calvino's new alternatives in writing as conflicted, the truth is that the author's dualistic fictional world was not as two-faced as it then seemed. True, the author was now writing across several genres, but significantly he was no longer writing at cross-purposes, as he had in the *Path*. Whether embroidering elaborate fables or spinning small private dreams, Calvino's fifties fiction was united—if not in style, then certainly in direction. Whether comical or sad, magical, or moodily pensive, all of Calvino's work now took an analytical look beneath exterior circumstance, examining not just the social issues involved but the philosophical as well; all emphatically probed the nature of man's being, soberly meditating on life's significance. This metaphysical inquiry would be as much a part of Calvino's fantasy trilogy (to be considered in the next chapter) as it was a part of the introspective personal dramas considered in the present one.

Today, hindsight confirms that such Calvino fifties tales as "Stories of Love and Loneliness," once mislabeled "realism," actually had little more in common with the "concrete" than did the author's fantasy novels. Instead, these curious slices of life correspond more pointedly to Malcolm Bradbury's useful definition of modernism in that they represent "less a style than a search for a style in a highly individualistic sense."[3] In other words, they are, as some recent critics observe, evolutionary tales, stories that mark one more step in what can now be easily recognized as the general dynamic of Calvino's work: its restless movement from the tangible to the abstract, or better said, from the mundane to the mythic.[4]

Almost without exception, these armchair travels—novellas including *Smog* and *The Watcher*, for example—rely on modernist storytelling practices. Their dependence on stream of consciousness, the seemingly unedited flow of the protagonist's thoughts, is paramount. Such disjointed outpourings fly in the face of realism's penchant for "fixed" characters and illustrate instead the modernist canon that human nature is "not to be contained," that it "instead is elusive, indeterminate, multiple, often implausible," and hence given to cognitive wanderings (McFarlane 81). Together these new Calvino characters ramble through their personal underworlds and postulate questions about the private whys and hows of humanity's earthly journey, finding answers that at worst are melancholy and at best amusingly ambivalent.

Multifaceted, as is all the author's work, these same narratives reveal not just the dark side of Calvino, but the lighter side as well. Shadowy, for instance, are the novellas *Smog, The Watcher, The Argentine Ant,* and *A Plunge into Real Estate* [*La speculazione edilizia,* 1957], all black comedies. Brooding meditations, they, and other stories to be named from *Difficult Loves,* inevitably focus on the inconsistencies of human reason and dramatize a hearty disregard for the usually tidy causal sequence to narrative events. In their modernist drive they aim at the "disestablishing of communal reality," and instead advance the validity of subjective fictions (Bradbury 27). In other words, they question the very premise of verity, challenging the reader to define it for him- or herself and to isolate whatever solid truth may be there.

Lighter, on the other hand, are the author's more sentimental tales, the whimsical Chaplinesque Marcovaldo stories, for example. These, and others we will look at, often still bear traces of a conventional, albeit sketchy, plot, and may even end on a tentatively upbeat note. But even these tales are polemical. Amusing though they are, they in no way subscribe to traditional humor. For example, Bergson's old-fashioned definition of comedy as indifferent, devoid of feeling, "a fringe of snow-white foam, feathery and frolicsome" finds no place even in Calvino's funniest stories. Nor does Bergson's conservative theory that the function of humor is socially remedial sit well with Calvino either.[5]

However funny the story is, discordant notes are not harmonized in Calvino the way they are in conventional comedy. All simply does not end well, because even Calvino's humor is never without its dark side. Farcical moments betray uneasy sentiments, gloomy life discrepancies that cloud the protagonist's peace of mind. Thus, laughter in Calvino often gives way to disillusionment when the reader comes face to face with the typically ambiguous posture of contemporary humor: that blend of comedy and pathos, of sad smiles and sobering afterthoughts.

Beginning with a seemingly simple tale from *Difficult Loves,* "The Adventure of a Bather" ["L'avventura di una bagnante," 1951], we see illustrated the equivocal nature of Calvino's humor, as well as certain existential undercurrents (197–208). The tale concerns Signora Isotta Barbarino who, amusingly enough, has suffered the misfortune of losing her bathing suit while swimming. Although it is still early in the day and there are plenty of bathers and boaters at the beach, given the awkwardness of her situation, she finds herself quite alone. Having just arrived at the seashore, she knows no one, nor does she see anyone nearby who inspires enough confidence to call for help. What is worse, modesty prevents her from raising a cry of distress or lifting herself out of the water to be seen. Fortunately she is a good swimmer and soon finds a nearby buoy that temporarily saves her from this embarrassing predicament.

Time passes as the reader follows the zigzag path of the water-logged protagonist's modernist life review. Subtly, but perceptively, both the sky and the story darken as the signora ponders not only her present dilemma, but her very existence as well. To her mind both situations are parallel: her nakedness and vulnerability in the water, her existential, naked defenselessness on shore. Here in the water, just as in life, there are others around her but none of them are trustworthy. Surmising her embarrassing situation, men in boats pass by, presumably to rescue her. But they are jesters and, as luck would have it, "her need for trust was met by these rising barriers of slyness and *double-entendre,* a hedge of piercing pupils, of incisors bared in ambiguous laughter, of oars pausing, suddenly interrogatory, on the surface of the water; and the only thing she could do was flee" (201–2).

At last, just when Signora Isotta is turning blue with cold and feeling deserted by the world, she is finally saved (205). For a few moments on the boat ride to shore she is able to warm herself both in the clothes her saviors have brought her and in the evanescent solidarity of their company. Thus ending on a cautious note, this early, seemingly innocent Calvino vignette is gently amusing yet quietly disconcerting. Beneath the surface of Signora Isotta's laughable situation lies a quandary more lasting than the loss of a swimsuit: namely, her existential frailty, her fear of exposure to the Other, of baring, not just her body, but her naked soul to those who may not comprehend her and whom she, in turn, does not comprehend. The lone individual, a society of one, is a late-modernist theme in the work of Calvino, who no doubt gained inspiration from other modernist characterizations, including some of his own earlier wartime figures. Bittersweet reflections on the loss of community and the isolation of the individual intrude in all Calvino's works from this decade, even those where one might expect humor emphatically to prevail: namely in the delightful, ever-popular collection *Marcovaldo, or, The seasons in the city.*

The first, and probably best of these stories, were written in the early fifties (1952–56), some appearing initially in serial form years before they were published together in one volume. They focus on the life of an unskilled laborer, Marcovaldo, whose name Calvino has ironically borrowed from Italian Renaissance epic literature.[6] Like many Italian workers of the fifties, Marcovaldo is hardly a hero. Rather he is a modern-day migrant, at heart a small-town rustic living awkwardly in the big city where he hopes to better himself and his family. Like most Calvino characters since Pin, he is an existential misfit, a "man-boy" (as Calvino characters have been called) whose limited childlike worldview clearly separates him from others (Bonura 136–37). Despite his chivalric name with its allusions to grand deeds, he is at bottom not one of life's doers but a typical Calvino spectator, a solitary observer who tentatively tests his simple dreams only to see them come to naught in the indifference of the city's cement jungle.

At the time of their writing, the motivations behind the Marcovaldo stories were surely not without social import. Through humor Calvino meant to expose the predicament of the Italian working class of the fifties, those who toiled in the cold impervious cities of northern Italy only to be discriminated against financially and socially. He also undoubtedly meant to examine, through his protagonist's eyes, the changing rapport between man and nature in our epoch of environmental abuses. Today, however, the Marcovaldo stories survive not just because of the topical relevance they enjoyed during a given moment in Italian history, but because of their larger contemporary and philosophical significance.

Marcovaldo, like his prototype in Chaplin, is a twentieth-century archetypal comic figure not entirely different from some seen in present-day novels (and films).[7] Plucky but ineffectual, he personifies the paradoxical role of today's dark-comic hero. His humor, always a mixture of pratfalls and pathos, directly evokes Chaplin's "little fellow,"[8] and inevitably elicits a dual response from the reader when initial laughter at his antics falls prey to the misgivings associated with his small but tragic disappointments. Humor mixed with pain always places extra demands on the reader because it forces him to reflect more seriously on the character's plight than he might care to. Too often and too uncomfortably, the reader sees Marcovaldo precipitously poised on the edge of some trivial disaster, a beggar snatching at scraps of happiness, an innocent who falls victim to sudden reversals whenever his slim fantasies collide with the larger indecipherable events around him.

One example of such an ignoble defeat occurs in the very first story, "Mushrooms in the City" ["Funghi in città"]. Here one quickly sees how ill-suited this perpetual adolescent is to life in today's urban world. It is a pleasant day and, while waiting for the tram that takes him daily to his dreary job, Marcovaldo, ever on the lookout for some relief from the dismal world around him, suddenly spies beneath him an unexpected delicacy perfect for his meager dinner table. So hopeful is he that while "Bending to tie his shoes, he took a better look: they were mushrooms, real mushrooms, sprouting right in the heart of the city!" (2). Unable to contain his childlike glee, he unwisely lets the news slip to both family and passersby. The end result is that he, his family and his neighbors eat the toadstools only to finish in the hospital emergency room having the toxic remains pumped from their stomachs. This story is clearly one of Calvino's most gently humorous; others, however, are significantly more poignant.

For example, the later and decidedly more Chaplinesque "City Lost in the Snow" ["La città smarrita nella neve"] finds Marcovaldo at work shoveling snow for his employer, yet somehow managing to make fun out of this tedious job. First, he challenges the city shovelers to a silent contest to see whether their street or his sidewalk will be the snow's final resting place. Next, from a snow bank he fashions an auto that in turn is momentarily mistaken for the real thing when his nearsighted director tries to get into it. At story's end he is himself literally buried in an avalanche falling from the roof and is subsequently mistaken by children for a snowman. An untimely sneeze clears him and the courtyard of snow, destroying his magic realm instantly. A forlorn reality intrudes, when "to his gaze there appeared [once more] the familiar courtyard, the gray walls, the boxes from the warehouse, the things of every day, sharp and hostile" (20). Lest the reader laugh too comfortably here, the author, in a typical Calvinian touch, has deliberately sabotaged the happy ending, reminding the reader that reality is probably less the stuff of dreams than of disappointments.

In another story, "A Journey with the Cows" ["Un viaggio con le mucche"], the reader is first amused by the opening scene, which finds Marcovaldo sweaty and sandwiched in one bed with his wife and children, and then disconcerted when confronted by the character's dire poverty and sleepless speculations. His debts, the weight of his large family, and the meagerness of his salary are misfortunes that precipitate the chronic insomnia of this touching figure and that feed his desire for the solitude of dreams. Indeed, the more one reads of Marcovaldo's crowded family, the more one is struck by his loneliness and emotional distance from wife and children. Underscoring this remoteness are the strangely empty cityscapes, the fragmented modernist world in which we frequently find him. The tortured nocturnal vigils, punctuated by night sounds, "the whistle of someone who felt alone," only serve to delineate more sharply the character's modernist estrangement from an industrial society in which he, despite his best efforts, invariably finds himself a trespasser (45).

Perhaps the story that best sums up Marcovaldo's losing battle with the transitory world around him is "Park-Bench Vacation" ["La villeggiatura in panchina"] wherein late one night he abandons his hot apartment in order to catch a breath of fresh air, a glimpse of nature, and a restful sleep on a park bench. As ever in his adventures, even these modest plans are thwarted by man, machines, and nature itself. A lovers' quarrel, garbage trucks rumbling, fountains bubbling, and finally chirping birds keep him from a well-deserved night's rest. This wakeful night, however, does afford our frail eyewitness (and the reader) food for thought, when in a pensive, philosophical moment, this small, solitary figure pauses to gaze at and compare the moon to a nearby traffic light. "The light flashed yellow, yellow, yellow, constantly blinking on and off," reminding Marcovaldo of the incessant grind of his daily life (7). The moon is another constant light, but her pallid color affords no better sense of well-being, as she too is aloof and inexplicable, representing a higher order, more remote and even less knowable than the mechanical contrivances around him. Characteristically for Calvino, the tale ends on an inquiring note, questioning the means of coping with the enigma of life and with the Other, whether earthly or celestial.

Ultimately armed only with his bewilderment, Marcovaldo can boast of two diametrically opposed choices for living, both of which highlight a well-known existential dichotomy. His first option is to put aside his existential ignorance and hurl himself into life's fray in the courageous Promethean stance once advocated by philosopher Jean-Paul Sartre.[9] His second option is simply to endure: to suffer stoically and silently the global confusion around him in the posture of what philosophers today refer to as "the existential Job."[10] True to his ambivalent portraiture, Marcovaldo tests both choices, but with contrary results. From the standpoint of laughter, his humor obviously springs from the absurdity of his Chaplinesque, little Promethean stance. His foolish exploits—his mushroom farming and snow shoveling—like Chaplin's frequent misadventures, afford a welcome relief from the angst that often accompanies larger existential decisions.

But laughter is not all there is to this slight, pathetic figure. Also sadly lurking within Marcovaldo is much of the makings of the modern Job—enough anyway to recall clearly characters from any one of Samuel Beckett's tragicomedies, but especially Vladimir and Estragon, who would patiently spend eternity "waiting for Godot." In the absence of final answers, Marcovaldo, like these two well-known theatrical characters, must content himself with losing battles and rely childishly on magical thinking and petty fantasy for spiritual nourishment and deliverance.[11] Whether these fancies involve camping on park benches or making snowmen, Marcovaldo would (like Pin) sooner trust his meager, unrealized dreams than face the impersonal absurdity of the alien reality about him. Such an emphasis on "small worlds" in Marcovaldo and in much of today's literature, philosophers tell us, bespeaks of twentieth-century man's insecurity within his universe and of his hesitancy to come to grips with issues outside of his own limited sphere. This reluctance, so apparent in the abbreviated vision of Marcovaldo, and in other characters we meet in Calvino, carries with it the subtle implication that the dynamics of life, its big picture, are no longer within human grasp.[12]

Turning now to some of the darker Calvino stories of this decade reinforces the portrait of the modern individual uprooted from community, alone and defenseless. Enhancing the sense of displacement in these tales is the frequent abandonment of the traditional fictional markers so essential to the grounding of conventional realism. Names, times, and locales now often fall by the wayside in what Ihab Hassan characterizes as "the modernist assault on forms."[13] An existential wasteland opens before the reader's eyes, foreign, frightening, and often inhabited only by anonymous figures. Unlike the gentle humor of the Marcovaldo cycle, these darker tales are laced with heavy irony, representing moments in Calvino where humor is eclipsed in shadows.

In this black comedy we most emphatically see the mutuality of spirit and direction that Calvino shares with Conrad and Beckett, modernist and late-modernist writers who, like Calvino, perceive reality as anything but solid and who contest the sacredness of transcendental Truth. It is Conrad's sense of the "dreamlike unreality of experience"[14] and

Beckett's "metaphysical clowns. . . . cripples, impotents" we now often encounter in Calvino's delusional characters (Hassan 217). Splintered are the dreams of the naive rube once named Pin, changed is his visage as, older and less hopeful, introverted and alone, he examines his uncertain existence through dreary and depressing diatribes. Selfishness and self-deception are just some of the unfortunate traits multiplying in the existentially crippled characters we next meet. All of these are individuals who find themselves lost to a modernist sense of the "power of unreason" (Bradbury 41). Firm truths no longer their option, they go it alone, curtailing their outer lives in order to preserve the few scanty private illusions left to them.

In the very early "Adventure of a Soldier" ["L'avventura di un soldato," 1949], we already see a shadowy Calvino figure materialize (*Difficult Loves* 185–96). Here we encounter nothing of the war or neorealism, but only Private Tomagra, a lowly young infantryman on leave and traveling by rail. On the train, a lady dressed in black, apparently a widow, enters his compartment and sits down right next to him even though there are other spaces available. To Tomagra, whose imagination is richer than his impoverished life, this simple gesture on the lady's part is provocative. Appraising her physicality, he finds her not unappealing despite her square, rather matronly frame and unexpressive face. With some trepidation, he decides to look into an opportunity for a fleeting dalliance. Almost as if they had a life and mind of their own, his legs first and then his hands tentatively span out to explore the presence so close to him and yet so far away.

First he tries a simple ruse, merely grazing the lady's nearby leg with his. Next, he tries to communicate with her wordlessly by tapping his calf against hers. Although these acts elicit no response from the widow, Tomagra, caught up in his own fancy, is encouraged and decides on more audacious action. Keeping his hand in the pocket near her, he hesitantly examines the lady's thigh through layers of garments. Pretending to be asleep, he then lets his hand fall casually (and presumably by accident) on the lady's knee. Interpreting the lady's lack of objection as compliance, the ludicrous one-sided sexual play goes forward until the inevitable moment when, in a darkened tunnel, the seduction arguably becomes a fait accompli. Although the lady herself remains inert beneath him, Private Tomagra is pleased with himself and with his conquest. Even while he perceives himself as no more than a coarse and unworthy nobody in the world, here at last in matters of *amore* he has surpassed himself, or has he?

What indeed is to be assumed from the events of this bleak comedy? One superficial but valid reading suggests that the story is simply a silly spoof, a demystification, of the cliche image of the Latin lover. The objectification of the female supports this observation, indicting Tomagra for emotional impotence. A second possible reading, however, hones in on the barrenness of existential relationships in general and further reveals that even the youthful Calvino possessed a gift for presenting the reader with several options to understanding any story: the surface events as well as various subtexts. For example, could it be that within the story's fiction there is no action and no Other? Could it be that the incident takes place only within the imagination of one emotionally starved and vacuous individual?

Given the mechanical depiction of the events and the fact that the author has seen fit to strip the lady both of her person and conversation, this last explanation seems as likely as any other. If the circumstances are indeed as illusory as implied, then the reader has met here an early example of those Calvino characters who, according to the author, portray contemporary man, the spiritual cripple bereft of human integrity.[15] Like Tomagra, such personalities are dreamers who, out of fear of community, feed on make-believe, substituting private truths and small worlds for whatever reality may be out there. Unlike the amiable Marcovaldo, these quirky introverts, more often than not, deliberately choose to avoid involvement, preferring instead the safe haven of what one critic aptly calls Calvino's "inner landscape" (Ricci *Games* 106).

In "The Adventure of a Reader," ["L'avventura di un lettore," 1958], we encounter a second elusive personality, Amedeo Oliva (*Difficult Loves* 254–71). He, like Tomagra, is also burdened by egocentrism and emotional impotence. As the story opens, he has found an isolated spot at the seaside with the express intention of ignoring the world by reading. Before relaxing he goes through an inordinate amount of carefully outlined preparation, signaling the reader that both character and writer love details, and that Amedeo is a compulsive individual given to inflexible and ritualistic behavior. After checking the wind velocity, meticulously folding his clothes and blowing up his beach cushion, he is finally ready to get down to serious business, books being the occupation he prefers to other more Promethean endeavors:

For some time Amedeo had tended to reduce his participation in active life to the minimum. Not that he didn't like action: on the contrary, love of action nourished his whole character, all his tastes; and yet, from one year to the next, the yearning to be someone who did things declined, declined, until he wondered if he had ever really harbored that yearning. (256)

Amedeo's aversion to active life apparently extends itself to involvement with people as well. Spying a lone, attractive woman on the beach and finding her appealing, he nonetheless initially decides not to speak to her. Speaking to her could mean a romantic tryst. That possibility, weighed against the chance of a interminably boring evening filled with mundane talk, makes him decide to go on reading—but not for long.

Though choosing not to admit it, Amedeo is drawn to the lady and all his protestations are lies designed to defend himself from anything more than cursory entanglements. Before long, despite himself, he arranges to meet and speak to the woman, but (as he allows) only out of common courtesy. A little later he swims with her, but (according to him) not because he wants to, only because he would have gone for a swim anyway. After the swim he joins her on her beach mattress, but warns her that he is there only to read. Eventually, he seduces the lady too, not out of healthy passion, but because he deems it inescapable. The conclusion finds Amedeo as practical as ever. During love's embrace, he strategically manages to free one hand in order to place a bookmark at the spot where he left off reading. After all, "nothing is more irritating when you're eager to resume reading than to have to search through the book, unable to find your place" (270).

The snigger provoked by this farce in no way endears the central character to the reader. Amedeo is not Marcovaldo; the author has seen to it. Calvino's ironic humor here has capitalized, not on pipe dreams gone awry, but on the character's neuroticisms. Amedeo's fears and self-deceit account for a goodly share of the grim humor the story evokes. In the eye of the writer, Amedeo is a pathetic figure who has acted in bad faith. Shut off from human warmth, like the earlier Tomagra, he plays the observer even during moments of life's greatest intimacy. Once again, there is little rapport between him and the other character. Instead, events move mechanically, as if they were furtive dreams taking place only in the privacy of the protagonist's mind.

Many of these issues above are reiterated when examining the selfish behavior of Quinto Anfossi in *A Plunge into Real Estate*. A self-styled speculator, Quinto foolishly believes that he can combine two diametrically opposed facets of his life: his Communist affiliation and his capitalist aspirations. Sacrificing a piece of family land in his native Liguria in order to erect high-rise apartments means paying back taxes, but it also happily means making a quick profit in the bargain. Never mind that in reality Quinto knows nothing of the machinations of business, that the deal struck with an unprincipled builder clearly spells anguish for his family, and that the new building goes against his own highminded contempt for "the fever of cement taking over the Riviera."[16]

Putting aside his scruples, Quinto soon becomes embroiled in a losing situation. Caught up in legal tangles, conspiracies, personal animosities, and his own paranoia, he finally flees the scene. Shifting his attentions to other frivolous projects, he hides away in Milan and elsewhere, disassociating himself from a repugnant reality, blaming others for his own bad judgment, and shamefully abandoning the messy business details to the person least equipped to handle them: his naive and aged mother. In this story, side by side with an indictment of capitalistic exploitation, Calvino offers the reader another sad example of modern man's inadequacy both to himself and to others.

In this ironic tale, as in other stories yet to be discussed, one observes an ever-widening distance between the central figure and his surroundings. His role as an onlooker has ostracized him from the society of the Other, exemplifying one of the more negative aspects of the modern existential situation. We see these same attributes in all of the author's passionless protagonists. Increasingly prevalent within them is an aversion to (or perhaps fear of) intimacy, the strong repression of emotion, and an aloofness that finally and definitively separates Calvino's youthful idea of humankind from his later cynicism.

Turning now to the author's three important novellas from *The Watcher and Other Stories*, one encounters again, particularly in *Smog*, another unsympathetic persona, his psychic situation worse than that of the others described earlier. So acute this time is the estrangement of the narrative's central figure that he is distanced not only from his peers, but from the reader as well, who never even learns his name. In retrospect, the gentle cordiality of Marcovaldo now suddenly appears no more than an agreeable memory. Instead, in *Smog*, one of the author's darkest comedies, a now-familiar Calvino character reemerges, a protagonist who epitomizes Franz Kuna's description of the Conrad man, that isolated individual caught up in "the irreconcilable antagonism between egoism, the moving force of the world, and altruism, its essential [assumed] morality."[17]

As the title suggests, the story is supposed to be about the perils of smog. The narrator, managing editor for an ecological magazine titled *Purification,* has observed firsthand the grievous effects of pollution and indeed has done research to inform himself more precisely of its evils. The reader might then assume him to be an activist in the humanitarian campaign for a cleaner environment, but such is not the case. Missing in the storyteller is any sense of goodwill or commitment to a cause. Instead, as is true in all Calvino's more compelling modernist tales, there remains a cowardly gap between the narrator's apparent intentions and his sullen, isolated behavior. Stripped of Marcovaldo's better intentions, this narrator, even at the start, perceives the ecological predicament as hopeless and retreats apathetically to his own superficial and self-absorbed world.

External events are mostly suppressed, the story instead focusing on the narrator's erratic modernist monologue, a discourse that the reader soon fears borders on insanity. In the first pages one learns most of what little there is to know of him: namely, that he really does not "give a damn about anything" (77) and that he has no wish to be well-established either in his new job or in the unidentified, smoggy, industrial city in which he has chosen to live. The new city for him is nothing more than a train station, the job for *Purification* generic, and home is merely a sparsely furnished room (77). Dominating his life is the symptom of a serious mental disorder: an obsessive-compulsive need to wash his hands incessantly (78–85).

In fact, all the circumstances of the character's existence revolve around this hand-washing ritual. Whether at home or at work, things are not different: dust and smog, real or imagined, cloud his surroundings, his thoughts, and his personal relationships. At work, he faces so many dusty papers that he feels constantly impelled to wash. At home, he spends hours secluded in his room unable to read because he dare not touch his books. Books collect too much dust and each reading means going back to the basin to wash his hands. Indeed, it is only after washing them that he feels in control again, as if he has "regained the use of them" (86).

His personal relationships are as murky as the atmosphere he lives in.

Appropriate to his "small world" lifestyle is his one-sided rapport with his deaf landlady who requires no words from him because she can barely hear. More provocative, however, are his associations with other males who, at minimum, require his acknowledgement and who, at times, unfortunately force him to face those unpleasant disparities in life that he so studiously seeks to avoid. Personifying the horns of the city's pollution dilemma, for example, is the narrator's duplicitous boss, who, paradoxically, is both the owner of *Purification* and one of the industrial magnates most responsible for the smog in the first place. Also awkward for the storyteller is his friendship with a Communist activist who makes it his irksome duty to remind the protagonist of his civic responsibilities.

But the most problematic relationship in the narrator's life is that with his mistress, Claudia, who, like some other female portraits in Calvino, touches a misogynistic chord. Through no fault of their own, Calvino's female characters often represent a troublesome Other. To the narrator, Claudia is a contradictory and most unknowable quantity, in that, more than any other person, she personifies the threat posed by close, human bonds. In fact, the love-hate relationship he shares with her dramatizes his childishly impotent and dishonest rapport with the whole world. A fearful threat to his insulated ego is the intimacy he shares with her, a liaison that he (recalling Amedeo in "Adventure of a Reader") feels he can only justify by self-deception, passing off a moment of sexual passion as a supremely humanitarian sacrifice:

> her skin was smooth, cool, undefiled; and as I saw in the lamp's cone of light a little shower of dust specks floating in the air, soon to be deposited also on Claudia, I threw myself upon her in an embrace which was chiefly a way of covering her, of taking all the dust upon myself so that she would be safe from it. *(113)*

The reader smiles, but ruefully, at the narrator's perverted account of his love tryst, a misrepresentation so implausible as to undermine once and for all the storyteller's credibility. Dubious at best are the "facts" of the fiction as narrated by this obsessive personality, and they are clearly to be taken with a strong dose of doubt. Early critics who complacently read *Smog* for its "moral tone" were surely substituting their own personal, social program for the author's decidedly more uncertain agenda.[18] The truth is that while *Smog* does provide commentary on one of society's very real ecological dilemmas, it does not pontificate. In fact, judging from the story's satiric twist, the fifties Calvino is suspicious of "good causes," viewing with caution both moral crusades and their perpetrators.

For Calvino, the story's focus is not merely on social issues, but on the exploration of one more impaired spirit, and his "befogged," but, perhaps for Calvino, not entirely invalid perception of life. This darkly drawn clown, like other Calvino characters, including Marcovaldo, has the same two opposing choices: he can do battle against life's inconsistencies as would the Conrad man, or else he can withdraw. Having rejected Conradian virility outright this time, the hero's tale simply trails off vaguely, while he waits patiently as the existential Job for life to unfold around and without him. This apathetic resolution typifies the ultimate direction of Calvino's modernist short stories, thus marking the author's own recalcitrant withdrawal from the literature of social engagement, toward a more remote philosophical surveillance of the passing scene.

A second novella, *The Watcher*, finished later (1963), but appropriately placed by the author in the same collection with *Smog*, substantiates the author's existential misgivings, his growing conviction of life's melancholy Beckettian cast. Even though this tale is tangibly more realistic than *Smog* in its wealth of practical details, it is modernist in other more significant ways. Once again, the story concentrates on a single center of consciousness, using interior monologue to minimize, or at least mask, authorial intrusion. It concentrates on what Charles Newman describes as the modernist "certitude of despair," at times tacitly suggesting that art may be the last and only bastion of morality.[19] More openly philosophical than *Smog*, this story directly poses certain key Beckettian questions such as "What is existence? or, What is Man?"[20]

Probably inspired by the author's personal experience, the story revolves around a day in the life of a Communist poll watcher, Amerigo Ormea.[21] Not the crusading political activist he once was, Amerigo is a bit skeptical about the day ahead of him, a day to be spent monitoring the voting at Cottolengo, a Turin institution for the physically and mentally handicapped. Nonetheless, when he receives his Party's call, he dutifully takes on the task. Once there, however, he plays little or no active role in the day's proceedings. The bickering among the other poll watchers and the blatant voter fraud he observes are repugnant to him, but they fail to engage him passionately. Several dull telephone conversations with his mistress produce the same wary response toward women as seen in other of Calvino's male protagonists. Yet, even in the face of these many annoying distractions, he strives to keep to himself. More than any other character, Amerigo the "watcher" personifies the Calvinian Everyman, the existential Job, awash in thought, waiting, looking, but inevitably failing to act.

The voters—deaf mutes, idiots, and even the comatose—all pass under Amerigo's incredulous gaze. The result is a circus parade of sorts, a spectacle of freaks and monsters who (at Mother Superior's insistence) "vote" with mouths ajar, eyes staring, and strange gasps and whistles emanating from their throats. A cruel comedy is this one, unabashedly evoking certain Beckettian figures, in particular that author's character, the Unnamable, who passively spends his life living in a jar.[22] Occasional uneasy giggles are elicited from the reader, even as the author deftly draws comparisons between those empty Cottolengo lives and Amerigo's own (31–35).

At first Amerigo is unaware of these parallels, fancying himself lucky to be "different" from the unfortunate inmates he meets that day at the asylum. But as the day wears on, both he and the reader come to question whether in fact he actually *is* different. From exposure to bits and pieces of his private life away from the hospital and his noncommittal rapport with his mistress, we soon learn that Amerigo is as crippled spiritually as the inmates are physically. Fearfully, he moves through life as a cautious stranger, isolating himself from contact and keeping a safe space between himself and the others. Even in matters of love, Amerigo (like Calvino's other watchers) tactfully limits his involvement by way of the now-familiar "small world" expediency. Accordingly, he sorts out the different bits and pieces of his life and carefully places them in small, manageable, but separate parcels.

Unlike the protagonist in *Smog*, however, Amerigo, despite himself, is suddenly seized by flashes of disquiet that ultimately find expression in the stark comparison he is finally forced to make between the rest of humanity and the Cottolengo residents. What have we, he finally cautiously asks, that makes us superior to these maimed individuals? "Limbs a bit better turned, a somewhat better proportion in our appearance, a somewhat greater capacity for co-ordinating sensations and thoughts . . . not much, compared to the many things that neither we nor they manage to do or know . . . not much, compared to our presumption that we can construct our history . . ." (37).

Having asked these painful questions and found no response within him that is not overwhelming, he suddenly feels "the vanity of everything yawning at his feet. Was this what they called a `religious crisis'?" (38), he asks himself. Trapped within his fear, Amerigo is figuratively reduced (like Beckett's Unnamable) to a pair of eyes, peering stupidly at the world without. He has come close, too close, to recognizing the emptiness of his existence, toward weighing its futility and wondering at the barrenness of life. He has also come closer than other Calvino watchers toward penetrating the thin crust of the author's dark comedy, to reveal a Beckettian cosmos in which man's birth is "his tragedy and his sin" (Jacobsen 105). The day done, his metaphysical imbroglio narrowly averted, Amerigo, like a child, crawls back into the shell of his small world, hopefully to think no more about it.

Not so the author, who will never retreat, but rather will pursue this so-called religious crisis throughout his literary career. Although it is also true that *The Watcher* directly assails the misguided direction of the Communist Party in 1950s Italy, this topical issue ultimately has less relevance today than the metaphysical questions Calvino raises here. Of more lasting significance in the author are the somber Beckettian questions that the novella poses regarding "the possibility that Cottolengo might be the only possible world," and that any man or woman may be just one more of its maimed, incoherent, fearful, and wretched residents (23).

The Argentine Ant, the final, but earliest-written, of the three tales collected in *The Watcher,* is perhaps the most innovative. In this story the author explores another Cottolengo world, this time a nightmarish Kafkaesque realm that, by its merger of two distinct and separate worlds—reality and science fiction—anticipates Calvino's postmodern work of the following decade. With unseemly tranquillity, the author interjects the bizarre into day-to-day events, pitting the possible against the impossible in order to create an otherworld faraway yet dangerously near. "Hideously funny" are the apt words that Gore Vidal chose to describe this dark comedy wherein even at the start the reader has few illusions about the gloomy fate of its protagonists.[23]

In fact, hope is extinguished at once in the story's opening lines, which already hint at an arcane menace waiting to strike the storyteller and his family in the new land to which they have just immigrated:

When we came to settle here we did not know about the ants.
We'd be all right here, it seemed that day; the sky and green looked

*bright, too bright, perhaps, for the worries we had, my wife and I—
how could we have guessed about the ants? (141)*

The storyteller's submissive tone uneasily coupled with a subtle un-
dercurrent of danger is characteristically Kafkaesque. Ominous, too, is
the storyteller's feeble attempt to reassure himself that, despite the ants,
"We'd be all right here," only to follow that statement with his curious
observation of the sinister sky. The hallucinatory "too bright sky" effectively cancels any notion that things are all right, creating a setting for
the supernatural. Banal narration inappropriately juxtaposed against bizarre events puts the reader on edge. As in Kafka, the confrontation of
such disparities serves to heighten suspense and drive home a sense of
fatality.

The story events unfold relentlessly, offering no chance of deliverance
from misfortune. The narrator and his small family have come to this
place seeking a fresh start and an end to their poverty only to find themselves victimized by an absurdly small, but implacable foe. Ants, the
couple learns, are everywhere in their home: on the walls, in the kitchen
sink, in the bed, on the food, and even in the baby's ears. They are beyond
extermination, as testified by the maniacal efforts that the neighbors
have already made to stem the invasion. All manner of poisons and
strange contraptions are meticulously described in order to underscore
the hopeless lengths to which the local population has gone to rid themselves of this relentless evil. All is to no avail: the ants are a force beyond
human reason, an otherworld incursion into the mundane business of
reality.

This unreasonable force is finally made flesh by Signor Baudino, the
man from the Argentine Ant Control Corporation. It is his task to exter-
minate the pests, but his appearance and attire—his black suit, bug-like,
red-rimmed eyes and twitching nose and mouth—ironically suggest to
the narrator that Baudino is one of the enemy (169). He appears a life-
sized ant himself, perhaps come to feed the pests rather than kill them.
This image of Baudino in the shape of a vermin quietly recalls Kafka's
novella *Metamorphosis* and its luckless protagonist Gregor Samsa, a
character who awakes one day to find himself amazingly transformed
into an enormous, unsightly insect.

Though ultimately different in direction, both the Kafka and Calvino
stories have several themes in common. Both meekly address terrors

that are beyond human control and comprehension; both timidly speak of the erosion of man's prowess by an indifferent and, in this case, lesser power. This image of man cowed by his own insignificance anticipates Calvino's later postmodern vision and his antihumanist perception of man displaced in his own world. Moreover, man's humiliation before the ants in the Calvino story once again recalls the author's discernment of contemporary man's maimed authority. The most powerful difference between *Argentine Ant* and other of the author's stories discussed here is that this time Calvino pushes the question of man's worth beyond the metaphysical issue of Amerigo in *The Watcher* and into the realm of the ontological. This time the issue is not man's place on this Earth, but his place in whatever strange worlds the cosmos may yet offer.

Although Weiss is surely correct when he says that the author intended *Argentine Ant* to "dramatize modern society's fragile character and impotence" (70), Calvino has, with sinister philosophic flair, gone beyond social commentary. The Kafkaesque implication of man penalized here for no explicable reason surpasses even Beckett's gloomy view of man's dull fate. Not only does the story question life's meaning, but it presents the human situation as a cosmic prank. This Kafkaesque portrait of man, the comic victim of an indifferent heaven, will pursue Calvino's watcher into the author's future works, most notably *The Castle of Crossed Destinies*, where universal, arbitrary damnation is an essential theme.

Calvino's modernist travels invariably trace the author's relentless move from the everyday world to an inner realm of ideas and existential ruminations. Although the author of the fifties remains interested in sociopolitical questions, he is already, as Weiss observes, "constantly drawn to consider universal ones as well" (81). Exercising the eyes of the modernist narrator and tracing his stream of consciousness, the author studies the human condition and finds both it and the protagonist wanting. Admittedly flawed is the cognition of the Calvino watcher, a dark clown figure, whose metaphysical shortsightedness limits his epic deeds to meager observations, mere conjectures, and amusing pratfalls in the arena of the inscrutable universe.

4.

FANTASY ADVENTURES

The publication of the fantasy saga *The Cloven Viscount* (1952) seemed an eccentric departure for Calvino, both from his first novel and from the so-called realistic short stories and novellas he was writing concurrently. As if this oddity were insufficient, the first fable was succeeded by two others, *The Baron in the Trees* (1957) and *The Nonexistent Knight* (1959), both obviously cut from the same magic mold. In ostensibly one leap, Calvino had moved beyond neorealism, catapulting his quest for profounder truths out of the everyday and into the fabulous. This undertaking, actually a more natural progression than it first appeared, would not only produce some of Calvino's best loved works, but would alter the entire course of his career.

In these new fables, the pioneer Calvino tested the fertile narrative field of cross-genre play: the spirited interaction of realism and fantasy, the irreverent merger of the past and present. Genre constraints, as politely observed by earlier fable-makers including two Calvino mentors, Lewis Carroll and Mark Twain, would enjoy less respect in Calvino's trilogy. Parameters between the "real" and "unreal," as outlined by literary theoreticians as diverse as Georg Lukács and Tzvetan Todorov, would no longer serve an author whose future literary explorations would be consistent in philosophic scope, even when they would be equivocal in form. Postmodern irregularities surface in Calvino's three fantasy novels, expressly in the author's growing impiety before the shrine of History and in his darkly amusing parodies of Man, the maker of "sacred" events.

Calvino's turn to fantasy, a literary mode out of step with the Italian realistic tradition, posed a new challenge to his readers. Once-admiring leftist critics now became openly alarmed at the author's abandonment of the conventional novel. It seemed that Calvino had turned his back on reality and on sensitive social problems, which should have been his first concern. He was growing frivolous, forgetting the didactic function of literature, especially within Communism. For these critics the trilogy, therefore, marked a grievous split in the author's work.

To other critics, there was plenty of room for hope, perhaps even a method to Calvino's new madness. Maybe through fantasy the author was approaching political or moral ideology from a fresh angle. To this last group political loyalty, or at least customary social dictates, still dominated Calvino's new trio of novels. As these last critics were quick to observe, all three fantasies touched on communal concerns, even if their discourse was sometimes perplexing and contradictory; all three posed provocative questions about man's personal integrity, as well as about his responsibility to himself and to the public.[1]

The Cloven Viscount, the first novel of the fantasy trilogy, appeared particularly straightforward.[2] Unlikely as it seems now, to J. R. Woodhouse then, this novel, despite what he calls its "sick humor" and fondness for the grotesque, was nonetheless an "optimistic" Calvino work. It was designed purely to identify social ills for which the author sought speedy repair (43, 60).[3] As time would tell, however, Woodhouse's routine perception of literature as morally instructive was not exactly what the author had in mind. Closer inspection of the novel's allegorical basis, in fact, proves decidedly more problematic and Calvino himself would later be the first to point this out in his insightful essay "Nota 1960."[4]

Controversy aside, *Viscount* begins entertainingly and holds the reader's attention both because of its dark humor and its aura of the supernatural. The time is the sixteenth century, the event, the Turkish wars, and the place, Bohemia, where Medardo, the young Viscount of Terralba, throbbing with life and humanity, has just arrived to savor for the first time the inhumane thrill of bloodshed. Dampening his spirits only slightly en route to the battlefield are the puzzling and sinister sights he spies along the way. Unusual, for instance, are the vast number of storks that, finding the fields stripped of crops and the streams dried by drought, are making their way toward the battlefield desperately seeking food. Similarly macabre is the baffling spectacle just ahead, where "over the bare plain were scattered tangled heaps of men's and women's corpses, naked, covered with plague boils, and, inexplicably at first, with feathers, as if those skinny legs and ribs had grown black feathers and wings" (146).

What could this mean? Medardo wonders aloud, only to be informed briskly by his practical squire, Kurt, that "these were carcasses of vultures mingled with human remains" (146). Naive questions and snide retorts continue along the way as Kurt further enlightens Medardo and the reader on the senseless slaughter that is, for Calvino, the essence of war—even in fairy tales. Dialogic banter, in this novel specifically, establishes itself as a hallmark of all Calvino's writing. Calvino always enjoyed teasing his readers, enticing them with queries, which, in standard novels, eventually find orthodox answers, but which, for this author, of course, do not. His is an acid humor, more appropriate to today's interrogative wit that is never bent on saving the world, but rather on raising doubts and challenging the reader. The *Viscount* only confirms these intentions of the author.

Once lured into the novel's dark-comic drama, the reader naturally expects the humorous worst to happen and of course it does. The next day, Medardo's first and last in battle, finds him immediately unhorsed by a small but wily enemy and then literally blown in half by a single cannon blast. The surviving part is subsequently declared a medical miracle and for that reason, and that reason alone, fascinates the field doctors. Self-righteously they decide to sew and patch what is left of him. "Now he was alive and half a man," and so Medardo went home, a cloven, disfigured spirit made flesh (156).

In the next chapter the narrator introduces himself and proves to be a new, yet curiously familiar character to any reader who has already met Pin in Calvino's first novel. Like Pin, the nameless storyteller, known to the reader only as Medardo's nephew, is a *fanciullo*, a child observer, presumably naive and completely at the mercy of the grownups around him. Unlike Pin, however, he is not a fresh creation. He is not the same boy who, according to the author of *Path*, was a character happened upon and then used by the writer to free himself of the embarrassing job of storyteller (*Path* 23). Rather, in *Viscount*, the young narrator is a deliberate and well-thought-out contrivance. The older, more artful Calvino is fully aware at this point of the boy storyteller's potential as a dark-comedy tool. Thus he wields Medardo's nephew as he would a weapon designed to manipulate the reader and to prick at him. (But more later about the narrator's task in Calvino.)

Although only seven or eight years old at the time, Medardo's nephew recalls vividly the day that the viscount, now halved or, as Calvino puts it, "*dimezzato*," returns to his castle. A bitter and vengeful spirit, bent on doing evil to any who cross his path, he soon becomes the scourge of the countryside. An obnoxious villain, he delights in terrorizing his family, the household staff, and the populace alike. He is no sooner home than he breaks his father's heart and precipitates his death; he drives away his faithful old nanny, Sebastiana; he pursues and torments the young narrator and the court physician, Dr. Trelawney; and he forces the court carpenter, Pietrochiodo (Peternail), to invent horrible devices of torture that he then tests liberally. When not at home he rides out to menace the locals: bullying a shepherdess, Pamela, whom he professes to love, harassing a nearby leper colony, and molesting an eccentric religious band of Huguenots. That some of these clusters of society, especially the misusers of the faith, medicine, and justice have been carefully targeted by the author for a thorough lampooning is clearly evident.

An intriguing scenario is no sooner firmly established than events suddenly reverse themselves—a common happening in Calvino's at-odds fiction. All at once noble deeds replace evil ones: the nephew-storyteller is saved by Medardo from a poisonous toad; Pamela and her flock are shielded from the rain by the viscount's cloak; and swallows once wounded by his crossbow are seen amusingly winging their way with their spindly legs splinted (206–14). Realization soon follows within the small community. Medardo lives, true enough, but not as just one person. Now there are two separate and distinct halves: the good one and the bad one (unfortunately translated as the "Good 'Un and the Bad 'Un" in this the novel's only English version).

It seems Medardo's better half was not lost in battle after all and he too has returned home, hopefully to set the world right again. But no such luck. Before long the good half with his cloying sense of rectitude proves as repugnant as the bad. The Huguenots, for example, despise his generosity when it means sharing their food with the poor; the lepers loathe him when he asks them to give up their lascivious ways; and Dr. Trelawney prefers pure science to dirtying his hands on the sick, as the Good One would have him do. And "thus the days went by at Terralba," the narrator cynically observes, "and our sensibilities became numbed, since we felt ourselves lost between an evil and a virtue equally inhuman" (235).

But this intolerable situation could scarcely continue for long. Inevitably, at novel's end Medardo's two opposing halves collide violently and a duel is set that facilitates the fairy-tale conclusion. In the subsequent melee both halves of the viscount are gravely wounded, their once-sutured sides rent asunder from head to toe. Quick to the rescue is Dr. Trelawney. He sees to it that all opposing members of the two half-men correspond and then he binds the viscount together with miles of bandages until he looks "more like an ancient embalmed corpse than a wounded man" (244). A nervous vigil follows but in the end Medardo is miraculously alive and, more important, in one piece again. He marries Pamela, has a family, and enjoys a long life. This seems like the perfect happy ending until the narrator offhandedly observes that "some might expect that with the Viscount entire again, a period of marvellous happiness would open, but obviously a whole Viscount is not enough to make all the world whole" (245).

Playful as it appears, this last cryptic remark inevitably blemishes the novel's happy ending as well as the narrator's seemingly innocent facade. Ambivalence like this has no place in fables, much less in traditional humor, both of which favor tidy endings and conventional wisdom. By contrast here in *Viscount*, the narrator's wry comment never comes off as morally directive, at least not in the positive sense Woodhouse and other early readers contended. If, in fact, the storyteller's sly innuendos are instructive at all, it is by their negativity. Clearly, the boy's words speak of the crueler lessons learned in childhood. It is no wonder that artist Paul Klee's childlike scratchings, his small tortured portraits of tarnished innocence, have been used to adorn Calvino book jackets.[5]

No wonder either that Calvino openly scoffed when critics misread

Viscount as a variation of Stevenson's Jekyll and Hyde tale with its facile choice between good and evil. The author knew his work to be fundamentally less naive than that. In fact, he admitted to having deliberately led the critics down the garden path, implying a moral standard in the novel where he meant none. As he acknowledged later, the issue of good and evil, at least in the traditional moral and religious sense, had, in fact, never entered his mind, "not even for a minute" ("Nota" 415). For him the story's characters—Dr. Trelawney, the Huguenots, Pietrochiodo, and Uncle Medardo's two halves—whether they represent the failings of modern medicine, the hypocrisy of empty religious rites, the catastrophic inventions of today's science, or the ticklish distinction between good and evil, never serve a purely cautionary function. Instead, these individuals are intended to dramatize what Calvino sadly identifies as typically dismal slices of the modern world's fundamental *"disumanità"* ("dishumanity"; see "Nota" 417).

This last perspective expressed by Calvino has come to be shared in more recent years by other readers as well. Gore Vidal, for example, commenting on the moral issues addressed in the author's work, states quite simply that *Viscount* is something less than Christian (19). Reinforcing the same observation is John Gatt-Rutter, who observes that in Calvino there is a perception of "the non-existence of evil, or `moral wrong-doing,' the impossibility of moral judgements."[6] Elementary as these observations may be today in the light of the author's later works, they still bear repeating. In the denial of a priori values, Christian or ethical, as expressed by the author in his own words about the novel, the reader recognizes the overwhelming presence of an existential perspective. This point of view purports a morality in which definitive traditional choices such as right and wrong (while ironically postured) are finally inconceivable. It embraces a world where, in the absence of God and Mother Reason, there reigns no sense of true and false, but only confusing fragments of information, doubt and indecision.

In *Viscount*, therefore, the ethical debate over which Medardo is right and which is wrong is never resolved. It seems clear that for Calvino in today's society neither of the two halves represent a "Good" choice, or anyway, one that coincides with the customary perspective of Jekyll and Hyde. Medardo therefore emerges, not as a conventional exemplum of morality, but instead, as a playful parody of the Victorian image of the divided self or doppelganger. As personified in this figure, such ironic doubling is enjoying new vogue today, especially in postmodern literature where the doppelganger's role customarily serves both to gibe at traditional morality and to dramatize the modern individual's lost integrity and splintered values.[7] Bearing in mind the viscount's contemporary function, one can now better understand why even the final welding together of his two halves does not, for the author, constitute the novel's happy ending, and why, in the final paragraphs, the storyteller feels it only wise to alert the reader to life's less fortunate compromises.

The author's cynical view of the central figure Medardo applies just as readily to the novel's narrator, who, as a character in the novel, cannot be excluded from Calvino's darkening assessment of humankind. While Olken originally noted certain felicitous "parallels" between the narrator of *Viscount* and Twain's *Huckleberry Finn*, her observations are both tardy and erroneous when applied to a transitional work like this particular Calvino novel (Olken 39). In reality there is much less of Twain in Medardo's nephew than in the author's earlier, more traditional focalizer, Pin. The innocence of Calvino's narrator in *Viscount* is a more calculated fiction than it was in *Path*, a work written by the author when he himself was more naive, more uncertain of his convictions, and like Twain, still going through the motions of conventional morality. Not so in *Viscount*.

In *Viscount*, if Medardo, Trelawney, and the others are examples of what Calvino called his flawed characters, in short, "the exemplification of . . . contemporary man's mutilation" ("Nota" 415), so too is the narrator. Born with the same inadequacies, the same existential ignorance as the others, the narrator's naive role in the novel is clearly perceived by the author as less of a blessing than a bane. Like Marcovaldo and Amerigo, or any of the Beckettian characters who have left their impression on Calvino's short stories, he too is another of life's misfits, an onlooker not a doer, a spectator—and not by virtue of youth alone, but more precisely because to Calvino, this is man's lot in life.

Similar observations can be made of the characters and their existential situation in Calvino's next fantasy, *The Baron in the Trees*.[8] This time the story takes place in eighteenth-century Italy and begins with an imaginative twist when one day young Cosimo Piovasco di Rondò, the twelve-year-old son and heir of Baron Piovasco di Rondò, refuses to eat his supper and seeks refuge in a nearby tree. The narrator, his younger brother Biagio, tells the reader that Cosimo's escape is precipitated by a disgusting dinner of snails that their wicked sister has prepared and that their parents have forced them to eat. Events soon take a second turn, when, in defiance of his conventional father, the stubborn but agile

Cosimo vows to live permanently in the trees, and to his family's utter amazement, keeps his word.

The next several chapters detail Cosimo's adventurous new freedom. Evident in these scenes is the author's own familial grounding in natural science, his unique mastery of flora and fauna, both as it exists today and as it must have existed centuries ago before the industrial age decimated the European landscape. The author takes obvious delight in inventing ingenious ways to facilitate Cosimo's adaptation to life in the trees. He relishes depicting the young baron's fearless confrontations with savage beasts and enjoys detailing the elements of nature, of forest creatures large and small. He also delights in contriving Cosimo's treetop comforts, including his Daniel Boone wardrobe and fur sleeping bag. Nor does the author overlook the hero's social life (such as it is), for brother Biagio insists that, even from a perch in a nearby tree branch, the otherwise isolated Cosimo could nonetheless still do his lessons, occasionally dine with family and friends, and even make new acquaintances in the person of the neighbor's daughter Viola, who would one day grow up to be the love of his life.

Later chapters, however, grow moody. The years roll by and Cosimo grows up alone and mostly lonely. Family ties falter (except for Biagio) when the hero's sister moves away and both parents die. Love misfires too when it falls victim to Cosimo's paranoid suspicions of Viola. News of his eccentric arboreal life spreads, bringing him fame, or more precisely notoriety. For those who know him (especially his brother), "he [Cosimo] was a solitary who did not avoid people," a treetop Good Samaritan (*Baron* 64). He is also a cosmopolitan who has met Napoleon personally and whose reputed lifestyle is admired even by that great Enlightenment philosopher Voltaire. By others, however, he is more realistically viewed as a recluse, a wild creature garbed in leaves who lives like a monkey (143).

This contrary portrait of Cosimo is surely nurtured by the seductive innocence of the narrator in the novel. In fact, duped by the narrator's reasonable facade, early readers were quick to attribute Biagio's soothing voice to the author himself, forgetting that it is Biagio who is the typical eighteenth-century man imbued with the perspective of the Enlightenment, not Calvino. The result was that they proceeded to attribute other of Biagio's qualities to the author as well, including his optimistic worldview. Out of brotherly love and an affinity to his own historical ambience, Biagio figures Cosimo's decision to live in the trees as a healthy one, indeed the correct moral choice based on Jean-Jacques Rousseau's model for the natural man. But Biagio's account, like that of Medardo's nephew before him, is not trustworthy.

Biagio's emphasis, as the Enlightened Narrator, is necessarily (and ironically) on his brother's viable fraternity with man (albeit at great distance) and he takes great care to document such moments. His examples are often deceptively appropriate too, as is the instance when Cosimo, from his vantage point in the trees, is able to alert the farmers to the threat of fire (104–9). At other times, however, Biagio's examples strain the possibilities of treetop humanitarianism and appear ludicrous, precisely because of the purported solemnity in which they are framed. Such is the case with Cosimo's deathbed ministrations to his mother from a nearby tree branch outside her window (144–46). Innocently locked as he is into his eighteenth-century attitudes, Biagio is simply blind to the contradiction that the contemporary author has here with conscious forethought planted in the novel. Biagio cannot therefore conceive of the twentieth-century moral and philosophical discrepancy of his brother's life: Cosimo's very real existential dilemma in deciding between the passive isolation of his arboreal existence and his role as an active social being.

For all Biagio's goodwill, or perhaps largely because of it, his story is misleading. Nor, for that matter, should it be assumed that it mirrors the author's mind. To learn about Cosimo's actual drama and the nature of his existential choices in *Baron* it becomes necessary to remove the narrator's rose-colored glasses and take a hard look at the central character's life as it finally evolves in the novel. At the same time it is also wise to pause for a moment to consider Calvino's own observations of Cosimo's character, for these are telling. Beginning with the author, one soon learns that Calvino's conception of Cosimo's life in the trees does not coincide with the storyteller's. The author is not subject, as is Biagio, to the "enlightened prejudices" of the society depicted in the novel, at least not at the time of his later writing on the trilogy. Here Calvino tells the reader clearly that he chose the eighteenth-century ambience for *Baron* not because he necessarily identifies with Biagio and Enlightened social reform, but rather because he empathizes with Cosimo and admires him essentially as a character whose eccentricity would fit nicely in that "great century of eccentrics" ("Nota" 419).

Furthermore, Calvino acknowledges that Cosimo's arboreal life *is* a lonely choice, one motivated not by sociability, but by the character's deeply felt sense of "singularity and solitude" ("Nota" 418). If the author admires Cosimo, therefore, it is not especially for his Enlightened Voltairean traits, as once thought, but rather because existentially the character represents to him "a person [who] willingly sets himself a difficult standard and follows it to its ultimate consequences, because without [doing so] he could not be himself either for himself or for the others" ("Nota" 417). This attitude toward Cosimo is of course Sartrean, as Calvino himself readily admitted in an interview (Paris 1978). It reflects not only the philosopher's paradoxical position on man's freedom of choice but even his very words.[9]

It is Sartre who, early in his career, advocated the heroic existence and decisions made boldly and even in defiance of the Other. In fact, it is this Sartre's too-emphatic denial of the Other that, by the end of his own life, fractured the facade of his humanism, precipitating a serious conflict in the philosopher's thoughts on man's obligation to self versus his responsibility to others.[10] At novel's end when Cosimo opts to speak no more, Calvino (like Sartre) has finally put forth as primary the peculiar existential emphasis on self and personal freedom, relegating Cosimo's other role as a social do-gooder, along with Enlightenment ideals, to second place. It might be added that, even where Calvino's portrait of Cosimo does coincide with the moral model of Biagio's Enlightened philosophy, this connection is superficial and more related to the way Voltaire's thinking anticipates Sartre's than to the specifics of Voltaire's own reasoning.[11]

Turning now to the person of Cosimo himself in the novel, one sees beneath the author's humorous gloss marked evidence of a sobering perspective. Terrible solitude, not social amenability, ultimately predicates Cosimo's existence. Caution colors his relationships with his fellows, including family and lovers. Flamboyant gestures but not great deeds characterize his actions (or rather, nonactions). Although the storyteller Biagio may figure Cosimo a vigorous molder of society, events in the novel do not bear this out. Rather, in this character, as in many other Calvino characters, the reader witnesses a retreat from human community, a withdrawal from decisive action, and a tangible existential reluctance to choose definitively, and not without good reason.

From the existential point of view, the issue of freedom of choice (or the crossroads, as Calvino calls it in his later work, *Castle*) has, in practice, come to be regarded as more alienating and less positive than it once appeared to be in Sartre's original descriptions of the *homme engagé*.

Instead of being a liberating, dynamic experience, a clear judgment between good and evil or between self and communal service, choosing by existential standards has proven, as portrayed in this novel, to be an awesome either/or dilemma whereby any choice spells a loss of other freedoms.[12] Indeed, today existential philosophers perceive this dread of the loss of other options as a very real source of human anguish.

In contemporary literature this agonizing over either/or by the hero, in fact, accounts for much of the curious suspension of action that is seen in novels and plays by such postmodern precursors to Calvino as Kafka, Beckett, and Sartre himself. The hero cannot act merely because he cannot choose rightly. In the absence of clearly definable alternatives, a placid inertia sets into the character, exactly like that earlier observed in the protagonists of Calvino's modernist short stories. This inaction, in turn, has provoked the dismay of literary critics who frequently lament that in this kind of fiction (including some of Calvino's) not much is happening.

From this anguish of indecision emerges the quandary of Cosimo Rondò's life and character in the *Baron*. Any decision he makes involves the loss of other choices: if he chooses to live on earth with others and have substantial family and community ties, he will have companionship, but he will have to endure the dreaded encroachment of his private space by people like his perverse sister, his eccentric mother, and his oppressive father. On the other hand, if he chooses to live alone he will retain his sense of self, plus a measure of peace of mind, but he will ultimately have to sacrifice the comforts of love in the person of his lady Viola. Much as Cosimo tries (and he does try), he cannot not have it both ways. His espoused belief "that anyone who wants to see the earth properly must keep himself at a necessary distance from it" is in no way a viable option for the *homme engagé* (144). Instead, this alienated posture neatly sums up the hero's existential dilemma, the double bind of all Cosimo's (and Calvino's) choices.

Cosimo's death similarly confirms the negativity that is the true essence of his freedom of choice. At novel's end, simply by *not* choosing the company of men, Cosimo has chosen anyway, opting for abject solitude. "In one sense choice is possible, but what is not possible is not to choose. I can always choose, but I ought to know that if I do not choose, I am still choosing," says Sartre and apparently the author here agrees with him.[13] Cosimo's withdrawal to his arboreal realm, his final balloon exit from earthly life, represents nothing more than the same ambivalent "non-choosing" already observed in *Viscount*. No sense of heroics, Rightness, or even personal gratification touch this last decision (or nondecision). Instead, there is only grim resignation and at last silence.

In this way Cosimo's end portrays the typical, pessimistic and alienated direction taken by the hero of many late-modernist and postmodern novels, including those of Calvino's literary colleagues like Robbe-Grillet. That is to say, Cosimo's choice reflects what many existentialists see as the inevitable result of pursuing Sartre's thoughts on freedom to their logical conclusion. This conclusion finally posits man's freedom not as liberty at all, but as condemnation, his social role not as an aggressive heroic act but as a passive withdrawal, personal and auto-destructive. While playfully treated, these dismal Calvinian speculations in *Baron* on the nature of freedom of choice have merited the close attention that they receive here primarily because this urgent theme, life's binary dilemma, will reemerge in the author's later postmodern works, where it is even more vigorously addressed.

Of the trilogy's three novels, the last one, *The Nonexistent Knight*, is both the most contrived and therefore the most postmodern. Its comedy depends more on slapstick, humorous disguises, and extravagant high jinks and less on the subtle play of ideas one sees in the first two works. As is often the case in Calvino, the reader's attention is captured at once by the introduction of a unique presence, this time in the shape of Agilulf, an empty suit of armor pretentiously masquerading as one of King Charlemagne's medieval knights. Encased as he is in protective vestments, Agilulf's nonbeing might easily go undetected were it not for an evening inspection, at which time the king insists that he raise his visor only to discover that Agilulf's helmet is empty and that "No one was inside the white armor with its iridescent crest" (6). When the doddering king next asks him to explain how, if he does not exist, he performs his duties to the realm, Agilulf responds, "By will power. . . and faith in our holy cause!," an answer that readily satisfies the senescent King Charlemagne, if not the bemused reader (7).

Unencumbered as he is by human necessities, including eating and sleeping, and lacking such human faults as laziness and lust, Agilulf ought to be in every way a peerless example of knighthood, but such is not so. Deprived of humanity, he is competent but officious, living by the book and feeding on rules and regulations instead of food. Pompous and condescending, he is an inflexible company man who knows nothing of love or camaraderie for he is incapable of emotion. Despite his gleaming white armor and perfect service record, something is missing within him, something that leaves him as lonely, isolated, and incomplete as many of Calvino's modernist characters.

As the farce opens, we see, this time in triplicate, a reworking of the *Viscount*'s doppelganger theme. In his squire Gurduloo, Agilulf encounters the opposite of himself in the shape of a humorously primitive and purely sentient creature. On the other hand, he also meets a third character: an all-too-human Raimbaut, a knight as impassioned as Agilulf is passionless and as lusty as he is sexless. The plot thickens when, at a banquet, Agilulf's honor is seriously challenged by a young upstart, Torrismund, and he must leave to find fresh proof of his worthy knighthood. In departing, however, Agilulf is followed by Lady Bradamante, an Amazon warrior foolishly in love with the nonexistent knight. In a manner reminiscent of a silent film chase, Bradamante is in turn pursued by Raimbaut who, having seen the maiden at her toilet, has become smitten with her. Not surprisingly, most of the major characters eventually converge at one point where the plot is conveniently resolved by deus ex machina.

Unable to justify his empty knighthood and having no other reason to exist, at novel's end Agilulf simply vanishes, bequeathing his armor to Raimbaut. Raimbaut in turn replaces Agilulf in the service of Charlemagne, thus uneasily conjoining the nonexistent knight's iron will to a defective human essence in order to shape one whole and arguably more serviceable knight quite reminiscent of the final Medardo in *Viscount*. Unable to find Agilulf, Bradamante accepts Raimbaut as her lover, in the interim blithely confessing to the reader her dual identity in the novel. Not only is she a part-time Amazon who gallops across fields of battle, but she is also a sometime nun and narrator, Sister Theodora, who spends her days in the convent writing down this very story (140).

Although more frenetic than either of the first two novels of Calvino's trilogy, *Knight* nonetheless remains faithful to Calvino's social agenda. An enemy of all forms of hypocrisy, the author, by way of Agilulf's example, is quick to attack the vain conformism and lost integrity of modern humans smothered by bureaucracy, or what the author here wryly dubs "the Superintendency of Duels, Feuds and Besmirched Honor" (16). Religion, or rather religious duplicity, also receives its usual number of playful blows from the author, who, in this work, takes on the Knights of the Holy Grail, a league that, in the novel, uses faith to manipulate the masses and performs evil in God's name.[14] Other social institutions are eventually blasted as well, significantly (from a postmodern view) historical truth, not nearly so reliable in the author's eyes as textbooks tell us. But most of all, Calvino assails his arch-nemesis, war, and mocks the sheeplike Raimbauts who execute it in the name of the vain Charlemagnes who invent it.

Both philosophically and structurally, *Knight* is always on course with *Baron* and *Viscount* in that, through the narrator's conversation, the novel goes on to explore both social issues and man's metaphysical situation or raison d'être. Given that this novel is overtly more theatrical than the other two, the task of the storyteller as an ironic tool is also more obvious. In the dual personality of Sister Theodora, Amazon-warrior and chatty, cloistered nun, the reader this time knows he has met a trickster figure. She is an explicit fraud, most likely a liar writing what appears a counterfeit history. But these faults, rather than detracting from her significance, actually enhance it.

It is her lively banter, so like Biagio's before her, that sets up a dialogue among the characters. With feigned simplicity she submits for the reader's consideration several hypothetical ways of being: Agilulf, the mechanical man, efficient and unfeeling, Gurduloo, the base, instinctual savage, and Raimbaut, the everyday man, an uneasy hodgepodge of good intentions and considerable faults. Together the three characters test life's options from their own perspectives and it is here, as in the earlier two works of the trilogy, that the novel's happy ending falters and that a philosophical tug-of-war ensues. Once again, there is no perfect hero and no ideal ending to the novel. Once again, the dialogue ends, leaving questions unanswered, moral issues unresolved, and the reader abandoned to his own uncertain conclusions.

In *Baron*, Cosimo's final aerial departure from the world is picturesque but evasive, leaving the riddle of his life and the novel's primary existential dilemma of man's social role versus his obligation to self not settled but sidestepped. In *Viscount*, Medardo's final merger offers no firm answer to the question of what constitutes right and wrong. In *Knight*, the bestial Gurduloo is easily rejected as the image of the ideal man, while Agilulf, the empty knight, provides no answer either, as he symbolizes the empty souls inhabiting this industrial age. In fact, at a metaphysical level, even the very construct of Agilulf, the disembodied mind, spoofs mortal intellect, subtly undermining humanist faith in man's direction as a species. In the end, the reader is left by default with Raimbaut, an altogether fallible solution to the problem of what humankind ideally ought to be.

Although it is undoubtedly true that *Viscount, Baron,* and *Knight* are three novels born out of the author's sense of helplessness in the face of the Cold War, the threat of the atomic bomb, and the disintegration of community and moral values, the implications of these works do not stop there. Disappointed with man's hypocrisy and skeptical anyway of humanity's ultimate importance in the global scheme of things, Calvino turns away from the ordinary, day-to-day doings of people for literary inspiration. In the trilogy one now sees the writer make his most definitive change in direction thus far: the author's ironic eye roving resolvedly from issues purely practical to the more expansive realms of the metaphysical, and finally, the ontological. This conversion in the trilogy from a fiction that pertains to the real world to a literature that documents other ways of being in otherworlds is characteristically postmodern.

In fact, before moving on to the seasoned writer that is the Calvino of the sixties, a summary of the postmodern subtleties that have quietly infiltrated the trilogy should be drawn. Some of these tendencies, especially the author's early experiments in self-reflexive writing, are best substantiated in the trilogy's most avant-garde novel, *Knight.* Other of his postmodern inclinations, however, including the author's antihumanist sentiments, his penchant for either/or dialogue and double coding, his reliance on parody, and his chameleonlike facility for slipping in and out of historical realism are already conspicuous in the first two works as well.

Regarding his postmodern turn, Calvino provides his own best testimony in the "Nota" consistently cited here. In it the author himself specifically undermines not only *Baron*'s Enlightenment itinerary but the efficacy of historical realism in general. In his discussion, Calvino maintains that historical novels per se do not interest him, but that what does interest him instead is "making a historical 'pastiche,' a repertoire of eighteenth-century images, supported by dates and correlations with famous events and personages; a countryside and a nature, imaginary yes, but described with precision and nostalgia; a happening . . . rendered justifiable and believable even at its unreal inception" ("Nota" 418).

These are already essentially the words of a postmodern writer, even though at the time the word "postmodern" itself scarcely enjoyed broad currency. Indeed, Calvino's musings here clearly anticipate the reflections of American writer John Barth in his later, respected postmodern manifesto, "The Literature of Replenishment. Postmodernist Fiction." Here, Barth defines the ideal postmodern author (including Calvino in his list) as one who "neither merely repudiates nor merely imitates either his twentieth-century modernist parents or his nineteenth-century premodernist grandparents." Instead, he is a writer who "aspires to a fiction more democratic in its appeal." His novels, in turn, are those that rise "above the quarrel between realism and irrealism, formalism and 'contentism,' pure and committed literature, coterie fiction and junk fiction."[15]

Though yet without benefit of Barth's definition, the fifties Calvino already clearly understood the basic ingredients of postmodernism, and in the same way in which Barth enumerates them. In the trilogy, he had already explored postmodernism's ambivalent blending of nostalgia and irreverence for the past, as well as its tendency to vacillate between the fictional realms of realism and fantasy. This last impropriety, namely toying with historical reality, was, and still is, easily one of the most audacious expressions of postmodernism to be found in Calvino and in his postmodern colleagues. In *Baron*, for example, in the fantastical France of the author's invention, the real-life figure of Voltaire not only appears but indulges in a bit of gossip with Biagio about the mythical figure that is Cosimo. In *Knight*, Calvino does not hesitate to poke fun at venerable King Charlemagne, transposing his kingdom to an impossible world populated by Amazons and nonexistent knights. But mild genre transgressions like these are not unheard of in other writers, such as Lewis Carroll and Mark Twain, for instance, and in Calvino might easily go unnoticed were it not for a sly difference in the present-day author's attitude.

Calvino's trilogy is neither *Alice in Wonderland* nor *A Connecticut Yankee in King Arthur's Court* and its author is neither Lewis Carroll nor Mark Twain, even if the three writers share palpable similarities.[16] In his works, Carroll takes great pains to firmly establish his real world in Victorian England and his fantasy realm elsewhere, in Wonderland; nor do these two territories collide. As is usually the case in traditional fantasy, in both *Alice* and *Yankee* realism and fantasy are discretely set apart from each other: fantasy safely designated to dreams where it poses no threat to the waking world, much less the presumably safe harbor of reality. Calvino's trilogy, on the other hand, waffles between fantasy and realism for the simple reason that no such tidy separation is ever put forth by the author. Like fairy tales, the trilogy assumes the bizarre; but unlike fairy tales (and like postmodernism), the trilogy often makes unannounced and unsettling incursions into reality, either by referring to tangible entities within the natural world or else by pointing to historical "facts" as we presume to know them. Carroll's tales, Twain's too, for all their eccentricities, thus espouse a conventional sensibility, respecting the boundaries of traditional fantasy; Calvino's fables, by contrast, already verge on the postmodern in that they indiscriminately conjoin real places and people to the chaotic realm of the incredible.

In like manner, Calvino also breaks with theoretician Tzvetan Todorov's popular structuralist concept of fantasy that, at bottom, is not altogether different from traditional definitions. For Todorov (like Carroll and Twain) there is a sharp line drawn between realism and the fantastic. Fantasy is unreal, but the world round about is solid enough, derived as Todorov insists from "reality as it exists in the common opinion."[17] Within postmodernism, however, this so-called common opinion of reality is severely tested, as will be the case in all Calvino's later works. Indeed, even in the trilogy the bastions of historical realism have already been shaken, and this is nowhere more evident than in the equivocal role of the narrator.

Although much has been written and said here and elsewhere about the role of the narrator in Calvino, there remains more to say, especially in the light of the author's impending postmodernity. In the trilogy, for example, it is the storyteller's "anything goes" attitude that frees the text and enables it to quietly slip from fact to fancy, from realism to fable and back again. The casual narrative tone, no doubt inspired by the storytellers of two very diverse Calvino models, Ariosto and Kafka, makes the most impossible situation seem plausible—even ordinary. At times, distinctions between what can be called real and what can be called fantasy dim, obscured by a Kafkaesque nonchalance, which, as critic McHale points out, Todorov would find altogether unacceptable and baffling (74–77).

In *Knight* expressly, it is the shocking banality of the narrator in the face of the extraordinary that finally drives the text to the brink of postmodernism. Storyteller Theodora absolutely dotes on addressing the reader directly, never concealing the author's irony as she all-too-innocently describes her limited life, confessing that "apart from religious ceremonies, triduums, novenas, gardening, harvesting, vintaging, whippings, slavery, incest, fires, hangings, invasion, sacking, rape and pestilence, we have had no experience. What can a poor nun know of the world?" (34).

Caustic and decidedly contemporary discourse like this goes beyond the gentler asides of Calvino's mentor poet Ariosto and determinedly advances Calvino's postmodernity. In postmodern writers such as Gabriel Gárcia Márquez or the earlier Kurt Vonnegut, to name only two, self-conscious narration of this type is meanly and calculatingly bent on shaking humanist faith, desanctifying the writer's task, and jolting the reader's casual submission to the written word, be it fantasy or recorded reality. The same can be said for Calvino's work.

In the author's lifetime two world wars had already effectively undermined human faith in self and in historical honesty, or what the author cites in *Knight* as that discrepancy between what actually took place and what is reported later (76). Questionable to Calvino in the aftermath of World War II was humanity's mastery of events, either political or artistic. We see this lost confidence openly acknowledged in his self-reflexive narrative mode wherein the author takes aim at the writer's ego by calling attention not to the genius of writing, but to its hit-or-miss nature and its dubious grasp of certitude.

Sister Theodora, for example, tells the reader naively that writing to her seems much like mechanically dotting the chronicle with maps, puckers, creases, and scratches, all of which are vainly intended to illustrate the ways of the world, to capture somehow its grace and sadness (106–7). She also confesses to being little more than a scribe, whose job is not to make fictional magic but to do "hard penance" by struggling to put words on paper (71). Essential to the task of the self-conscious narrator is this demystification of the art of writing, the spoofing of author and reader alike, elements that characterize postmodern parody.

Calvinian parody, for example, typically guides the reader down an already well-trodden literary path only to reverse directions or abandon him in a forest of contradictions. The author feigns a traditional Manichaean allegory on good and evil in *Viscount* and then methodically dismantles its univocal meaning; takes an exalted theme like chivalry in *Knight* and then levels it; chooses a genre like the historical novel and, as in *Baron*, skews it by affecting Enlightened reason where there is actually modern-day existential polemics.[18] This playful, postmodern attitude is obvious in the duplicitous conversations of Calvino's trickster narrators whose subversive hedging in the trilogy significantly accounts for the uncertain resolution of each novel. Such polarized, self-contradictory structures in Calvino's fiction, amusing as they may be, *do*, according to Umberto Eco, ultimately serve a purpose—namely to critique the world as the reader knows it by creating within him a "sense of logical uneasiness and of narrative discomfort."[19] They also serve to test the so-called tried and true morality of traditional ethics and, above all, to launch the text beyond history's confines.

Both thematically and technically, the trilogy marks a significant change in Calvino's literary direction as he now strides decisively away from the world of realism toward the imaginative frontier of postmodernism. All three Calvino fables reveal postmodernism's irreverence for boundaries: boundaries between genres, boundaries between the past and present, and especially boundaries between fictional fact and pure fantasy. All three look sideways at the feeble worlds humanity has made, already seeking new venues more exhilarating and unfettered.

This tension between the everyday and otherworlds accounts for three of the author's best-loved and most enduring novels and sets the stage for his future writing. Contradiction, reversal, and paradox will shape Calvino's new plural, postmodern landscape. Making and unmaking the text will form the dynamics of his future storytelling, shaping a labyrinthical path through fictional otherworlds still uncharted.

5

OTHERWORLD EXPLORATIONS

In many ways Calvino and postmodernism came of age together. Not
only do they share a common worldview, but they share the same birthday. If postmodernism was born out of the tragedy of World War II, the
Holocaust, and the atomic threat, so too was Calvino the writer; if its
fiction expresses a loss of faith in mainstream literary forms and heralds
a search for more relevant means of expression, so too does Calvino's.[1]
Furthermore, just as postmodern philosophy sets out to explore life's
tenuous journey, so does Calvino, whether he is portraying a spiral trek
from cradle to grave in *t zero*, an infernal labyrinth descent in *The Castle
of Crossed Destinies*, a mystical tour of *Invisible Cities*, or a galactical
expedition in *Cosmicomics*.

Establishing Calvino's birthright in postmodernism, however, does not automatically make him a member of the club. More serviceable once again are the words of John Barth who, together with John Updike, early on identifies the author as a "true postmodernist," because Calvino's unorthodox inquiries into literature "are as modern as the new cosmology and as ancient as folktales," or to put it more succinctly, because Calvino "keeps one foot always in the narrative past—characteristically the Italian narrative past of Boccaccio, Marco Polo, or Italian fairy tales—and one foot in, one might say, the Parisian structuralist present; one foot in fantasy, one in objective reality."[2]

This 1980 reference to Calvino as a heretical postmodern writer may well be one of the first. Furthermore, much as this early description concentrates primarily on the "hows" rather than the "whys" of Calvino and other postmodern writers, Barth's and Updike's observations are as valid today as they were then. Postmodern art is a brashly antithetical craft: savoring duplicity and reveling in the juxtaposition of old and new, order and disorder, fact and fancy. Equally at home with the latest literary theories as well as with old-fashioned storytelling, postmodern narrative, Calvino's not excluded, is democratic, perhaps even to excess.

In fact, enlarging on the just-quoted definition, some critics would call postmodern art disruptive and downright anarchic. Impudently, its literature bridges historical and ontological boundaries, merges unrelated landscapes and events and amalgamates disparate genres. Randomly, it leaps from text to text, purloining plots and characters to be twisted into cunning parodies. Exuberantly, it baits the reader, self-consciously making a game of reading and erecting elaborate scams to hoodwink and astonish its audience. More controversially, postmodern fiction frequently elevates language above its users, reducing the writers' and protagonists' roles to that of dull reporters, amazed spectators before the conundrum of the universe.

For these and other unruly pranks, postmodern fiction has been disparaged. Perceiving art as sacred, the artist as seer, and recorded history as the march of progress, past critics distrusted postmodernism with its trickster scribes, emblematic characters, and "yo-yo" concept of time, suspecting it of having no foundation in serious thought. Accused, as Calvino was in the sixties, of consorting with low-life literature like science fiction and fantasy, postmodern fiction was early labeled kitsch and, thus, bad art. Even today, despite its respectable bonds with Robbe-Grillet's *nouveau roman* and a wide range of highly diverse and respectable theorists, including Vladímir Propp, Ferdinand de Saussure, Roland Barthes, Jacques Derrida, Jacques Lacan, and others, postmodern narrative is still occasionally called folderol. Not excused from censure either are some of Calvino's late works, which have been ridiculed as verbal gymnastics.[3]

The opinion that postmodern fiction is serious literature has, however, over the years gained credence. That postmodernity derives its impetus from the cataclysmic events of this last half-century and from the somber philosophy born of these events is now a viable assertion. Since Barth's breakthrough article, it has also been substantiated that Calvino and writers like Borges, García Márquez, Robbe-Grillet, Vonnegut, and the precocious Kafka, all of whom will be mentioned in this chapter, are writers joined in postmodernism.[4] Once labeled a caprice, postmodern literature today is assuredly anything but that.

Calvino was never a writer given to caprice or literary fads anyway. Postmodernism was not a fashion imposed on him from without but a force arising from within. It was for him an authentic portrait of late twentieth-century life, an impassioned appraisal of humankind's fragile existential situation—living, as Calvino puts it, in a "period in which [one] feels less faith in directing the course of things" (*Pietra* 41). Furthermore, such reflections as these were, and are, scarcely unique to Calvino. According to William V. Spanos, even at its genesis, postmodern literature carried leftover existential baggage from earlier times.[5] These issues, as we have seen, hounded Calvino just as they had dogged certain of his forerunners, most notably Kafka and Sartre. The demise of faith in a universal order and the tension between individual and communal values were philosophical dilemmas that had arisen with World War I and that had not been laid to rest by World War II. Temporarily assuaged by the 1945 peace and the enthusiasm of rebuilding, these old anxieties were prompt to resurface after the second war, as readily evidenced by Calvino's first novel.[6]

To many, including Calvino, the new postwar society, or what he called "living between Buchenwald and the H bomb," was unsatisfactory (*Pietra* 14). More importantly, the recent existential crisis went deeper than circumstances of war and peace. This time the angst, as Spanos observes, hit at the very heart of man: specifically at his inflated idea of self and at old-fashioned humanist faith in progress and causal relationships (18–19). Discordant voices would be heard, Calvino's among them. Postmodern philosophers such as Gianni Vattimo openly scoffed at man's egocentric and outmoded Galilean humanism. In writing his epitaph to leftover Renaissance pride, Vattimo would say simply that "humanity maintains its position as the 'centre' of reality, as the current notion of humanism suggests, only through reference to a *Grund* [final cause or foundation] that verifies this role" (33). Or to put it another way, "the true substance of the crisis of humanism is the death of God" (32).

Jacques Derrida, Michel Foucault, and other postmodern thinkers would be no more reassuring than Vattimo in their perception of the contemporary human situation. Speaking of the apocalyptic threat to our Western philosophic system, Derrida cites a "radical trembling. . . . played out in the violent relationship of the whole of the West to its other."[7] Expressing himself even more bluntly, Foucault observes cynically that "man is an invention of recent date. And one perhaps nearing its end."[8] Thus, in the loss of divine models (Christian or Platonic) in this century, humanism, according to many observers today, has effectively been deprived of its transcendental base, and humanity in turn stripped of its mastery of the universe and of history.

That Calvino early intuited this somber philosophic turn, and that he understood what Andrew McKenna calls the new "post-Auschwitz," "post-Christian,"[9] and decidedly antihumanist mentality of our times is demonstrated by his own words on the matter. As early as 1958, while speaking at a San Remo conference, the writer sounded like a philosopher himself when he talked of "the defeat, the vanity of history, the impossibility of understanding life according to a rational scheme," especially in our epoch where "the absurd atrocity of the world becomes a common point of departure for almost all literature" (*Pietra* 25).[10]

Calvino's own personal crisis in humanism, his own cognizance of life's fearful fragmentation, insinuated first in his modernist stories and in the fantasy trilogy, was more emphatically expressed afterward in his postmodern works. In these writings, one sees conclusively a rejection of the utilitarian, material world with its firm sense of History. At an aesthetic level, one further observes the subsequent and logical rejection of Aristotelian poetics with its notion of well-made plots and final solutions. Instead, in all Calvino's postmodern works there is an impatient striving on the author's part to liberate himself from the shackles of time and place. Like his postmodern colleagues Borges and García Márquez,

Calvino seeks freedom in new "ontological zones," or otherworlds, there to create apocryphal histories that are new, stimulating and more flexible (see McHale 43–94).

Calvino's novels of the sixties onward take full advantage of these new horizons, investigating alternate ways of being in places other than what is known to this world. These would be Calvino's most ambitious enterprises, the fruits of his most productive period and the high point of his postmodernism. Even in their physical construction, none of these works resemble traditional novels. Postmodern literature favors short works and Calvino's are no exception. All his new fictions would be groups of short pieces gathered under a common frame or cornice. Allegory, metafiction, and parody would feed the author's new subversive dialogues as he looked into being Other in remarkable heterotopias of his own invention.[11]

Among these heterotopias, several works including *Cosmicomics*, *Invisible Cities*, *If on a winter's night a traveler*, and *Mr. Palomar* are especially harmonious. These last-mentioned novels find the author more forbearing of life's inherent contradictions and therefore represent what might be dubbed the "provisionally supportive camp" of Calvino's postmodern fiction. Earlier, however, he would write *t zero* and *The Castle of Crossed Destinies*, contentious works that more rightly belong to postmodernism's "radically antagonistic" camp, but that deserve equal attention here.[12] *Castle*, in particular, is both a technical and poetic tour de force which has sometimes been overlooked, both because of its complexity and because of it melancholy worldview.

Examining in order the author's postmodern narratives, we begin necessarily with the earlier *Cosmicomics* and *t zero*, two works that at first appear companion pieces but then take separate paths. Both begin as fanciful galactical explorations but cannot be called space operas, as, in form and content, they defy such an elementary description. The cosmicomics may romp through space and time but they are not science fiction. Partly inspired by writer Raymond Queneau and his literary group, the *Ouvroir de littérature potentielle* (Workshop of Potential Literature, or Oulipo), they are instead ventures in integrating humor into science and mathematics.[13] None of the hardware accompanying science fiction is in place. Rather, there is a good deal of amusing play with semiotic principles (the study of language signs) and with mathematical concepts which serve as parodies of the usual dramatis personae.

Like all Calvino works, both sagas still involve social, philosophical, and now linguistic issues, the difference being that this time the author has often looked outside the human, urban civilization for both his questions and his answers. In keeping with postmodernism's democratic attitude, in *Cosmicomics* creatures usually presumed less significant than humans—amphibians, dinosaurs, slugs and the like—merit the same attention as people and astronomical phenomena. Characters range in variety from Mr. Hnw "who later became a horse" to "Uncle N'ba N'ga," a fish of the Coelacanthus family, who embodies the reptilian evolution from aquatic to land creatures (19, 71).

Most amusing is *Cosmicomics'* irrepressible narrator, Qfwfq, a cosmic Huck Finn and nostalgic link to Calvino's past storytellers in *Baron* and *Viscount*. Different from those, however, Qfwfq as a talking equation is free of time, space, and earthly cares. As JoAnn Cannon rightly observes, he is not "a single, coherent character," but rather a phenomenon who incongruously tosses atoms with his playmates and whizzes around the galaxy at the speed of light.[14] In other words, Qfwfq is the quintessential postmodern Other. Except for his sense of humor, he is unencumbered by the human ties that proved so burdensome to many earlier Calvino characters, for instance, Amerigo the poll watcher. A cosmic eye, Qfwfq engenders (or perhaps parodies) Robbe-Grillet's idea of de-anthropomorphic narrative—and yet, how very much his thoughts can, and often do, reflect our own. Endearing are his cosmic, tongue-in-cheek reminiscences in "The Spiral" ["La spirale"] as he ponders the simplicity of bygone eons, moments made happy simply because "when you're young, all evolution lies before you, every road is open to you, and at the same time you can enjoy the fact of being there on the rock, flat mollusk-pulp, damp and happy" (142).

This incongruous wedding of the forces of evolution to folksy simple pleasures is, of course, resoundingly postmodern. It involves a perspective on fantasy drastically different from the earthbound ideas of structuralist Todorov, as mentioned earlier. In *Cosmicomics* the reader encounters something akin to (if not identical with) García Márquez's so-called "magic realism."[15] Like García Márquez's *One Hundred Years of Solitude*, *Cosmicomics* takes place in infinity, in an ontological zone where "the centuries flow by as if they were minutes" (19).[16] History in García Márquez, and in Calvino here too, is perceived as an outmoded humanist habit. Thus, in *Cosmicomics*, navigating through space, we see Time obliterated; we see past and present merged. With postmodern alacrity, Qfwfq juxtaposes the celestial against the earthly, the marvelous against the mundane in a Never-Never-land where "moon-milk was very thick, like a kind of cream cheese" (5).

In one of *Cosmicomics'* first and most engaging episodes, "All at One Point" ["Tutto in un punto"], Calvino plays with scientist Edwin P. Hubble's theory that the universe originally expanded from one point. Building on this notion, he fabricates a delightful postmodern parody, modeling the cosmos after a chaotic Italian neighborhood and poking fun at neorealism (and perhaps particularly at actress Sophia Loren). Blithely, Qfwfq describes spaghetti-making in outer space and also Mrs. Ph(i)Nk$_0$'s bosom as she industriously kneads her flour and eggs for a distant future of noodle-making (45–47).[17] Clotheslines, too, are strung across the one-point universe, already hopelessly cluttered with beds, mattresses, and all manner of paraphernalia suitable for future galatical generations (44).

With the nonchalance of a Kafka storyteller, but with substantially more goodwill, our heavenly watcher crams the vast cosmos into a one-point, earthbound reality, leveling the universe down to the reader's size simply by recalling that:

> *Naturally, we were all there,—old Qfwfq said,—where else could we have been? Nobody knew then that there could be space. Or time either: what use did we have for time, packed in there like sardines? (43)*

Naturally? What could be more incongruous here than the word "naturally," since there is nothing whatever natural about the story. Ironic word play like this, grounded in otherworld intellection and not in conventional comedy, is the very hallmark of the best postmodern humor. Coolly sophisticated is the scientific basis of much of Qfwfq's humor, yet many of his observations are curiously homey, furnishing the reader with a glimpse of postmodern humor at its most reassuring. His observation that "we were all there," silly as it may be, is cheering, conveying a sense of unanimity within the universal scheme of things, if not the earthly one.

Because of his talent for camaraderie, Qfwfq remains to this day one of Calvino's most lovable watchers. A universal chronicler, he invites the reader not only to speculate with him on cosmic events, but to participate with him in them as well—a unique and tempting offer, one affording the reader the chance to be Qfwfq's companion in the leap from the ordinary to otherworlds more amusing and intellectually challenging. Perhaps the reader will reason, as one sensitive critic of *Cosmicomics* already has, that "reality is not *the* world . . . but merely one of many modes of experiencing it" (Ricci "Introversion" 338). Indeed, exchanging, even for a brief time, the transience of this sphere for the eternity of Qfwfq provides a delightful respite from the reader's own more confined space.

In the last analysis, however, one must be cautious of Qfwfq's good-natured celestial speculations, since they do not make him wiser or more immune to fortune's outrage than any other postmodern protagonist. In fact, considering his celestial flounderings, the giddy Qfwfq is often curiously reminiscent of Kurt Vonnegut's Billy Pilgrim, the daft, time-traveling, postmodern hero of that author's *Slaughterhouse-Five.* For all his wit, Qfwfq, like Billy, is a powerless heavenly traveler who is always coming "unstuck in time" and who is eternally at the mercy of the cosmic ebb and flow.[18] Despite his hyperreality, Qfwfq thus participates more in mortal man's frailty than one might initially suspect. In fact, the very things this superhero and Vonnegut's all-too-human Billy Pilgrim share and ironically will never master are "the past, the present and the future" (Vonnegut 60). In like manner, Qfwfq also recalls, once more, Beckett's characters Vladimir and Estragon, in that Qfwfq too is "waiting for Godot," and for the answers that will never come because there is, as he puts it, "nothing to do but wait" (19).

Another example from *Cosmicomics,* "A Sign in Space" ["Un segno nello spazio"], deserves mention here for it underscores not just Calvino's philosophical reflections but his new experiments with language as well. In the story, Qfwfq tells the reader that he wants to create something uniquely new by hanging a sign in space which would be "like a name, the name of that point, and also my name that I had signed on that spot; in short, it was the only name available for everything that required a name" (33). To his chagrin, however, not only is his sign usurped and adulterated, but before long other signs grow so numerous that his loses originality.

At surface this game with signs appears no more than a silly cartoon, but there is more to it than that. Hidden in the diversion lies the author's serious purpose, as, by this play, Calvino determines to teach the reader a lesson both in living and linguistics. The game is meant to demonstrate linguist Ferdinand de Saussure's work in semiotics. According to Saussure, no sign (that is, word or symbol), including Qfwfq's, is inviolable. Instead, all language signs (including those galactical) are mutable, their meaning varying according to the social and linguistic setting in which they are read.[19] Poor Qfwfq, if only he could find a place more solid than space to hang his sign, a place where it could enjoy lasting meaning—but then that is not possible given the arbitrary nature of words—and worlds. Subtly implied in Qfwfq's anguished struggle for self-identity, therefore, is a metaphysical question that should not be overlooked. Could it be that humanity too, is merely a sign and hence itself an entity of no uniqueness?

One final cosmicomic story, "The Dinosaurs" ["I Dinosauri"], should also be mentioned in this discussion, for although it emphasizes the crisis of self in today's world like the previous tale, it does so in more poignant, human terms. In this episode, Qfwfq, spokesperson of every evolutionary age, recalls an ancient time when he was a mighty dinosaur, at first proud of his power, then later ashamed and reviled as part of a disparaged and dying breed. A quaint survivor and the brunt of cruel prejudice, he cautiously mingles with the "New Ones," hoping to pass unnoticed and therefore unmolested. His attempt succeeds, ironically not because he is accepted, but rather because he is easily ignored (102).

Unrecognized, Qfwfq goes disrespected. Once the dinosaur was a creature at least feared, but now Qfwfq, deprived even of that singularity, is no longer an individual. He is known only as the "Ugly One," a useful beast of burden, otherwise insignificant. Who is the dinosaur and what is his meaning beneath the surface of this postmodern allegory? In this story, according to Calvino, the dinosaur is any creature "Different, a Foreigner, and therefore Untrustworthy" (102). He is then, at one time or another, any one of us—black, white, old, obsolete, anyone who holds opinions or assumes shapes alien to the Other, and who, for these differences, is contemptuously labeled or ostracized. Keeping the above observations in mind, one understands why Siegel contends that, despite its sophisticated mathematical and scientific dabblings, the true emphasis of *Cosmicomics* rests not on physics but on metaphysics (44). Appreciated too are the words of Antonio Illiano, who, unlike many critics, finds *Cosmicomics* more polemical than amusing and a disquieting commentary on humanity's meager role in history.[20]

t zero, the sequel to *Cosmicomics*, begins as a delightful continuation of Calvino's celestial romp, but then two-thirds through, the work suddenly digresses. With no explanation, the Qfwfq stories simply stop and the book takes a decided turn towards a flatter and notably less embellished style. This final section, from which the second book derives its title, is intended to pay homage to French theorist Roland Barthes and his concept of writing degree zero, or what Susan Sontag has called "post-novel prose narrative."[21] Going a step beyond *Cosmicomics*' whimsy, Calvino tries his hand here at what Barthes calls a "writerly" work, or a psychological narrative of social and historical disengagement. In these texts the reader, deprived of fictional trademarks like plot and character-ization, is challenged to participate actively in the story's making by adding his own suppositions. Also detected here is the more important stylistic influence of Robbe-Grillet whose *nouveau roman* coincides with the writerly text for its emphasis on phenomenology, or the neutral reportage of objects and events.[22]

Today many recognize both the *nouveau roman* and zero-degree writ-ing as early manifestations of postmodernism. In fact, it has been ob-served that Robbe-Grillet's own tangled, ruminative tales mark "a wa-tershed between modernist and postmodernist poetics," and surely there is truth in this statement.[23] In both postmodernism and the *nouveau roman* there is a cynical de-emphasis of human motivation and an alto-gether bland delineation of story circumstances. With plot obscured and the protagonist treated perfunctorily, seeming inconsequentials such as color and texture leap to the surface. This recourse to the safe ground of pure description, along with the new accent on language, discerning crit-ics see as yet another symptom of today's rejection of moral humanism, a rejection that both postmodernism and the *nouveau roman* undeniably share. As Ben Stoltzfus observes, once the vicissitudes of humans have been put aside, abstract elements, like language, become "the protago-nists of the new fiction," which self-reflexively points out its own liter-ary devices to the reader, leaving him the responsibility of filling in the narrative blanks.[24]

Another significant bond between the *nouveau roman* and postmodern literature is the labyrinth metaphor, an image of life shared by Robbe-Grillet and Calvino that is often less than uplifting. Robbe-Grillet's *Jeal-ousy* and *In the Labyrinth* take place like bad dreams in a disorienting time warp.[25] Obsessive thoughts and a preoccupation with minutia sub-stitute for cause and effect, action and character. The same can be said for the last tales in *t zero*, dominated as they are by the same nightmarish aura and by a slavish devotion to particulars, to portraiture in language, and to circular thinking.

For example, *t zero*'s "The Night Driver" ["Il guidatore notturno"] is a mind-locked maze in which an anonymous narrator is driving from A to B seeking his estranged lover Y. At a roadstop, he phones her, but Y is not home. As a result, he is alternately tortured by thoughts that Y may be with his rival in love or else that Y, sorry about their recent tiff, may actually be on the opposite highway speeding towards him. In fact, any car coming the other way might be hers, but who is to say which, and furthermore, whether the couple will ever meet again. Characteristically postmodern is the narrator's passive reaction to these dismal reflections, and similarly typical is his subsequent behavior. Because nothing is certain, he focuses on the only sure things at hand, precisely the same consuming details often portrayed in postmodern novels.[26] His tranquillity is premised not on his certain knowledge, but rather on his certain ignorance and on knowing only that:

> as long as we can check our telephone numbers and there is no answer then we will continue, all three of us, speeding back and forth along these white lines, with no points of departure or of arrival to threaten with their sensations and meanings the single-mindedness of our race, freed finally from the awkward thickness of our persons and voices and moods, reduced to luminous signals, the only appropriate way of being. (136)

A sad commentary on humanity is the night driver, and a classically impotent Calvinian watcher. Past bewailing his sorry fate, he exists as a nonentity, his peace of mind founded not on escaping the highway maze, but rather on foregoing human contact and staying safely hidden.

Significant here is the repetition of the car metaphor, yet another satirical symbol in Calvino of man's victimization by outside forces, in this instance machines: mechanisms designed to liberate humanity but that enslave instead. Highways also spell prison in *t zero*; they embody the random sterility of the no-man's land that is life's roadway today. As if to underscore his grim commentary on the modern mortal's crippled essence, Calvino has deliberately substituted letters of the alphabet for places and names, lest the reader develop an affection for the character entirely out proportion to his or her importance.

At least one more labyrinth story, "The Count of Monte Cristo" ["Il conte di Montecristo"], deserves attention here, not only because it is the most challenging tale in this last section of *t zero*, but also because it is the most postmodern. An impeccable example of metafiction (stories about stories), "The Count" willfully tampers with the original Dumas novel by boldly borrowing its principal character, Edmond Dantès. For all its postmodernity, this tale, like the others in *t zero*, is once again, by the author's own admission, stylistically indebted to Robbe-Grillet (Paris 1978). In it one does not follow the original adventure, but rather the maddening trail of Dantès's twisted thoughts. His neurotic schemes to escape his circuitous prison in the Chateau d'If serve to underscore the pointlessness of the entire endeavor, since, as he indicates:

> *The search for the center of If-Monte Cristo does not lead to results that are more sure than those of the march toward its unreachable circumference: in whatever point I find myself the hypersphere stretches out around me in every direction; the center is all around where I am; going deeper means descending into myself. You dig and dig and you do nothing but retrace the same path. (147)*

This last ingenious otherworld, stripped as it is of external events, is clearly Calvino's most extreme labyrinthical exploration. As Capozzi points out (79), Calvino calls upon the image of a molehole to conjure up the frantic mental digging depicted in "The Count," and certainly this metaphor is apropos (*t zero* 143). With its mania for introspection, this particular voyage suggests that there can never be any rapprochement between the entombed protagonist and the Other, the gap between his inner and outer reality can never be bridged, and the subterranean world, at least for him, represents a *huis clos* [no exit].

In recent times, Newman, a sometime antagonist of postmodernism, has disparagingly indicted its literature as "inflation of discourse" (10). Another critic, Benussi, discredits Calvino's *t zero*, calling it "cerebral in the manner of Borges" (116). But remarks like these, though well-intentioned, are unfair. Benussi's observations especially reveal a misapprehension not only of Calvino and Borges, but of postmodernism and the new novel as well. The *nouveau roman*, its rhythmic monotone punctuated by novelistic fragments, is not just about literary games, but about life attitudes, and the same can be said of Calvino's work. His novels portray a postmodern landscape: a bafflingly twisted road in which there is little a person recognizes with certitude besides the geometrical surfaces often described in the *nouveau roman*. In fact, when Stoltzfus says that the labyrinth topos in Kafka, Borges, and Robbe-Grillet reflects modern humanity's "alienation, disorientation, and ennui," he might as well be speaking of Calvino. Calvino's literature too is about spiritual homelessness today. It is no wonder then that the theme of the wanderer, "a central image of our times," henceforth becomes an informing metaphor in much of the author's last works (Stoltzfus 118–19).

The tortuous search for a center, as portrayed in *t zero*, reaches a darkly dramatic climax in Calvino's next novel, *The Castle of Crossed Destinies* (1969, 1973), a collection of stories that is unique at both a technical and a fictional level.[27] As fiction, *Castle* provides a scathing parody of the traditional tale of the hero's quest: a topos inferred in much of Calvino's works. Cynically the author reverses the conventional story, juxtaposing its uplifting message against the dilemma of postmodern man's downhill slide and dubious life choices. At a technical level, *Castle*, like many postmodern works, can be a daunting novel. Not designed for passive reading, it warrants a thorough look below the events in order to be appreciated. Beneath the fiction lies a wealth of technical innovation, including a firm foundation in structuralist theory. Not to be ignored in a full reading are the input of Propp's and Saussure's respective narrative and linguistic research. It is precisely their precepts that the author means to test here as tools to create a grim satire.[28]

To execute his complex narrative strategy, Calvino first calls into practice Propp's theories on the repetitive patterns inherent to fables. According to Propp, there are consistent narrative parallels to be observed between one folktale and another, if not in their details then certainly in the generic characters and events which such stories share. For example, Propp indicates that typical fairy-tale characters usually include, besides the hero: the villain, the helper (often magical), and the princess (or some other sought-after personage). Some predictable, universal story functions, on the other hand, entail the hero's birth (often under extraordinary circumstances), his departure on a quest, the tests he endures during his journey, and finally his triumphal return, be it physical or moral.[29]

Confident of Propp's principles, and having elsewhere himself described these narrative parallels as "fixed structures" built into storytelling by oral tradition, Calvino now sets out in *Castle* to prove his observations ("Process" 94). Eagerly, he proceeds to show that the hero's mission (or monomyth), whether in the shape of a fairy tale, chivalric quest, or epic saga, is emphatically not excepted from Propp's theories on fable-making. In fact, following the theoretician's narrative paradigm and choosing his own heroes, the author creates sixteen separate tales in the novel that are both different in their details and yet analogous, at least in their overall plan.

As the cornice story indicates, each of *Castle*'s adventures begin as a seemingly innocent recapitulation of the conventional hero's journey:

> *In the midst of a thick forest, there was a castle that gave shelter to all travelers overtaken by night on their journey: lords and ladies, royalty and their retinue, humble wayfarers. (3)*

Typical of the traditional hero's quest is its beginning in error's dark wood, the place from which many a brave warrior has been called to depart on his mission. Like other traditional literary heroes, these earthly sojourners in the novel are tested, endure trials, do penance, and suffer harrowing misfortunes. Unlike the traditional hero, however, they are never redeemed, their calamitous fates sealed even before their stories begin.[30]

Driven by guilt to confess their sins, yet inexplicably cursed by muteness, the *Castle*'s adventurers recount their terrible travels as best they can by way of the only means available to them: a deck of tarot cards. As the other players stand watching, awaiting their turns, and guessing at the cards' meanings, each hero (or victim) lays down his tarot. As is postmodern custom, many of the stories have been borrowed from various sources, including Dante, Boccaccio, Ariosto, Shakespeare, and other great writers. Each story testifies vividly both to Propp's theories and to the author's versatile employment of the hero's tale, be it the Calvinian stories of Hamlet, Lear and Macbeth in "Three Tales of Madness and Destruction" ["Tre storie di follia e distruzione"], the Ariostesque "Tale of Roland Crazed with Love" ["Storia dell'Orlando pazzo per amore"], or the author's own stunning account of Parsifal in "Two Tales of Seeking and Losing" ["Due storie in cui si cerca e ci si perde"]. But the stories themselves, as well as Propp's implicit input, are only one part of the novel's narrative process.

By way of the tarot cards, Calvino takes his storytelling a step beyond Propp, imbedding simultaneously in the novel an even more elaborate and controversial stratagem: this time visual, and this time inspired by linguist Saussure's perception of language signs. As stated earlier, Saussure sees language, whether presented through words or other symbols as equivocal: a form of communication made up of two opposing factions. The first faction is *parole*, or the individual linguistic signs, whose meanings are entirely arbitrary when read out of context. The second is *langue,* or language system, the organizing social force that, from without, imposes order or consistent meaning on given sets of signs.[31] Hence, not just words, but traffic placards, chessmen, and most specifically here, tarot cards, all can function as language because all communicate meaning—that is to say, if the players or speakers share a common reading and know the rules of the game. The debatable issue in *Castle*'s card readings, of course, is this last gray area: the ever dubious question in Calvino of what the rules are—what is certain, and most importantly, what is not.

In the tarot deck Calvino has happened upon a darkly playful, theatrical tool. Via the cards and their mysterious emblematic images, the author means to dramatize not only Saussure's binary theory of language, but his own at-odds philosophy of living as well. Within the cards there already exist all the ingredients for a vigorous tug-and-pull drama both linguistic and narrative—though at the start of the novel this may not be apparent. For example, as the novel's characters silently lay down their tales in tarot rows, the cards readily shape themselves into a magical puzzle of intersecting stories that, when observed superficially in the text's illustration, appears an integral unit.[32] Viewing the tarot maze in this tidy rectangle temporarily rouses in the reader a deceptive sense of *langue,* or order, which reinforces the solidity of the traditional myth of the hero and likewise implies stability to the communicative process. Like the reader, the characters too are initially taken in by the card puzzle. In it they hope to discover a mantic code, an explanation of the events which might make sense of their future (or is it their past?).

These expectations, of course, are dashed at once since it is this same panorama of cards that precipitates the breakdown of *langue* and thus the undoing of the hero's journey. No sooner has the stage been set in the conventional forest setting and all the clues neatly planted in the reader's mind for the traditional monomyth, than things go awry and the reader learns that the integrity of the novel's tarot grid has been spurious from the start. Despite the seeming unity of the card arrangement, *Castle*'s individual stories defy definitive reading. Indeed, once the whole plan (*langue*) is suggested, the reverse dynamics of Saussure's theory come into play and the individual card signs (*parole*) haphazardly go their own way. The cards of Hamlet's story, for instance, read in the opposite direction, unpredictably become the story of King Lear; the story of Parsifal, read in reverse order, emerges as the story of a lesser character, the gravedigger; *The Two of Cups*, to one character, capriciously signifies an amorous encounter, and to another simply a toast; *The Star* in one tale represents psyche, in another a serving maid, and so on.

The Dantesque model of the hero's labyrinth descent with its orthodox religious content and promise of redemption is particularly targeted for deconstruction. With mock piety, stories like those of Faust conjure up in the pictorial cards religious icons such as heaven and hell, sin and damnation, only in the end to confound any discrimination between good and evil. Moral and metaphysical issues are raised and pondered; philosophical dialogues are initiated, touching on the meaning of the world and the sustaining principle of the universe, but the discourse leads nowhere. A tale begins as if it were a conventional fable, perhaps even the journey of a soul to God, only to be shattered. In the end, the archetypal drama falters disastrously when a key ingredient, the hero's salvation, is peremptorily jettisoned. In the polarized struggle between language system versus language as arbitrary signs, erraticism triumphs both dramatically and linguistically and the novel's expected allegorical message is meanly sabotaged.[33]

Two important stories in *Castle* explore unfinished metaphysical di-lemmas pertaining to Calvino's Sartrean impasse over free will and choice. "The Waverer's Tale" ["Storia dell'indeciso"] treats the difficult question of what is right and wrong begun in Calvino's earlier *Viscount*. "I Also Try to Tell My Tale" ["Anch'io cerco di dire la mia"] effectively concludes the discussion of the conflict between duty to self versus duty to the Other, as once explored in *Baron*. Both of the stories illustrate the negativity of Calvino's reasoning in this area: man's power to make vi-able choices perceived as a fruitless hoax.

As the title implies, in "My Tale," we encounter the central narrator's own story, which after a frustrating search he finally locates among the other players' scattered tarot cards. Critics readily detect the author's own voice in this tale, a likely assumption, because at the outset, the storyteller confesses to being a writer, one who has spent years impris-oned in his study watching the trail of ink from his pen (107–8). When questioned, Calvino did in fact admit that if one single story in *Castle* contained a "message" of his, it was indeed this one ("Fabulist" 79–80).

As the narrative opens, the storyteller finds himself at his own exis-tential crossroads, seeking a reasonable compromise between a life of blessed solitude and one of social involvement. Quickly, he isolates *The Hermit* and *The Knight of Swords*, two tarot cards that personify his dilemma. After naming the cards St. Jerome (the recluse) and St. George (the dragon killer), the narrator takes the reader on an imaginary tour of world art galleries, stopping here and there to examine portraits of these two different saints. Looking over the paintings, he admires St. Jerome for the quiet of his study, but not for his internal strife, his compulsive fixations (107). The narrator also admires St. George, an active man involved in life's fray, but rejects him for his lack of sensitivity, as "psychology is no use to the man of action" (109).

After a tortured journey of self-examination, and pondering the two saints' differences, our writer warmly assures the reader that he has found an answer, a compromise, the way to combine the best of both saints: preserve his private space and still acquit himself in the world. He congratulates himself on his solution, but then in a stinging two-line coda sarcastically refutes it, saying, "Thus I have set everything to rights. On the page, at least. Inside me, all remains as before" (111). In other words, the truce that the narrator sought, borrowing the best from both saints, apparently looks good, but only on paper, much the way Cosimo's active social role in *Baron* seemed feasible, but only in fairy-tale form. The truth is that for Calvino (as for Sartre) the twain here do not meet: the roles of the warrior and the intellectual remain incompatible. At story's end the quandary of the Other is left unresolved, the narrator/author acknowledging his personal failure particularly as a warrior—or perhaps in Calvino's case, as a political activist.

"The Waverer's Tale" is a second striking study in existential choice, this time focusing on the vexing definition of right and wrong in today's society. In the tale, the author mercilessly dissects the classical metaphor called the *bivium*, or crossroads of decision, and through the pairing of opposites, gibes at the comfortable definition of ethical choice.[34] Concurrently, he again elucidates his fixation with the Sartrean premise: "choice is possible, but what is not possible is not to choose" (Sartre *Emotions* 41). The end result is a deadly game wherein, by paraphrasing Sartre, Calvino pits the idea that choosing is necessary against the grim rewards for having done so.

The story concerns an evasive young knight with a cowardly distaste for decisions, who flees his hometown in order to avoid choosing between two brides. An agony of abortive decisions and hasty escapes follow as the hero faces an absurdist Saussurian list of archetypally paired opposites. Neo-existentialism, mythology, and dark postmodern play merge when, for him, every bend in the road, every simple gesture, exacts a penalty in choosing. When at a crossroads the hero cannot choose which road to take he leaves the decision to his two horses; when neither of them, left or right, can decide either, he flips a coin; when the coin lands on edge pointing skyward, he decides to take the easy way out and let heaven decide. But the Calvinian heaven offers no answers either, because, once up there, events continue to unfold, as one critic observes, in a veritable "binary obsession."[35] Ultimately, the young man meets his comeuppance in an encounter with an angel-devil in the City of God, or is it the City of Dis?

The preoccupation with pairing in this and other stories in *Castle* has received a good deal of critical attention, but often only for its structural significance rather than its existential meaning. Most critics have recognized in the book's polarized scheme the theories of Saussure on signs, and have, therefore, perceived the novel as merely a word game designed to illustrate the linguist's premise that language elements always exist as paired opposites (Saussure 120–22). Such critical observations, while valid, have underestimated our author, however. As always in Calvino, there is more to the story than what is obvious.

In the incessant coupling of contraries, in the struggle between thesis and antithesis, the author illustrates for the reader not just Saussure's linguistic theories, but also the very absurdity of ever choosing rightly at all. As options blur before the hero's eyes, as heaven and hell and devils and angels merge, right and wrong finally dissolve into a meaningless, amoral swirl of contradictions which spell a death to choosing. Thus, at the end of "The Waverer's Tale," we find that, unlike Dante or other model heroes, the young man has learned nothing. His postmodern quest has been neither redemptive nor instructive. Indeed nothing about his situation has changed, except the color of his hair, now prematurely gray from his ordeal (63).

This last image of the hero in *Castle*, beaten not by bad choices, but by the very act of choosing itself, further confirms Calvino's postmodern and existential worldview. Gone is the mask of the trilogy's naive storyteller. In his place, the reader encounters a world-weary watcher for whom the moral *bivium* is a dilemma in which conventional values are emphatically denied and any "middle road" excluded. The storyteller's torment at the decisive moment, his hands shaking, clearly recalls the existential angst, the misgivings at choosing experienced by the protagonists of Sartre, Kafka, Vonnegut, and other late-modernist or postmodern authors. Although "The Waverer's Tale" is not the last story in *Castle*, it does spitefully conclude the dialogue on free will which the author initiated in his earlier works.

One last story requires study, not just because it underscores the existential perspective of the two narratives above, but because it adds a distinctly postmodern nuance. "Two Tales of Seeking and Losing" presents the reader with a Calvinian adaptation of Parsifal's failed quest for the Holy Grail. Meaningfully, the details of the journey are of only secondary interest and quickly disposed of. Instead, the storyteller rushes on to what interests him more: the absurdity of the quest in the first place and the inevitability of its failure. Pitilessly he hammers at the unavoidable nature of Parsifal's errors, stressing that the hero's only mistake was simply "not knowing." To emphasize the irony of Parsifal's predicament, the narrator insistently juxtaposes Parsifal's complete innocence against the heinousness of his subsequent yet naive wrong doing.

Bereft of divine intelligence and guidance, Parsifal makes his way alone, a guilty victim, lost to desolate terrain. Even nature, we are told, has a clearer, if perverse, conception of Parsifal's destiny. These characteristics of Parsifal, borrowed from Greek tragedy, are also emphatically connected to the depiction of postmodern man in contemporary literature. Many authors in this Godless century have expressed similar attitudes of "not knowing." Kafka, to whom Calvino has often been compared, comes readily to mind. Parsifal's silence, his fatal habit of never asking questions, specifically recalls Kafka's protagonist in *The Trial* whose silent wait outside the court of justice is no different than Parsifal's mute, indecisive vigil over the tarot cards.

So profound is Parsifal's naiveté that, as the story tells us, he does not even know what questions to ask (96). His ignorance, like that of Kafka's characters, is existential. The end of his story finds Parsifal still searching for enlightenment amid the cards only to find that "'the kernel of the world is empty, the beginning of what moves in the universe is the space of nothingness, around absence is constructed what exists, at the bottom of the Grail is the Tao,' and he points to the empty rectangle surrounded by the tarots" (97).

Much attention has been devoted here to *The Castle of Crossed Destinies*, and for good reason. By the author's own admission, at one time it was the novel closest to him. In it, he acknowledged, he said more of himself than in any of his other previous works ("Fabulist" 80). As such, its bleak message serves as a summa of the author's darkest considerations of humanity and existence. In the novel life is portrayed as a card trick, a journey which, in youth, borrows its orderly ideals from Propp only to see them disintegrate into a Saussurian whirl of wild cards. Stripped of the keys of the traditional hero's journey, deprived of religious canon, and moving from thesis to antithesis, the work pursues a vindictive course. It reenacts a postmodern doomsday itinerary whereby the individual, like the characters in *Castle*, is sacrificed to a dystopian universe whose order or disorder he will never plumb.

Not only does *Castle* render the hero's quest meaningless, but it casts a pall over the essence of humankind. Unlike Dante or Odysseus, who learn from their mistakes, here the hero's faults are irremediable. This sinister Kafkaesque quirk, the idea of man's innate ignorance, refers the reader back once more to Calvino's earlier words on humanity's spiritual disfigurement. This time, however, the author treats the theme with devastating irony.

Important as the novel was once to its author, *Castle* is not Calvino's most popular fiction, and no wonder. Perched combatively on the edge of the metaphysical abyss, it is an either/or work intended to affront reader sensibilities and to challenge conventional complacency both in reading and living. In this regard, furthermore, it is eminently successful. Opportunely, *Castle* does not, however, represent the author's last thoughts on humanity or literature. Other novels followed quickly, more tolerant in their posture and yet equally daring in form and content. These later, conciliatory novels would not completely dispel the melancholy shadow *Castle* had cast on Calvino's work, but they would lighten it.

6

FINAL JOURNEYS

The Castle of Crossed Destinies was Calvino's darkest novel; he would not write another like it. Rather, the seasoned writer turned away from *Castle*'s antagonistic portrait of existence and, to commemorate his final years, made a truce with his postmodern misgivings. To his last works, *If on a winter's night a traveler, Mr. Palomar,* and *Under the Jaguar Sun,* fell the task of escaping the philosophical blind alley figured in the previous novel, of recuperating serenity and humor, and finding a middle ground for his fiction. Themes familiar in Calvino, specifically the double-edged dilemma of choosing, recur in all his last works, but are treated with new restraint. *Invisible Cities,* a novel written contemporaneously to *Castle,* already reveals a changed author, striving for a more compromising tone. In late life the older writer explores a postmodernism both more moderate and forgiving of twentieth-century humanity and its failings.

Like his darker postmodern pieces, however, Calvino's new conciliatory fiction finds no home in the arid land of everyday realism. The author therefore continues his explorations of more malleable, abstract otherworlds, tampering with the conventional novel as he had done in *Cosmicomics* and *Castle,* provoking and amusing the reader with his highly original dialogues on postmodern life. The results provide some of Calvino's most inventive and sensitive literary moments. Influenced by the works of Saussure, Derrida, and now psychoanalyst Jacques Lacan as to the precariousness of the spoken (or written) word, Calvino sometimes experiments with a prose inspired by what is unspoken.[1] He explores language at a subconscious level where, as Lacan observes, "the function of Language is not to inform but to evoke."[2] Scrutinizing the shifting meanings, the unexpressed emotions wedged in the "void" between words,[3] he seeks out a literature intuitive by nature, innately ambiguous and, for its mystical quality, discretely inspired by Borges.

The influence of Borges is observed early in *Invisible Cities,* the transitional work marking Calvino's turn toward a compassionate postmodernism. Like Borges' stories, *Cities* unfolds in the form of a fantasy parable: a soft-spoken, lazy colloquy endowed with rich allegorical allusions. A novel replete with recurring forms and inspired by the myth of the eternal return, it recalls such similarly visionary Borges tales as "The Circular Ruins" or "The Garden of Forking Paths."[4] Structural parallels to *Castle* persist in *Invisible Cities* in that it too possesses a determined framework. However, again in the manner of Borges, this architectural weight is lightened by the novel's lacy, delicate poetry.

Like *Castle, Invisible Cities* encapsules multiple stories that, in typical postmodern fashion, recover and revel in nostalgia for bygone times; like *Castle,* the cornice of *Cities* is modeled on a fixed grid, this time a chessboard instead of a tarot card maze. Unlike *Castle,* however, and more akin to the earlier *Cosmicomics, Invisible Cities* eludes the hard knocks of an either/or itinerary by slipping off to tranquil, alternate worlds where the grim necessities of choosing are mitigated by fantasy and where the omnipresent Calvinian spectator perceives the journey from cradle to grave as tolerable, adventuresome and wryly amusing.

The cornice story that frames the novel is imaginatively based on Marco Polo's *Il milione,* that author's remarkable thirteenth-century account of his sojourn in China. In the Calvino version, Marco Polo, a merchant and guest at the court of Kublai Khan, has been asked by the great leader to investigate and map the cities of the empire and then report back to him about them. In their meetings over chess, the two men muse together on these magical and exotically named places. Housed within this delicate frame story are more than fifty poetical vignettes that describe a variety of fabulous cities and wondrous sights. All of these places are filled with curious and contrary discoveries that the first modern tourist, Polo, ponders with the Khan in an ongoing travelogue, both quietly philosophical and playful.[5]

Tourism, or visionary travel, is characteristic of postmodernism's "supportive" fiction where "getting away from it all" is a priority both in film and literature.[6] Clearly, the intent of such works, including this one, is to offer relief from practical necessity and provide human freedoms not to be found either in this world or in the nihilistic labyrinths figured in other postmodern works. Through the migration in *Invisible Cities* from one magical oasis to the next, thorny metaphysical questions about the meaning of the world or of man's final end are skirted or magically transformed. Unpleasant queries are replaced by what McHale would amusingly perceive as typically postmodern and touristy questions, such as "which world is this? What is to be done in it?" (10).

The agonizing over the suspect Other has also been moderated in this novel. A human solidarity is inferred, despite (or, perhaps, because of) the Khan's Sartrean description of life as the hell *we* make and share by living together (165).[7] Furthermore, for the first time in Calvino, the pleasure, rather than the pain, of being an outsider is tacitly weighed. Like a visitor from another planet, the foreigner Polo takes solitary delight in exploring the beauties around him. A Calvinian watcher of rare equanimity, he puzzles unperturbed, and even delights in the author's description of life's spiraled twists and turns.

The choice of the city as the novel's focus is surely not without allegorical import. The city here (as in literatures past) is presented as a metaphor for life, or perhaps more expressly, human society. Such a topos is no doubt partly inspired by traditional treatments of the same theme as they are found, for example, in the Bible or in St. Augustine's *The City of God*.[8] Updated here by Calvino, the concept "city" focuses on today's problematic postmodern environment: a society ceaselessly vacillating between monotony and turmoil. His rancor of earlier works quieted, the mature author resignedly reassesses the paradoxical aspects of the contemporary world and human choices within it. Sometimes the novel focuses on the tension today between misfit man's drab sense of anonymity and his eccentric attempts at originality. At other moments, it sensitively pits the blessings of tedium against the ceaseless frenzy for change, both of which perspectives are alternately dramatized in our present-day fractured (*dimezzato*) society.

Two of the cities described, Trude and Eutropia, exemplify certain intrinsic postmodern contradictions. Trude, despite its tidy suburbs and shops, is a tiresome metropolis whose houses, hotels, and downtown are identical to any other Trude, unequivocally the same in all particulars. Indeed, the narrator might easily be alluding to any one of a number of drab American cities, bedecked with identical strip malls and fast food restaurants, when he slyly informs the reader that "the world is covered by a sole [generic] Trude which does not begin and does not end. Only the name of the airport changes" (128).

Eutropia, its name suggesting today's conflicted European community, is another of life's anomalous cities. Paradoxically revealed in Eutropia are both the growing congruence of today's world community and the desperate striving for diversity among its separate societies. Like Trude, the story of Eutropia is a parable of life, concurrently implying both the oneness of Propp's Everyman fable and the many of the individual tales and unique existences within it. Eutropia, we are told, is a city literally on the go, transplanting itself hastily anytime its citizenry gets restless or sluggish. Yet despite its constant changes, its fresh vistas, new residents, friends, and wives, Eutropia nonetheless remains ironically unchanged simply because "the inhabitants repeat the same scenes, with the actors changed; they repeat the same speeches with variously combined accents; they open alternate mouths in identical yawns" (64–65). Housing Eutropia's diversity, therefore, is the blessed, if boring, oneness of humankind.

The tale concludes sadly, but wisely, when the reader is told that Eutropia, its enormous variety notwithstanding, is at best no more than an "ambiguous miracle" (65), a postmodern phenomenon, whereby the individual is incessantly assailed by what is enduring, on the one hand, and what is transient or faddish on the other (64–65). Like Calvino's early works, *Invisible Cities* inevitably reminds the reader of life's contradictions. It reprises, but now with quiet composure, Calvino's *Castle* where the predictability of existence as depicted in the tarot card puzzle incongruously rested on the unpredictable behavior of its individual cards.

Both the frantic pace and transience of postmodern existence are perhaps best captured by the metaphoric city of Fedora, a multifaceted (or perhaps, as the name implies, multi-hatted) city where, according to Marco Polo, any or all of the city's facets, plans or models are merely suppositions. "The one [model] contains what is accepted as necessary when it is not yet so; the others, what is imagined as possible and, a moment later, is possible no longer" (33). Via Fedora, Calvino alludes to the tempo of postmodern society, to the race for novelty, and to the alarming flux that undermines confidence in self and community today. Going a step further, the author encourages the reader to seek peace of mind by building his own private Fedora, the city that corresponds to his own imaginary model (32). This last advice is typically postmodern and proposes a distinctly Borges-style alternative to life's realities: fantasy.

Fantasy, dreams, imagination . . . these are the remedies to humanity's restless ennui. It has been said of Borges that imagination is "the most positive force in his universe, capable [as only it is] of probing the abyss of being."[9] The same observation can be made of Calvino's last works. For this author, too, dreams are now the stuff of life, humanity's supreme consolation in the face of ongoing uncertainty. Whereas reality may be conjecture and appearances deceiving, fantasy never lies. Furthermore, fantasy is a dream city larger than life because, as Polo suggests, "everything imaginable can be dreamed" (44). Only in the mind's eye, therefore, can the reader/author truly experience unlimited choices, enjoying there (and only there) the liberty of taking apart his fantasy, disassembling his dream cities, as would the Great Khan, only to rebuild them in other new ways merely by shuffling their parts (43). In imagination, where the universe is infinite, the reader emancipates himself from earthly constraints to merge time and eternity, truth and fiction, and thus find a contentment seen neither in real life nor in Calvino's earlier novels, particularly in the sobering *Castle of Crossed Destinies*.

According to the Khan (Polo's dialogic doppelganger in the novel), dreams are better than words anyway. Words (like arbitrary tarot cards) fail. However, in the crevices between words, there exists an unspoken (Derridian/Lacanian) "space"—or corner of the mind—reserved just for dreams (38). For Calvino, it is in this unlimited expanse that man's ultimate freedom lies.[10] A uniquely postmodern autonomy is this harmonious city of the mind, an otherworld of the imagination that is never boring or false because here man's thoughts are both dependable and yet as changeable as "grains of sand" (22).

In *Invisible Cities*, Calvino has found (at least on paper) an alternative to reality's either/or dilemma. He has penetrated what McHale calls the "excluded middle," those otherworlds that defy both the confines of fictional verisimilitude and life's nitty gritty reality (McHale 106). Recuperating this generous arena, the author creates there his own personal poetry, carving a private literary oasis where there are no boundaries and where ambiguity is not only tolerated but embraced. Many readers have enjoyed the freedom Calvino garners in this novel, not to mention the return ticket out of the labyrinth which the novel buys. It is scarcely surprising then that *Invisible Cities*, with its small snatches of poetry in prose, remains a favorite among the author's works. While offering no firmer answers to life's mysteries or to its fatal end than does *Castle*, the novel emphatically adopts a more free-wheeling attitude towards living, advising the reader to make the most of his aimless sojourn on earth, to travel, see the sights, dream dreams—but not bother to ask questions.

After *Invisible Cities*, Calvino personally published only two more completed works, *If on a winter's night a traveler* and *Mr. Palomar*, and these appeared only after a lengthy hiatus of more than five years. This silence did not mean, however, that the author was idle or had given up his literary journeys. An edition of short stories, *Numbers in the Dark and Other Stories*, and a last fragmented work, *Under the Jaguar Sun*, begun earlier but published only after the author's death, provide ample examples of Calvino's work both during this interim period and also during times previous.

Numbers in the Dark is a hodgepodge collection of stories written over a lengthy time span from 1943 to 1984 and, for this reason, many of the early stories have no place in this present discussion of the author's final works. Some of the later (and certainly most rewarding) stories, however, do belong here. Two particularly thought-provoking postmodern tales are "The Mirror, the Target" ["Lo specchio, il bersaglio," 1978] and "The Last Channel" ["L'ultimo canale," 1984]. Both, not surprisingly, treat of life's choices and of alternatives lost. Obeisance, if not acceptance, now plays a decisive role in the older author's encounters with destiny. As a result, customary Calvinian themes are often treated playfully with little trace of the author's former truculence.

In the amusing "Last Channel," the narrator is obsessed with the remote control of his television set. According to him, switching channels is the only means to discover the True Story amid the myriad of programs available. "I am convinced," he tells us, "that there is a sense in the happenings of this world, that a coherent story, explicable in all its series of cause and effect, is going on somewhere at this very moment, and is not beyond our capacity to verify, and that this story contains the key for judging and understanding everything else" (255). Nonetheless, there remains the dubious task of finding it. The real program is "out there" somewhere, but, as he ironically allows, it must be on another channel somewhere amid "the dustclouds of a fragmented world" (256).

His story might end harmlessly there if he could keep his itchy finger aimed solely at the television set, but he cannot. Instead, as dissatisfied with the choices of worlds around him as he is with those on television, he turns his remote on the passing scene, hoping to effect some changes in his wife, his father-in-law and, finally, in the chiefs of government. This last ill-conceived act is naturally misinterpreted by the police and, as a result, the storyteller finishes in a padded cell at the sanitarium with his finger still spasmodically pushing an imaginary button. A judge has declared him insane, but he knows better. He knows that it is things around him that are awry, and that even the smallest choice, even the tiniest "yes" or "no," the flick of a switch, for instance, might alter circumstances and at last put him in touch with the right channel. At its conclusion, "Channel" slyly pokes fun at the so-called validity of the concrete world and its technology, and like *Invisible Cities*, offers (at least to this character) an alluring "middle road," a fantasy escape from an insufferable reality.

More poetical, but just as philosophical, is "The Mirror, the Target," a bittersweet tale of forsaken dreams. While he is young, Fulgenzio lives with his face in the mirror where every once in a while he catches a glimpse, however fleeting, of some unattainable other self in a bewitching otherworld. But the voices of reason offer him no rest and never leave off giving him practical advice:

> Fulgenzio, you can't always be so vague about your plans! Fulgenzio, you must set yourself an end to achieve—an objective—an aim—a target—you must press on to your goal—you must learn your lesson, you must win the competition, you must earn a lot and save a lot! (213)

Though smitten as he is by the hidden depths in the mirror and fascinated by the secret, poetic side of everything he sees, Fulgenzio nonetheless succumbs to reality, thereby short-circuiting his dreams and eventually, in later years, even forgetting the otherworlds of his youth. Like "Channel," this Borges-style tale posits a freer and more enticing middle ground to life, one that exists elsewhere in fancy. More pragmatic than the other tale, however, "Target" quietly implies that growing up and growing older often means compromise, choosing with silent dignity from what is before you rather than what might have been.

Under the Jaguar Sun, published late as an entity, but conceived and begun much earlier (1972),[11] was apparently intended as a probe (perhaps Lacanian in inspiration) into the five senses. As such, it marks a surprising indulgence for the rational Calvino into the Freudian realm of the instinctual or pre-linguistic. In it Calvino sets himself the challenging task of delving into the primitive, unspoken emotions of human experience, those psychic events that precede the conscious word and therefore defy the superficial contrivances of conventional language. Incomplete at his death (the chapters on sight and touch unwritten), *Jaguar Sun* is a slender yet uncommon expression by the author.

For example, the droll title story, "Under the Jaguar Sun" ["Sotto il sole giaguaro"], devoted to the sense of taste, reveals a side to Calvino rarely glimpsed in his other works: the erotic. A visit to Mexico, its tropical climate, romantic ruins, lush vegetation, and evenings spent feasting has had a powerful effect on the narrator, reawakening him to his wife's charms by way of her seductive eating habits. Sitting across from Olivia and watching her devour her dinner suddenly arouses him sexually. Hungrily, he begins to see himself as her dinner, musing lustfully:

> It was the sensation of her teeth in my flesh that I was imagining, and I could feel her tongue lift me against the roof of her mouth, enfold me in saliva, then thrust me under the tips of the canines. I sat there facing her, but at the same time it was as if a part of me, or all of me, were contained in her mouth, crunched, torn shred by shred. (23)

As voluptuously textured as the narrator's sexual fantasy are the exotic meals he verbally concocts: the pungent *"chiles en nogada,"* or small pleated peppers succumbing to a savory sauce, the appetizing *"gorditas pellizcadas con manteca,"* small spherical delicacies whose names he sensually translates as "plump girls pinched with butter," not to mention the *"tamal de elote"* and other succulent morsels named that make the reader's mouth water (5, 26–27). A tale bubbling with sauces and simmering with lechery, Calvino's "Jaguar Sun" opens the reader's eyes (or rather taste buds) to a reassuring postmodern realm where food is the primary sexual metaphor and banal sexual signs (that is, lips and breasts) incredulously take second place to flavorsome cues like *"sopa de frijoles"* (29).[12] Calvino, an author who usually prides himself on frostier humor, surprises the reader here with a delightfully earthy digression. By combining a pinch of erotica with a dash of plot, he has created a clever spoof of today's libidinous society, inventing a delicious otherworld escape in which solid food replaces the melancholy implications of some of his past works.

A more effective, but decidedly less humorous, story from the same volume is "A King Listens" ["Un re in ascolto"], a chilling examination of the psychology of hearing and of the paranoia it can breed in one who might (or might not) have good reason to fear. By rights this less-than-comforting tale belongs with Calvino's darker postmodern fiction, particularly with *Castle*. Only by virtue of its inclusion in Calvino's posthumous publication and because of its artistic importance as a stunning portrait of the psyche, do we digress to include it here.

A figurehead king sits alone on his throne, both empowered and enfeebled by his position. The symbols of his rank, his crown and scepter, chain him. He dare not move lest he lose them. Ironically, in gaining the throne, he has lost the very freedom he sought and, like many a Calvino character before him, his solitary life is defined by waiting, and in this particular instance, listening. Through sounds, the reader traces the despot's mounting suspicions and dissects the panic that gnaws at him in the night. "A door slams. Where? Someone runs down steps, a stifled cry is heard" (43). Such noises are enemy to the king for they embody the stultifying isolation and consuming terrors that cloud the tyrant's brittle victory. From where, the king wonders, does the threatened danger arise, from so-called faithful followers or from within himself? "Here the walls have ears," he thinks, and "spies are stationed behind every drapery, curtain, arras" (38). The tale never specifies the nemesis, choosing rather to focus on the unknown, the uncertainty and the obscure disquiet of human life.

"A King Listens" is an altogether brilliant study of an already well-established theme in Calvino: humankind the enemy of itself, lost, emotionally crippled, and inadequate to the task of living. Different from Calvino's consolatory postmodern works (and indeed different from postmodern fiction in general), the piece relies heavily on psychological speculations and on what prove to be the mature author's sure intuitions of the unconscious. Despite the Freudian considerations, however, story names and events inevitably remain shrouded in Kafkaesque obscurity. Abstract allusions to nameless people and places like these are not always dramatically effective, but in this instance they work extremely well, heightening suspense and universalizing the story experience. The tale's theatrical power is no doubt the reason that it inspired the libretto for Luciano Berio's successful opera *Un re in ascolto*.[13]

Of Calvino's last works, *If on a winter's night a traveler* (1979) is both one of the most successful and the most demanding. In fact, one of Calvino's postmodern contemporaries, a wary Salman Rushdie, calls the work "quite possibly the most complicated book you . . . will ever read." Author John Updike is even more skeptical, finding *Winter's night* "cool with few warm spots," a novel that "cannot sustain for its length so intricate an interplay of reader, author, and hero."[14] Such mixed reviews result from the fact that the work is not just amusing fiction, but a feat of postmodern engineering. So intricate is its construction that it could be safely assumed that this novel alone would have sufficed to busy the writer during the interval between its publication and that of his previous major work, *Invisible Cities.*

At the novel's beginning, the complexities arising from its structure are not much in evidence, however. Instead, the reader is thoroughly entertained by the initial interplay between the author's two opening characters: the unconventional second-person protagonist subsequently referred to as "you the Reader," and the singularly impudent narrator. An explicitly postmodern "I," who recalls the storytellers of other contemporary writers (Vonnegut, in particular), this narrator is easily one of Calvino's most colloquial spokespersons. He is not only affable, like Qfwfq in *Cosmicomics*, but he is also downright intrusive and thinks nothing of putting his nose into "you the Reader's" personal business. It is this fun-loving fellow who opens the work, addressing "you" too familiarly (using the Italian *tu* form), casually informing "you" that he is about to read Italo Calvino's latest novel, and then giving "you" explicit instructions on how to begin: "Relax. Concentrate. Dispel every other thought. Let the world around you fade . . . . Anything else? Do you have to pee? All right, you know best" (3, 4).

Presumably comfortable at last, the fictitious reader "you" opens the Calvino book and, as is almost universally true in the author's novels, things immediately go wrong. After a few pages, the story takes an unexpected turn and "you" discovers to his chagrin that the Calvino novel has been misbound with pages from a work by another author. Frustrated, he takes his complaint to the vendor where he is rewarded with yet another misbound book as well as a first glimpse of the Other Reader, Ludmilla, a damsel who shares his dilemma and will eventually share his bed. With this meeting in the bookstore, both the novel's complex frame and the hero's adventuresome search for the completed Calvino novel have now been put in motion. From here on *Winter's night* is a merry chase, one that will take both the reader outside the book and "you the Reader" inside the book on a labyrinthical quest across the pages of literature in an ongoing march from one unfinished novel to the next.

Integral to this quest is the novel's grander plan, a narrative design wherein the primary story, that of the protagonist "you," is playfully and repeatedly interrupted by secondary stories, specifically, the ten unfinished novels that "you" will begin reading in the hope of finding the missing Calvino work. Further complicating the novel's wandering itinerary is the fact that nestled in turn within the individual abortive novels there will be other entertaining and distracting subplots, these buried deep within *Winter's night*'s unstable fictional funnel, thereby creating a narrative effect commonly referred to as "chinese boxing."[15]

To understand what is meant by chinese boxing the reader need only turn to the chapter devoted to would-be translator Ermes Marana (115–31). At this point in "you's" quest for the lost novel, he is on the trail of Marana whose underhanded involvement in the confusion has been discovered through communications the scoundrel has sent to his publisher from different ports of call. Embedded snugly within "you's" presumably dependable account of things is the smaller, less reliable story of Marana himself as revealed through his dispatches. Nestled in turn within Marana's letters is the still smaller and even less stable fiction of Marana's reported interview with a novelist called Silas Flannery. This clever boxing of increasingly smaller stories within the larger ones dramatically jolts the fiction's verisimilitude, and, like its visual counterparts, mirror-imaging and trompe l'oeil, creates the illusion that the piece could continue ad infinitum.[16]

Subverted by this elaborate regressive system of nesting is any semblance of a solid fictional reality, one in which "we the readers" outside the novel might hopefully "lose" ourselves—and this, of course, is precisely as the author intends. Confounding the reader, undermining his servile reliance on literary convention, is the novel's strategy. None of the ten additional novels introduced in *Winter's night* are meant to be finished and this kind of tease is common in postmodern writing. Each story breaks off at a dramatic juncture as suddenly as a soap opera. Such self-reflexivity, or calling attention to authorial technique, again puts into practice Roland Barthes' ideas on the writerly text. It is a device designed to undo the reader's passivity and actively engage him in the creative process of literature by letting him discover his own solutions to the story. Besides the goal outlined above, however, the method just described also projects a philosophic message that is actually more important and should therefore be addressed. Implied ever so subtly by the novel's intricate form is the Calvinian observation that verisimilitude, whether in prose or in the reality we contrive ourselves each day, is equally fictitious.

Moving away from the complex design of *Winter's night* to its ten individual substories, one finds each characteristically postmodern: sly parodies of popular fictional genres, including sentimental love novels, convoluted spy thrillers, exotic oriental tales, and above all, detective capers—a natural target for much postmodern fiction.[17] As observed, the novel focuses on sleuthing and specifically zeroes in on the pop art features of detective fiction, including pasteboard figures, rigid emplotment, and the obscure clues that finally lead the "gumshoe" to the inevitable solution. At every opportunity the enterprising Calvino amuses himself by deconstructing this mystery formula, planting false clues, blind allies, and, of course, in the end providing no answers whatever. In this way Calvino again storms the citadel of formula fiction.[18] Likewise, by abandoning the placid comforts of happy endings, the author, as Cannon points out, also cunningly and obliquely questions the integrity of humankind's "well-made positivistic universe" (Cannon *Postmodern* 9).

Farce, with its convoluted plot and its dependence on witty repartee, in the past has been (and is once again here) a medium ideally suited to Calvino's subversive style. With high speed, the reader both within and without the novel is propelled through a series of incidents wherein multiple, diverse worlds collide, creating a hybrid ontological province well outside traditional fictional realities. In the interim, all kinds of tried and true farcical ploys are pulled out and exploited. These include outlandish disguises, banana peel slapstick, and bawdy innuendo.

For example, "you," in one of his forays after the "real" Calvino book, finds himself suddenly involved in a preposterous confrontation with secret agent Sheila. Seeking to discover her true identity, he strips off her smock to discover the police uniform of her alter-ego Alfonsina. Taking this off, he finds beneath it the anorak of Corinna. Pulling Corinna's zipper, "you" sees below it the chevrons of Ingrid. At last "it is she herself who tears off the clothes that remain on her," and all at once, "a pair of breasts appear, firm, melon-shaped, a slightly concave stomach, the full hips of a *fausse maigre,* a proud pubes, two long and solid thighs" (218). A wonderful example of postmodern high jinks, this Calvino parody of Mata Hari and James Bond pokes fun at spy thrillers and hackneyed language to create its own brand of contrary humor.

In another amusing episode, "you," once again thinking to have stumbled upon the missing novel, finds himself reading nothing more than a cheap gangster story, "Looks Down in the Gathering Shadows" ["Guarda in basso dove l'ombra s'addensa"]. In this abortive tale, set in Paris and probably meant as a parody of the French wave of gangster movies, the story narrator has just liquidated his rival in crime, "Jojo." Unfortunately, the defunct proves less cooperative dead than alive, and the narrator is hard-pressed to dispose of the body. Plastic garbage bags quickly prove inadequate for they either reach only to Jojo's neck or else leave his feet sticking out. Walking the corpse out the door is also a tricky business, not only because Jojo refuses to stand upright, but because he expels gas noisily, attracting the attention of two curious policemen. Worse still, riding with the well-dressed cadaver bolt upright in the car poses a curious inconvenience when the narrator's female accomplice insists on making love in their tiny vehicle with Jojo's body listing to one side and the dead man's open eyes staring at them. To the reader's chagrin, the escapade breaks off abruptly, leaving this particular secondary storyteller in a worrisome fix that the observer outside the novel would dearly love to see resolved.

Puzzling even to those familiar with Calvino's tireless literary innovations, however, is *Winter's night*'s final chapter, an abrupt and bookish departure from the novel's body. In this scene, "you," in one last mighty effort to locate the Calvino book, goes to the library. There he becomes involved in an unconventional conversation with other readers about the art and meaning of reading. Before long it is clear to the reader outside the novel that the ensuing dialogue is a pretext for the writer to elaborate openly his personal thoughts on literature and its significance for living. In the subsequent discussion, the author stresses once more the reader's role in making meaning, explaining in terms that would assuredly satisfy not only Barthes, but Propp and Saussure as well.

For example, according to a second reader with whom "you" converses, it is the reader himself who, in the Barthean sense, actually generates the fiction, simply by rereading, grasping a thought and then forming his own impressions. Before long other speakers interject themselves into the conversation. "'I, too, feel the need to reread the books I have already read,' a third reader says, 'but at every rereading I seem to be reading a new book, for the first time'" (255). For these readers (and obviously for the author as well), perusing a book more than once enhances the creative vigor of literature, enriching by its variety the uniquely personal experience that reading ultimately is.

Quick to modify the third reader's assertion, however, is another Calvino commentator/double who contrarily affirms that, even within the privacy of individual reading, there is still found in any volume traces of what is the Whole of literature. Explicating, he adds, "every new book I read comes to be a part of that overall and unitary book that is the sum of my readings" (255). In *Winter's night,* this totality, with its eternal components, also appeals to the author. Fragmented perhaps are men and women's separate stories, both in life and in *Winter's night,* but there is still comfort to be found in the archetypal fable described by Propp because it is this tale that promises everlasting continuity.

Shortly after this digressive library interlude, the novel concludes. Though less poetic and more pedantic than *Invisible Cities, Winter's night,* too, means to reassure the reader both of the resiliency of fantasy and of life itself. Like most of Calvino's late narratives, *Winter's night,* via its adventurous travel plan, seeks ways to deal with the doldrums of conventional existence and of standard fiction, to assail the nihilistic limitations of reality, and to circumvent the confines of time. Furthermore, the novel's recursive form, its interminable spiraling from one level of fiction to the next, hearteningly implies that books and, therefore their creators too, *do* participate in the eternal. This extension into the hereafter, this possibility of limitless tales, bespeaks once more of *Invisible Cities'* most perfect freedom. Against all odds, Calvino strives to liberate himself from history and opt for immortality's roundtrip. Here in *Winter's night,* if there will be no Calvinian *"via d'uscita,"* or way out of the labyrinth, then at least the hero will never see a *puntus terminus,* or dead end.[19]

As alluded to earlier, some disconcerted readers have looked askance at Calvino's storytelling process in *Winter's night*, finding it contrived.[20] A metafiction, or book about books, the novel figures life's journey as an encyclopedic literary tour. A self-reflexive endeavor, the work continually points to itself, deliberately calling attention to every artifice. Embracing the intellectual security of geometric shapes, mazes, and funnels, it is a book that marks a critical extreme within postmodernism and only time will determine its continued artistic success. As a statement on what Calvino sees as the role of fiction today, however, *Winter's night* represents the author's last word. Literature for Calvino is the citadel of man's independence, humanity's claim to eternity, and hence its ultimate blessing.

Just as *Winter's night* sums up the author's literary canon, so his final work, *Mr. Palomar*, effectively reassumes his metaphysical convictions. In this sense, the author's two closing works complement each other: the first mirroring the author as writer, the last, the author as man. Of the two works, *Mr. Palomar*, by virtue of its humanity, is the most touching and comprehensible. Begun as a series of newspaper vignettes that Calvino then collected into one volume, *Palomar* treats moments in the life of Everyman, moments that appear trivial but that are intensely philosophical and surprisingly intimate for a man as private as the author was.

It is an emphatically personal book, its autobiographical basis barely concealed. Though narrated in the third person, Calvino makes it abundantly clear that the nervous Mr. Palomar, who lives in a world the author views as crowded and frantic, has much in common with him (4). Like Calvino, he is older, married with one nearly grown child, and lives alternately at the seaside and in the city; like the author, perhaps, the retiring "Mr. Palomar suffers greatly because of his difficulty in establishing relations with his fellow man" (116). Although the reader never learns the protagonist's occupation, he does discover that Palomar shares Calvino's concern for detail as well as his love of nature and the sciences. Before long he also intuits that Palomar shares Calvino's soul for he verbalizes the same crucial postmodern and existential leitmotives which have been ongoing in Calvino's previous novels.

Paramount among these motives is the portrait of the novel's protagonist: Mr. Palomar himself, the definitive Calvinian watcher and the author's final and most compelling image of contemporary man.[21] Burdened by existential limitations, disabled by postmodern bafflement, but named (we are told) for the telescope at Mt. Palomar, his very name poses a postmodern contradiction (37–38). For instance, Mr. Palomar perceives life as a visual enterprise. With his eyes, he endeavors to penetrate the mysteries of the earth, to understand its rhythms and patterns, even though, by land and sea, it is apparent that "the surface of things is inexhaustible" and thus impenetrable (55). Worse still, while studying the stars at night Mr. Palomar feels no Galilean exhilaration at his discoveries. In fact, though a knowledgeable man, Mr. Palomar is just as overwhelmed by his ignorance as were some earlier, less-learned Calvino characters. Confronted by the universe, he stands dumbfounded and, like Marcovaldo (of the earlier novel by that name), he instead feels his stature diminish. So undone is he by the smallness of his wisdom that he is forced to admit that he actually mistrusts all he knows (47).

Before Palomar's perplexed gaze, the same Calvinian existential questions inevitably rear their heads: the reason for man's being at all in the face of his ignominious end, and the relevance, in such case, of his decisions here on earth. But being a peaceable postmodern hero, Mr. Palomar's response to these questions is decidedly more tempered than was that of the characters in the author's younger works. Existential choice, once an anxious life-and-death struggle in Calvino's *Castle, Baron*, and *Viscount*, is dealt with here on a small scale, its scope and seriousness limited to silly, small events tinged with the gentlest Marcovaldian touch of capricious humor.

For example, in "The Cheese Museum" ["Il museo dei formaggi"], Mr. Palomar visits a Paris *fromagerie* and while struggling simply to select one cheese out of the many before him, he soon finds himself face to face with a habitual Calvinian dilemma. Hidden among the cheeses is an incontrovertibly negative, but now-familiar (to any Calvino reader) existential axiom: choose we must even if every choice eats "the possibles which we project" (Sartre *Being* 598), and Mr. Palomar is suddenly aware of his absurd Sartrean quandary. As disconcerted as the hero in *Castle*'s "The Waverer's Tale," "Mr. Palomar's spirit vacillates between contrasting urges: the one that aims at complete, exhaustive knowledge and could be satisfied only by tasting all the varieties; and the one that tends toward an absolute choice, the identification of the cheese that is his alone, a cheese that certainly exists even if he cannot recognize it" (72).

Unable to decide and nervously aware that any one choice cancels another, he nearly loses his turn in line. Rather than miss out entirely, he finally does choose, a default choice like those of Cosimo in *Baron*. However, that choice, fraught with trepidation and uncertainty, in the end sums up the small world of small choices that (at least for Calvino) finally characterizes human existence. Striking, however, is one difference between Mr. Palomar and Cosimo. The wiser and more discerning Palomar, rather than rebel like Cosimo, gracefully accepts his limited prowess as a matter of fact and quietly surrenders to the inanity of postmodern decision-making.

In fact, Mr. Palomar's commentary on the trivial freedoms that are men's lot coincides with Calvino's anti-Renaissance worldview, or what critic Ferretti cites as the author's recognition of the "vacuity of [humanity's] anthropocentric presumptions" (143). It also coincides with Mr. Palomar's sensible observations that the standards by which humans live are, after all, only relative anyway and hence prone to error (52). Shrugging his shoulders submissively, Palomar therefore resigns himself, but not without frustration, to the one task that he and every other Calvino hero does best: watching.

In "Reading a Wave" ["Lettura di un'onda"], for example, Mr. Palomar is standing on the shore contemplating the sea. However, "it is not 'the waves' that he means to look at, but just one individual wave" (3), one separate and distinct from any other, one certain and definable. But this seemingly innocent experiment immediately proves fruitless. Similarly, in "The Gecko's Belly" ["La pancia del geco"], Mr. Palomar unhappily witnesses the inevitable transit from life to death when he sees a lizard pressed against the glass and through its transparent gullet he watches the passage of the gecko's dinner, and "the butterfly, fragile Eurydice, sinks slowly into her Hades" (60). Both tales above treat lightly, but resolutely, the vanity of human truths, the enigma that is existence and the fatality that is the earthly sojourn: salient themes that Calvino shares with postmodern colleague Borges and such significant precursors as Beckett and Kafka.

Best in this collection, perhaps, is the wistful story "The Albino Gorilla" ["Il gorilla albino"], a tale whose humor is muted by sober reflections. One day, while visiting a Spanish zoo, Mr. Palomar spots Copito de Nieve [Snowflake], a mountainous white ape whom he immediately recognizes as a spiritual kinsman. Not entirely different from other living beings including Mr. Palomar, this misfit is unique in some respects, yet ultimately just as ordinary as any other creature caught up in life's existential predicament. In the ape's listless, sorrowful glance, Mr. Palomar identifies his own mute resignation at being born the way he is and suffering for being merely a presence taking up space in this world (81).

The ape is a loner and so is Mr. Palomar. Like the ape, "He [Mr. Palomar] avoids and reduces to a minimum his association with his similars" (117). Like Mr. Palomar, the gorilla is a "watcher," the only amusing difference being that, while Mr. Palomar sees things from the outside in, the gorilla looks from the inside out, in his cage. A postmodern ape, the gorilla is yet another of Calvino's displaced beings and an undeniable postmodern parody of Palomar/Calvino himself. Poignantly clutching a rubber tire as if it were his sole raison d'être, Snowflake is a study in impotence, personifying a plight with which Mr. Palomar strongly identifies. Pausing as he leaves the zoo, Mr. Palomar reflects empathetically on his simian doppelganger and, acknowledging their bond, he observes to himself, "We all turn in our hands an old, empty tire through which we try to reach some final meaning, which words cannot achieve" (83). Life, he concludes, therefore, is a roundabout punctuated by uncertain curves and few, if any, answers.

One specific realistic touch distinguishes Mr. Palomar from Calvino's other earlier watchers and that is his age. Whereas Pin, Marcovaldo, Amerigo, and other Calvino characters remain forever young and are often comforted by slender hopes and sweet delusions, Mr. Palomar is notably older; he realizes that his dreams for the future are essentially over. Whereas Marcovaldo sees a hereafter in survival, Mr. Palomar has not even this small comfort. Through his backyard telescope he contemplates a limitless expanse, a universe whose future he will not know, and in an uncannily intuitive and deeply moving passage, "Learning to be dead" ["Come imparare a essere morto"], he foresees both the watcher's and the author's swift end.

"For some while he [Mr. Palomar] has realized that things between him and the world are no longer proceeding as they used to," and that the world and he no longer expect the same things of each other (121). He therefore determines that it is time to think on his coming end and to practice being dead. "This is the most difficult step in learning how to be dead," he reflects, "to become convinced that your own life is a closed whole, all in the past, to which you can add nothing and can alter none of the relationships among the various elements" (125). Modestly, he reassesses his existence and the negligible influence that he has had on the world. He derives some measure of consolation when, with Sartrean pride, he addresses his own identity. After all, "each individual is made up of what he has lived and the way he lived it, and no one can take this away from him" (125), not even death. Next, he stoically consigns himself to posterity, to his "genetic heritage" (125), to the centuries and millennia of the future, and dramatically "at that moment he dies" (126).

This abrupt epitaph concludes Calvino's fictional dialogue with the reader, ending a conversation initiated some 40 years earlier with *The Path to the Spiders' Nests*. Melancholy as the novel is at times, some critics have judged *Mr. Palomar* "an endless series of defeats" and the summation of a cultural climate characterized by crisis and uncertainty, but this pessimistic view is only part of Calvino's story (Cannon *Writer* 107). True, as the troubled years of the twentieth-century rolled past Calvino/Palomar's dismayed eyes, and the logical life plan he had envisioned was disfigured by war, technology, human shortcomings, and the chaos of reality, the author had, as he admits, lost trust in the progress of history and in humanist vanity (108). As a result, he renounced his role as a man of outer gestures, political or otherwise, and turned his inquiring mind inward toward the surer, eternal path of literature.

Across the years of his career, Calvino himself as "watcher" explored his own frustrations through writing: in the early years in terms of the political reality of wartime recollections, later in terms of modernist inquiries into the fragile and contradictory essence of man, and finally in terms of literary otherworlds personal in creation but yet more lasting than mortal life. It is in certain masterpieces, therefore, particularly in the insightful *Watcher*, the fabulous adventure trilogy, and the otherworlds of *Cosmicomics* and *Mr. Palomar*, that we find Calvino not lost to the reader but lasting. Free at last of small-world constraints and the insult of death, there he explores his "inner architecture" and aims audaciously for postmodern horizons where time and choices are limitless (124). It is in this secret realm that we find him most at ease, eager to laugh shrewdly at life's comic foibles, to investigate magic lands, and to carve new paths through the forest of conventional letters.

As a culmination of these explorations, *Mr. Palomar* thus testifies not to the end of the author's art, but solely to his personal demise. Through literature, and specifically through Palomar, Calvino comes home to himself, ultimately admitting both his own separateness as an artist and his inevitable place in the world of people. In *Mr. Palomar*, he chronicles human shortcomings, true, but he also makes peace with his warring Other and in this, his personal reckoning, he openly exposes his own human fallibility to the reader and then bids him a candid farewell.

NOTES

INTRODUCTION

The abbreviations ER and CR refer to Calvino's *Eremita* and "Cronologia" throughout the text and notes. In all Calvino titles, I have followed the capitalization style of the original editions, the titles of which tended to be traditional in the early years and lower-cased in the later years.

1. For his writerly agility, friend and mentor Cesare Pavese early dubbed Calvino the *scoiattolo della penna*, (literally, "squirrel of the pen"), implying that author Calvino was a writer, quick, dexterous, and busy. See Cesare Pavese, *"Il sentiero dei nidi di ragno," La letteratura americana e altri saggi*, 5th ed. (Turin: Einaudi, 1962), 273–74, hereafter cited in text as Pavese; trans. mine.

1. THE AUTHOR AND HIS WORKS

1. Calvino's regret at having no memory of Cuba and his amusement at being named Italo by anti-Fascist parents, at a time when such a name ironically resounded with Fascist pride, is expressed in *Eremita a Parigi. Pagine autobiografiche* [A Hermit in Paris: Autobiographical Pages] (Milan: Mondadori, 1994), 23–24. *Eremita* is a collection (in Italian) of Calvino interviews, articles, essays and

personal reminiscences gathered from newspapers, magazines, and personal journals. With the exception of several major pieces, primary sources will not be indicated and the volume will hereafter be cited in text as ER; trans. mine.

2. Calvino's words as cited from the detailed "Cronologia" [Chronology] of the author's life prepared by Mario Barenghi and Bruno Falcetto for the complete collection of Calvino's fiction, *Romanzi e racconti* [Novels and Short Stories], 2 vols, 2nd ed., ed. Mario Barenghi and Bruno Falcetto (Milan: Mondadori, 1993), LXIV. For major dates and events in Calvino's life, the present study is much indebted to this authorized chronology (vol. 1, LXIII–LXXXVI) and to the already-mentioned *Eremita*. Information from the chronology, without reference to primary sources, will hereafter be cited in text as CR; trans. mine.

3. The Waldensians are a puritan religious sect dating back to the twelfth century. They are perhaps the model Calvino used for the Huguenots who play a role in his novel *The Cloven Viscount*.

4. *The Road to San Giovanni*, trans. Tim Parks (New York: Pantheon Books, 1993), is a posthumously published collection of Calvino's autobiographically inspired short stories, hereafter cited in text as *Road*.

5. *L'entrata in guerra* [Entering the War] (Turin: Einaudi, 1974) was originally published in 1954 and is hereafter cited in text as *Entrata*. It includes three short stories: "Gli avanguardisti a Mentone" [The Advance Guard at Menton], "Le notti dell'UNPA" [Nights with the UNPA], and the title story. To my knowledge, these stories are not available in English.

6. A quote from Alexander Stille, "An Interview with Calvino," *Saturday Review*, March–April 1985, 37.

7. From Calvino's observations on Conrad in "Natura e storia nel romanzo" [Nature and History in the Novel], 29, an important critical essay on world writers found in the author's major collection *Una pietra sopra. Discorsi di letteratura e società* (Turin: Einaudi, 1980), hereafter cited in text as *Pietra*; trans. mine. Some of *Pietra's* essays (but not this one) are available in English in *The Uses of Literature: Essays*, trans. Patrick Creagh (New York: Harcourt Brace, 1986); whenever the English translation is available it will substituted for the Italian volume and cited in text as *Uses*.

8. Calvino told several interviewers of his struggle to get words on paper, describing how he wrote laboriously in longhand, wasting reams of paper. Some of these observations on the mechanics of writing took place during the interview published as "Italo Calvino: The Contemporary Fabulist," by Constance Markey, *Italian Quarterly*, 23 (spring 1982): 77–85, hereafter cited in text as "Fabulist."

9. According to the introductory paragraphs to *Ultimo viene il corvo* [The Crow Comes Last] (Milan: Mondadori, 1994), v–vi, the original edition of *Corvo* (Turin: Einaudi, 1949) was comprised of thirty short stories that Calvino wrote from 1945 to 1949. Of these, twenty were later republished in Calvino's *I racconti* [Short Stories] (Turin: Einaudi, 1958), hereafter cited in text as *Racconti*. In English many of the stories are found in *Adam, One Afternoon and Other Sto-*

ries, trans. Archibald Colquhoun and Peggy Wright (London: Secker and Warburg, 1983), and in *Difficult Loves,* trans. William Weaver, Archibald Colquhoun, and Peggy Wright (New York: Harcourt Brace, 1984), hereafter cited in text as *Difficult Loves.*

10. From Italo Calvino's "Main Currents in Italian Fiction Today," *Italian Quarterly* 4, nos. 13–14 (1960): 5, hereafter cited in text as "Currents." This article was taken from a paper read by the author in English 16 December 1959 at Columbia University in New York and then later republished in Italian in *Pietra* under the title "Tre correnti del romanzo italiano d'oggi," 46–57.

11. An earlier realistic current in Italian literature, *verismo,* parallels the French realism of the late nineteenth to early twentieth century. Its emphasis on the lives of little people and the use of everyday dialects also has bearing on neorealism. For *verismo's* relationship to neorealism, see Sergio Pacifici, *The Modern Italian Novel: From Manzoni to Svevo* (Carbondale: Southern Illinois University Press, 1960), or *From Verismo to Experimentalism: Essays on the Modern Italian Novel,* ed. Sergio Pacifici (Bloomington: University of Indiana Press, 1969), 3–34.

12. There are two available English editions of Calvino's first novel: *The Path to the Nest of Spiders,* trans. Archibald Colquhoun with preface trans. William Weaver (New York: Ecco Press, 1976), and *The Path to the Spiders' Nests,* trans. Archibald Colquhoun, rev. Martin McLaughlin and preface trans. Martin McLaughlin (New York: Ecco Press, 1998). Unless otherwise stated, the 1998 edition will be cited here in text as *Path.* It is important to observe that the 1964 preface (in the 1998 edition, comprising pages 7–30) was written much later than the novel's original publication (Turin: Einaudi, 1947) and therefore reflects hindsight on the author's part.

13. Lucia Re, *Calvino and the Age of Neorealism: Fables of Estrangement* (Stanford: Stanford University Press, 1990), 201, hereafter cited in text as Re.

14. In "Fabulist," 84, Calvino stated that if there was any one American writer to whom he would like to be compared it would be Twain. A critic who has observed similarities between Calvino's waifs and Twain's Huck Finn is Ilene T. Olken, *With Pleated Eye and Garnet Wing: Symmetries of Italo Calvino* (Ann Arbor: University of Michigan Press, 1984), 39. Hereafter only this volume by the above author is cited in text as Olken.

15. In *Letteratura americana,* 274, Pavese also related Calvino to the great Italian Renaissance epic poet Ludovico Ariosto and that author's *Orlando furioso,* a whimsically ironic Renaissance spoof of knighthood that undoubtedly influenced Calvino's fantasy trilogy and other later works.

16. See Beno Weiss, *Understanding Italo Calvino* (Columbia: University of South Carolina Press, 1993), 27, and Cristina Benussi, *Introduzione a Calvino* (Rome: Laterza, 1989), 24, hereafter cited in text as Weiss and Benussi respectively; any trans. mine.

17. Calvino's words, vii; trans. mine, are from his 1969 introduction to *Corvo,*

reprinted in the cited 1994 edition. In it, the author explains why he eliminated some of his earliest stories from subsequent publication. Since the author's death, the excluded tales have, however, been restored to *Romanzi e racconti*.

18. See Italo Calvino's "Il midollo del leone," [The Lion's Marrow], *Il paragone* (June 1955): 17–31, an untranslated article reprinted in Calvino's *Pietra*, 3–18.

19. From Calvino's letter of resignation from the Communist Party, reprinted in a posthumous collection of his writings, *Saggi. 1945–1985* [Essays: 1945–1985], vol. 2, ed. Mario Barenghi (Milan: Mondadori, 1995), 2190 and 2189; trans. mine.

20. These remarks appear in Contardo Calligaris, *Italo Calvino* (Milan: Mursia, 1973), 33, hereafter cited in text as Calligaris; trans. mine.

21. Gian Carlo Ferretti, *Le capre di Bikini. Calvino giornalista e saggista 1945–1985* (Rome: Editori Riuniti, 1989), 46. Only this Ferretti volume is hereafter cited in text; trans. mine.

22. The author's words from a late-life interview with Calvino by Maria Corti, published posthumously in *Autografo*, as "Intervista. Italio Calvino" 2 (6 October 1985),I and reprinted in *Eremita*, 273.

23. In addition to tales from *Ultimo viene il corvo*, stories from Calvino's *Racconti* and his later *Gli amori difficili* [Difficult Loves] (Turin: Einaudi, 1970) are also found in English in the earlier-cited *Difficult Loves*.

24. *Marcovaldo, or, The seasons in the city*, trans. William Weaver (New York: Harcourt Brace, 1983), is hereafter cited in text as *Marcovaldo*.

25. The words "Noble Savage" are from Ilene T. Olken, introduction to *Il visconte dimezzato* (New York: Appleton-Century-Crofts, 1968), 4. Critics who view Marcovaldo with a more skeptical eye than Olken include: Constance Markey, "The Role of the Narrator in Italo Calvino's Fiction," Ph.D. diss., University of Illinois at Urbana-Champaign, 1980; and Franco Ricci, "Introversion and Effacement in *I racconti* of Italo Calvino," *Italica*, 63, no. 4 (1986): 331–345. Hereafter cited in text are Markey "Role," and Ricci "Introversion."

26. In English *Smog, The Watcher*, and *The Argentine Ant* are found in *The Watcher and Other Stories*, trans. William Weaver and Archibald Colquhoun (New York: Harcourt Brace, 1975) and are hereafter cited in text from that volume as *Smog, Watcher*, and *Argentine Ant*.

27. Emilio Cecchi, *Di giorno in giorno* (Milan: Garzanti, 1959), 310–312. Some other early critics who concurred with the notion of Calvino as solely a sociopolitical writer and moralizer include J. R. Woodhouse, *Italo Calvino: A Reappraisal and An Appreciation of the Trilogy* (Hull: Hull University Press, 1968), and Germana Pescio Bottino, *Calvino* (Florence: La Nuova Italia, 1967), hereafter cited in text respectively as Pescio Bottino and Woodhouse, where necessary; trans. mine.

28. *The Nonexistent Knight and the Cloven Viscount*, trans. Archibald Colquhoun (New York: Harcourt Brace, 1977), as well as *The Baron in the Trees*, trans. Archibald Colquhoun (New York: Harcourt Brace, 1977), are hereafter

cited in text respectively as *Knight, Viscount,* and *Baron.* There are also one-volume editions of this trilogy: in Italian, *I nostri antenati* (Turin: Einaudi, 1960; reprint, Milan: Mondadori, 1991) and in English, *Our Ancestors,* trans. Archibald Colquhoun (London: Secker and Warburg, 1980). Hereafter these last two volumes are cited in text respectively as *Our Ancestors* and *I nostri.*

29. These are Calvino's words from the revealing "Nota" 1960 to *I nostri antenati,* 415, hereafter cited in text from the Milan 1991 edition as "Nota"; trans. mine. Unfortunately, this same essay does not appear in *Our Ancestors.*

30. Calvino describes his role in the volume's making in his introduction, trans. Catherine Hill, to *Italian Folktales: Selected and Retold by Italo Calvino,* trans. George Martin (New York: Harcourt Brace, 1980), xv–xxxii.

31. See Marc Beckwith's informative study of Calvino and Italian fables in "Italo Calvino and the Nature of Italian Folktales," *Italica* 64, no. 2 (1987): 244–62.

32. Important essays of that period, originally published in *Il menabò,* reveal the author's early hesitation about the new literature he saw emerging in Europe. Included among these are "Il mare dell'oggettività" [The Sea of Objectivity], 2 (1960): 9–13, and "La sfida al labirinto" [Challenging the Labyrinth] 5 (1962): 85–99: Both articles are reprinted in *Pietra,* but, interestingly, both are later excluded from the English translation, *Uses,* by Calvino the postmodern author.

33. See CR LXXIII and LXXVI. According to the same chronology, other operas on which Calvino collaborated with Berio in 1982 include *La vera storia* [The Real Story] and *Un re in ascolto* [A King Listens], CR, LXXXIV.

34. The pages of Calvino's often amusing, always informative "Diario americano, 1959–1960" (American Diary, 1959–1960) are found in *Eremita,* 26–138.

35. From Calvino's essay "Philosophy and literature," *Uses,* 45.

36. Alain Robbe-Grillet, *For a New Novel: Essays on Fiction,* trans. Richard Howard (New York: Grove Press, 1965), 44.

37. From Renato Barilli's article "My 'Long Infidelity' towards Calvino," trans. Franco Ricci in *Calvino Revisited,* ed. Franco Ricci (Toronto: Dovehouse Editions, 1989), 11, hereafter cited in text as Barilli. Other critics preoccupied with the apparent inconsistency in Calvino's writing—his vacillation between realism and fantasy—include Agata Piromallo, "Italo Calvino," *Il Baretti,* no. 42 (1966): 66–76, and Geno Pampaloni, *Il novecento* (Milan: Garzanti, 1969), to name but two spokesmen for a critical dilemma in Calvino that still disturbs some readers.

38. See Giorgio Pullini, *"Il barone rampante," Comunità* (November 1957): 101–102, and Claudio Varese, "Italo Calvino. *La giornata d'uno scrutatore," Nuova Antologia* (May 1963): 120–23, who chided Calvino about the dangerous direction of his work.

39. From Ferdinando Camon's interview with Calvino in *Il mestiere di scrittore. Conversazioni critiche* (Milan: Garzanti, 1973), 190, hereafter cited in text as Camon; trans. mine.

40. *Cosmicomics,* trans. William Weaver (New York: Harcourt Brace, 1977),

hereafter cited in text as *Cosmicomics*. Two other editions of Calvino's cosmi-comic stories, *La memoria del mondo e altre storie cosmicomiche* [Memory of the World and Other Cosmicomic Stories] (Milan: Club degli Editori, 1968) and *Cosmicomiche vecchie e nuove* [Old and New Cosmicomics] (Milan: Garzanti, 1984), testify to the continuing popularity of these otherworld journeys.

41. For an introduction to postmodernism's otherworlds, and how they relate to Calvino's work, see Brian McHale's discussion of "ontological zones" in *Postmodernist Fiction* (New York: Methuen, 1987), hereafter cited in text as McHale.

42. *t zero*, trans. William Weaver (New York: Harcourt Brace, 1976) is hereafter cited in text as *t zero*.

43. Calvino's words are from "Cybernetics and Ghosts," *Uses*, 12.

44. The words of Roland Barthes, *Writing Degree Zero*, trans. Annette Lavers and Colin Smith (New York: Hill and Wang, 1983), 76–77.

45. *The Castle of Crossed Destinies*, trans. William Weaver (New York: Harcourt Brace, 1979), and *Invisible Cities*, trans. William Weaver (New York: Harcourt Brace, 1978), are hereafter cited in text as *Castle* and *Invisible Cities*, respectively.

46. Italo Calvino's words from "Notes towards a definition of the narrative form as a combinative process," trans. Bruce Merry, *Twentieth Century Studies* (May 1970): 94, hereafter cited in text as "Process."

47. The author spoke of the importance of the Antonio Feltrinelli Prize to him at our last meeting in Rome (June 1985).

48. *Six Memos for the Next Millennium*, The Charles Eliot Norton Lectures, 1985–1986, trans. Patrick Creagh (Cambridge: Harvard University Press, 1988).

49. *Numbers in the Dark and Other Stories*, trans. Tim Parks (New York: Pantheon Books, 1995), and *Under the Jaguar Sun*, trans. William Weaver (New York: Harcourt Brace, 1988), are hereafter cited in text respectively as *Numbers* and *Jaguar Sun*.

50. *If on a winter's night a traveler*, trans. William Weaver (New York: Harcourt Brace, 1981), and *Mr. Palomar*, trans. William Weaver (New York: Harcourt Brace, 1985), are hereafter cited in text respectively as *Winter's night* and *Palomar*.

2. FIRST STEPS IN NEOREALISM

1. This is an early observation of Gian Carlo Ferretti, *La letteratura del rifiuto* (Milan: Mursia, 1968), 131; trans. mine. Those interested in the debate surrounding neorealism's definition can also see Re, 11–75, as well as Frank Rosengarten "The Italian Resistance Novel (1945–1962)," in *From Verismo to Experimentalism: Essays on the Modern Italian Novel*, 212–38, hereafter cited in text as Rosengarten.

2. Ignazio Silone, an early, ardent anti-Fascist, spent many years abroad in exile for his political sentiments. His novel *Bread and Wine*, which might be consid-

ered a forerunner to neorealism, was first published in America in 1937, but was not published in Italy till after the war. Vittorini's *Men and Not Men*, trans. Sara Henry (Marlboro, Vermont: Marlboro, 1985), was published in Italy in 1945.

3. For more about America's input into Italian neorealism see Donald Heiney, *America in Modern Italian Literature* (New Brunswick, N.J.: Rutgers University Press, 1964), 55–78, as well as Calvino's "Currents," 3–14. In Italian, see Pavese, 5–32, and Italo Calvino's Prefazione [Preface] to the already-cited Pavese volume, xi–xxxiii.

4. In Italian the proper title of Carlo Collodi's 1883 fairy tale is *Le avventure di Pinocchio. Storia di un burattino* and in English *Pinocchio: The Adventures of a Little Wooden Boy.*

5. Calvino's thoughts on his relationship to Twain are expressed in "Fabulist," 84. For observations about Calvino and Collodi, see Re, specifically 201–22.

6. Although the three "Riviera Stories" mentioned are not included in this discussion, those wishing to read them in Italian in Calvino's *Racconti* will find the original titles listed respectively as "Un pomeriggio, Adamo," 1947, "Il giardino incantato," 1948, "Un bastimento carico di granchi," 1947, and "Pesci grossi, pesci piccoli," 1950.

7. Interestingly, "Theft in a Pastry Shop," *Difficult Loves*, 131–140, inspired *Palookaville*, the recent American film directed by Alan Taylor that won the Best Feature Film Award at the 1995 Venice Film festival.

8. Much as the young Calvino admired Hemingway's hero for his savoir faire, he was suspicious that under that facade there lurked "a sense of the vanity of everything, of desperation, defeat, of death" (*Pietra* 32).

9. See George Prince's discussion of reader expectations in the conventional novel in *Narratology: The Forms and Functioning of Narrative* (Berlin: Mouton, 1982), 72.

10. Re sees the neorealistic writer's effort to shape his work into a "seamless" bildungsroman as highly problematic, however, given the complexities of the Resistance movement, 84.

11. For a lengthier discussion of Calvino's subversive tendencies in *Path*, see Re, 259–63 and Markey, "Role," 7–74.

12. From "Right and Wrong Political Uses of Literature," *Uses*, 99, originally a paper read by Calvino at Amherst College, 1976. The same article appears in *Pietra* as "Usi politici giusti e sbagliati della letteratura," 286–93.

13. One of *Path*'s most idealistic readers is surely Giuseppe Bonura, *Invito alla lettura di Italo Calvino* (Milan: Mursia, 1972), 136, hereafter cited in text as Bonura; trans. mine.

14. See Markey, "Role," 34–36, and Re, 210 for further discussion of Pin's idiosyncratic role within neorealism.

15. For her complete discussion of Calvino and fairy-tale emplotment in *Path*, see Re, 201–22. In these pages she outlines structuralist Vladímir Propp's theories

on the underlying consistency of the narrative process, a topic that will be taken up here in a subsequent chapter.

16. The story of the hero's rite of passage or maturation has other connotations besides the social, historical, and political messages we often speak of today. Other models of this timeless story of a religious, mythical, and metaphysical nature (like those in Dante, Virgil, and the Bible) antedate by good measure the modern bildungsroman to which Re refers. In fact, in Calvino's later works it is these metaphysical paradigms that eventually come under critical scrutiny.

17. Both Ferretti, 3–41, and Markey, "Role," 47–48, perceive existential alienation as a fundamental motive in Calvino's *Path*.

18. "I-thou" is a term used by existential philosophers like Martin Buber and Paul Tillich to describe the nature of existential interpersonal relationships and this theme is discussed in Maurice Friedman's introductory words to Part 4, "Existentialism and Psychotherapy," in *The Worlds of Existentialism: A Critical Reader*, ed. Maurice Friedman (Chicago: University of Chicago Press, 1973), 365–68.

19. Paul Tillich, in *The Courage to Be* (New Haven: Yale University Press, 1952), 68–70 and 76, describes small world withdrawal as the individual's "narrow castle of certitude which can be defended and is defended with the utmost tenacity." Hereafter cited in text is Tillich. Rollo May, in "Existential Bases of Psychotherapy," *Existential Psychology*, 2nd ed., ed. Rollo May (New York: Random House, 1969), 72–83, refers to this same syndrome as the "shrinking world" (72) and describes it as a means of "blocking off aspects of the environment so that he (the individual) may be adequate to the remainder."

20. Mark Twain, *The Adventures of Huckleberry Finn*, ed. Peter Coveney (New York: Penguin Books, 1985), 176, hereafter cited in text as Twain.

21. For several illuminating discussions of this well-documented personal and narrative conflict in Twain, see Peter Coveney, introduction to *The Adventures of Huckleberry Finn* by Mark Twain (New York: Penguin Books, 1985), 33–37; James L. Johnson, *Mark Twain and the Limits of Power* (Knoxville: University of Tennessee Press, 1982), 90–91; and Leslie Fiedler, "Faust in the Eden of Childhood," in *Mark Twain's Wound* ed. Lewis Leary (New York: Crowell, 1962), 280 and 284–291.

22. Franco Ricci, *Difficult Games: A Reading of "I racconti" by Italo Calvino* (Waterloo, Ontario: Wilfrid Laurier University Press, 1990), 50, hereafter cited in text as Ricci *Games*.

3. MODERNIST TRAVELS

1. James McFarlane, "The Mind of Modernism," *Modernism 1890–1930*, ed. Malcolm Bradbury and James McFarlane (London: Penguin Books, 1992), 80, hereafter cited in text as McFarlane.

2. From the author's brief introduction, trans. Isabel Quigley, to the already-cited *Our Ancestors*, ix.

3. From Malcolm Bradbury and James McFarlane, "The Name and Nature of Modernism," again in *Modernism, 1890–1930*, 29, hereafter cited in text as Bradbury.

4. Discussions of this Calvinian tendency toward abstraction are found in Albert Howard Carter, III, *Italo Calvino: Metamorphoses of Fantasy* (Ann Arbor: UMI Research Press, 1987), 83, and in Rocco Capozzi's "*Cosmicomiche vecchie e nuove*: Keeping in Tune with the Times," in *Calvino Revisited*, ed. Franco Ricci (Toronto: Dovehouse Editions, 1989), 65–84, hereafter cited in text respectively as Carter and Capozzi.

5. A quote from Henri Bergson's discussion of humor, in "Laughter," from *Comedy: "An Essay on Comedy" by George Meredith, "Laughter" by Henri Bergson*, ed. Wylie Sypher (Baltimore: Johns Hopkins University Press, 1980), 189.

6. Marcovaldo is the name of the giant slain by Knight Roland in Luigi Pulci's epic work *Morgante*.

7. For example, Woody Allen, in his various modernist film characterizations of the perpetual loser lost in the indifferent forest of the big city, was a Calvino favorite.

8. The "little fellow" is the name Chaplin himself affectionately applied to his tramp character.

9. Sartre's views on man in action are incongruous. See his major work, *Being and Nothingness: A Phenomenological Essay on Ontology*, trans. Hazel E. Barnes (New York: Washington Square Press, 1977), 559–711, hereafter cited in text as Sartre *Being*. According to Sartre, man (in the Promethean sense), must act because it is only by doing so that he defines himself, 574. Contrarily, however, Sartre acknowledges the inherent negativity of taking action, as any decision one makes cancels other options and is therefore fraught with risk, 598–99. We will examine this Sartrean dilemma in Calvino's writing more closely in the next chapter.

10. An excellent contrast is drawn between the existential Job and the existential Prometheus in Maurice Friedman's *Problematic Rebel: An Image of Modern Man* (Chicago: University of Chicago Press, 1973), 437–85.

11. Submissively waiting and hoping for the better tomorrow that never arrives is as characteristic of Marcovaldo as it is of Beckett's clown figures in his renowned play *Waiting for Godot* (New York: Grove, 1954).

12. Once again we refer here to Tillich's thoughts, 76, on modern man's existential tendency to reduce his life to a small, manageable fantasy. See also Marjorie Grene, *Introduction to Existentialism*, 11th ed. (Chicago: University of Chicago Press, 1970), 52, for a discussion of the existential terror of choosing.

13. Ihab Hassan, *The Dismemberment of Orpheus: Toward a Postmodern Lit-*

erature, 2nd ed. (Madison: University of Wisconsin Press, 1982), 9, hereafter cited in text as Hassan.

14. From Morton Dauwen Zabel's comments on Conrad in his introduction to *The Portable Conrad*, ed. Morton Dauwen Zabel, rev. Frederick R. Karl (New York: Viking Penguin Books, 1976), 34.

15. Here we recall the words of Calvino from his "Nota" to *I nostri*, 415, where he characterizes contemporary man as "*dimidiato*" or "*dimezzato*," that is to say, incomplete and figuratively inadequate to modern life. In Calvino's fantasy novel *Viscount*, we will meet this same character again, this time dramatized literally in the physically cloven protagonist.

16. *A Plunge into Real Estate*, the inaccurately translated title for *La speculazione edilizia* [The Building Speculation], is a novella found in English in the Toronto edition of *Difficult Loves*, trans. D. S. Carne-Ross (Toronto: Lester and Orpen Dennys, 1984. The quote here, however, is from the original Italian, *Racconti*, 386; trans. mine.

17. From Franz Kuna, "The Janus-faced Novel: Conrad, Musil, Kafka, Mann," in the already-cited *Modernism, 1890–1930*, 446.

18. Marco Forti's observations in "Temi industriali della narrativa italiana," *Il menabò* 4 (1961): 213–39.

19. For his summary of modernism's values, see Charles Newman, *The Post-Modern Aura: The Act of Fiction in an Age of Inflation* (Evanston: Northwestern University Press, 1985), 25, hereafter cited in text as Newman. According to this author, modernist principles include the idea of "art as a sanctuary" as well as a sense of "elitism," 26, 37–38, all sentiments reflected in the intellectual snobbism of Calvino's narrator in *Watcher*.

20. From Josephine Jacobsen and William R. Mueller, *The Testament of Samuel Beckett* (New York: Hill and Wang, 1964), 103, hereafter cited in text as Jacobsen.

21. According to both Benussi, 88, and Claudio Milanini, *L'utopia discontinua. Saggio su Italo Calvino* (Milan: Garzanti, 1990), 95, the events in the story may well have been inspired by a day in the life of Calvino himself during the time of the controversial Italian elections of 1953.

22. The voters, as described in *Watcher*, bear a palpable resemblance to the grotesque, immobile creature described in Beckett's tale *The Unnamable* (New York: Grove, 1958). Other critics who have remarked on this similarity include Kristi Siegel, "Italo Calvino's *Cosmicomics:* Qfwfq's [*sic*] Postmodern Autobiography," *Italica* 68 (Spring 1991): 44, hereafter cited in text as Siegel.

23. See Gore Vidal, "Fabulous Calvino," *New York Review of Books*, 30 May 1974, 14, whose timely article helped establish Calvino's name in America.

4. FANTASY ADVENTURES

1. See both the already-cited Barilli article as well as Tommasina Gabriele's *Italo Calvino: Eros and Language* (Teaneck, N.J.: Fairleigh Dickinson University Press, 1994), 26–35, for a summary of Calvino's reception by Italian critics during the fifties and sixties.

2. *The Cloven Viscount* comprises half of the two-novel volume *The Nonexistent Knight and the Cloven Viscount*, as already cited.

3. Some additional writers who quickly chose to interpret the pessimistic undercurrents of Calvino's trilogy positively are: Ferdinando Virdia, "Calvino e i paladini," *La Fiera letteraria* 3 (January 1960): 1–2, who constructs an elaborate allegory of history and the perennial flux of good and evil out of Calvino's trilogy, and Sebastiano Addamo, "Italo Calvino. *Il cavaliere inesistente*," *Il Ponte* no. 3 (1960): 416–18, who weaves elaborate symbols around the working man and his neglected social role out of *The Nonexistent Knight*. Critics who misread him this way exasperated the author who objected to the idealized views they espoused and said so in our conversation at his home in Paris (18 June 1978), hereafter cited in text as Paris 1978.

4. Specifically his ""Nota" to *I nostri antenati*, as already cited, and to be cited again in this chapter; trans. mine.

5. For example, both the Italian paperback edition of Calvino's *Path* (Turin: Einaudi, 1974) and *Marcovaldo* (Turin: Einaudi, 1966) appropriately feature Klee's work on their covers.

6. John Gatt-Rutter, "Calvino Ludens: Literary Play and Its Political Implications," *Journal of European Studies* 5, no. 4 (1975): 324.

7. Thoughtful discussions of the doppelganger or double in literature past and present are to be found in Richard Kearney, *The Wake of Imagination* (Minneapolis: University of Minnesota Press, 1988), 53–61; T. E. Apter, *Fantasy Literature: An Approach to Reality* (Bloomington: Indiana University Press, 1982), 49–66; and Karl Miller, *Doubles: Studies in Literary History* (Oxford: Oxford University Press, 1987).

8. Some of the discussion of *Baron* below has appeared in another form in my article "Calvino and the Existential Dilemma: The Paradox of Choice," *Italica* 60, no. 1 (1983): 55–70.

9. These words mirror explicitly Sartre's discussion of freedom in *Being*, 559–711, and especially, 667–70, where the author elaborates the issue of the Other-as-object and discusses why the "for-itself [the individual] must be free; . . . must choose itself." (667).

10. In his discussion of human responsibility in *Being*, 707–711, Sartre, like Cosimo, tries to have the best of both worlds, asserting first that "each person is an absolute choice of self," 709, and next insisting that all of us "carry the weight of the world," 710, and are thus responsible for the Other. This conspicuous contradiction in Sartre has made philosophers (and Calvino too, as seen in *Baron*) question the workability of Sartre's humanism. How can the hero, whom

Sartre describes by nature as self-centered and free of Godly or ethical constraints, still be morally accountable to the Other?, asks James Collins in his discussion of Sartre's conflicted humanism in *The Existentialists: A Critical Study* (Chicago: Henry Regnery, 1968), 77–87.

11. As is readily observed, Sartre and Voltaire do have things in common: both are polemical moralists who stress humanitarianism and the freedom to doubt. But their similarities begin and end there, because in Sartre social compromise is in the last analysis an uneasy issue while Voltairean Utopia is never even figured.

12. Sartre admits that his definition of freedom of choice constitutes the "horns of a dilemma": free will in the last analysis being conceived as torment, as "in anguish we do not simply apprehend the fact that the possibles which we project are perpetually eaten away by our freedom-to-come" (*Being* 598).

13. Jean-Paul Sartre, *Existentialism and Human Emotions*, trans. Bernard Frechtman (New York: Philosophical Library, 1957), 41, hereafter cited in text as Sartre *Emotions*.

14. So striking is the similarity between Calvino's portrait of the Knights of the Holy Grail in this novel and the depiction of the knights in the later postmodern film *Monty Python and the Holy Grail* (directed by Terry Gilliam, Great Britain, 1974), that one cannot help but wonder if the Calvino work had any role in inspiring the screenplay.

15. In *Atlantic*, January, 1980, 70; hereafter cited in text as Barth.

16. For a discussion of the similarities between Calvino and Lewis Carroll, see Gianni Celati, "Il racconto di superficie," *Il Verri*, no. 1 (1973): 94–95. Calvino and Twain are discussed together here in Chapter 2.

17. Tzvetan Todorov, *The Fantastic: A Structural Approach to a Literary Genre*, trans. Richard Howard (Ithaca, N.Y.: Cornell University Press, 1980), 33 and 41.

18. Excellent summations on the nature and function of postmodern parody are found in Kearney, 251–98, McHale, 57–58 and 144–145, as well as in Linda Hutcheon, *The Politics of Postmodernism* (London: Routledge, 1989), 93–117. Any further in-text reference to this last author will be only from this volume, hereafter cited in text as Hutcheon.

19. See Umberto Eco, *The Role of the Reader: Explorations in the Semiotics of Texts* (Bloomington: Indiana University Press, 1984), 234.

5. OTHERWORLD EXPLORATIONS

1. A basic definition of postmodernism in M. H. Abrams, *A Glossary of Literary Terms*, 4th ed. (New York: Holt, Rinehart and Winston, 1981), 110, supports the description of postmodernism given here, defining the movement as a response to World War II that reveals itself through an expression of "lost faith" in mainstream traditions and literary manners.

2. Although this quote is from the already-cited Barth article, 70, some of the

words (source unidentified) are attributed to John Updike. Today, this identification of Calvino as a postmodernist is scarcely new. The author's name appears regularly in studies of postmodern fiction, including the already-cited McHale, 43–44 and 113–14, Kearney, 125 and 303, as well as Linda Hutcheon, *A Poetics of Postmodernism: History, Theory, Fiction* (London: Routledge, 1991), 127–128.

3. Detractors of postmodern art and literature range from those who deny its existence (an unwitting acknowledgment) to those who grudgingly grant it merit. The most vitriolic critic is perhaps John Gardner, *On Moral Fiction* (New York: Basic Books, 1978). Others who find fault with the term postmodernism or with its literature include: Gerald Graff, *Literature Against Itself: Literary Ideas in Modern Society* (Chicago: University of Chicago Press, 1979); Jürgen Habermas, "Modernity: An Unfinished Project," in *Postmodern Culture*, ed. Hal Foster (London: Pluto Press, 1985), 3–15; and the already-cited Newman.

Some early critics who reproved Calvino for his postmodern tendencies include: Walter Pedullà, "Calvino alla corte di Lacan," *Il Caffè* 5/6 (1972): 77–85; and the already-cited Claudio Varese, who cautioned Calvino about drowning in his own "sea of objectivity," 122; trans. mine.

4. See both Steven Connor, *Postmodernist Culture: An Introduction to Theories of the Contemporary* (Oxford: Blackwell, 1992), and Brenda K. Marshall, *Teaching the Postmodern: Fiction and Theory* (London: Routledge, 1992), two recent volumes that place Calvino among his colleagues.

5. See William V. Spanos's discussion of the existential heritage within postmodernism in "The Detective and the Boundary: Some Notes on the Postmodern Literary Imagination," *Early Postmodernism: Foundational Essays*, ed. Paul A. Bové (Durham: Duke University Press, 1995), 17–39, hereafter cited in text as Spanos.

6. For thoughts on the difference between early existentialism after World War I and the renewed (antihumanistic) existential crisis of this present era, see Gianni Vattimo, *The End of Modernity*, trans. Jon R. Snyder (Baltimore: Johns Hopkins University Press, 1991), 31–47, hereafter cited in text as Vattimo.

7. See Jacques Derrida, *Margins of Philosophy*, trans. Alan Bass (Chicago: University of Chicago Press, 1982), 134–135.

8. See Michel Foucault, *The Order of Things: An Archeology of the Human Sciences*, trans. unknown (New York, Vintage Books, 1973), 387.

9. These apt expressions were coined by Andrew McKenna in "Postmodernism: Its Future Perfect," *Post-modernism and Continental Philosophy*, ed. Hugh J. Silverman and Donn Welton (Albany: State University of New York Press, 1988), 235.

10. This informative talk became the nucleus of the earlier-cited essay "Romanzo," reprinted in *Pietra*, 19–38.

11. "Heterotopia" is a term apparently coined by Foucault and used to define "the kind of space . . . capable of accomodating many incommensurable and mutually exclusive worlds" (McHale 44).

12. It is Hutcheon who defines these two attitudes of postmodern fiction (and film) in the already-cited *Politics*, 17.

13. Those interested in Queneau and Oulipo can see Jane Alison Hale, *The Literary Encyclopedia of Raymond Queneau* (Ann Arbor: University of Michigan Press, 1989), Weiss 90–94, as well as Calvino's own words in *Uses*, 28–31.

14. From JoAnn Cannon, *Italo Calvino: Writer and Critic* (Ravenna: Longo Editore, 1981), 52, hereafter cited in text as Cannon, *Writer*.

15. García Márquez's own brand of postmodernism, sometimes called "magic realism," focuses on the primitive religious rituals and superstitions associated with third-world countries and thus finally distinguishes itself from Calvino's world of ideas. See Kathleen McNeary, *Understanding Gabriel García Márquez* (Columbia: University of South Carolina Press, 1989).

16. See García Márquez's *One Hundred Years of Solitude*, trans. Gregory Rabassa (New York: Avon Books, 1971).

17. This scene, perhaps intentionally, recalls the opening moments of Vittorio De Sica's film, *The Gold of Naples* [*L'oro di Napoli*, 1954], in which an eye-catching Sophia Loren rolled pasta.

18. Kurt Vonnegut, Jr., *Slaughterhouse-Five* (New York: Dell, 1975), 23, hereafter cited in text as Vonnegut.

19. Ferdinand de Saussure's theories of language are found in his seminal work *Course in General Linguistics*, trans. Wade Baskins, ed. Charles Bally and Albert Sechehaye (New York: McGraw-Hill, 1966), hereafter cited in text as Saussure.

20. Antonio Illiano's sentiments are expressed in "Per una definizione della vena cosmogonica di Calvino: Appunti su *Le cosmicomiche e Ti con zero*," *Italica*, 49, no. 3 (1972): 291–301.

21. The observations of Susan Sontag are from her preface to *Writing Degree Zero* by Roland Barthes, trans. Annette Lavers and Colin Smith (New York: Hill and Wang, 1983), ix.

22. See Roland Barthes, *S/Z: An Essay*, trans. Richard Miller, (New York: Hill and Wang, 1974), 3–15, where the author defines a writerly text as a flexible "perpetual present, . . . *ourselves writing*, before the infinite play of the world" (5). Also see the already-cited Robbe-Grillet's *For a New Novel* for that author's own manifesto on apsychological writing, 25–47.

23. It is McHale, *Postmodernist Fiction*, 13, who notes specifically the affinity between Robbe-Grillet and postmodernism, offering examples of that author's use of postmodern technique, 118–119. See also Stefano Tani, *The Doomed Detective: The Contribution of the Detective Novel to Postmodern American and Italian Fiction* (Carbondale: Southern Illinois University Press, 1984), 22, who similarly relates Barthes's writerly text and Robbe-Grillet's *nouveau roman* to postmodernism.

24. From Ben Stoltzfus, *Alain Robbe-Grillet: The Body of the Text* (Teaneck, N.J.: Fairleigh Dickinson University Press, 1985), 17, hereafter cited in text as Stoltzfus.

25. Alain Robbe-Grillet, *Two Novels by Robbe-Grillet: Jealousy and In the Labyrinth*, trans. Richard Howard (New York: Grove, 1965).

26. For example, in the García Márquez novel *Chronicle of a Death Foretold*, trans. Gregory Rabassa (New York, Ballantine, 1984), the narrator substitutes insignificant references to fictitious folios, clock time, clothing, etc. for hard facts that inevitably remain obscure throughout the entire novel.

27. There are two English editions of *Castle*. The first, short version, *The Castle*, appears in *Tarots: The Visconti Pack in Bergamo and New York*, trans. William Weaver, ed. (New York: Franco Maria Ricci Editore and Rizzoli International Publications, 1976). The second, expanded edition, trans. William Weaver (New York: Harcourt Brace, 1976), is the edition used here, with citations from the 1979 printing.

28. Some of the discussion of *Castle* below appears elsewhere in another form in Constance Markey, "The Tarot Cards as a Subversive Tool in Italo Calvino," *Aspects of Fantasy*, ed. William Coyle (Westport, Conn.: Greenwood, 1986), 181–86, and Constance Markey, "The Hero's Quest in Calvino," *Quaderni d'italianistica* 4, no. 2 (1983): 154–66.

29. Propp's narrative functions are explicated in V. Propp, *Morphology of the Folktale*, trans. Laurence Scott, 2nd ed., ed. Louis A. Wagner (Austin: University of Texas, 1979), particularly 19–86.

30. Others have identified story parallels in the hero's tale, specifically Joseph Campbell in *The Hero with a Thousand Faces* (Princeton: Princeton University Press, 1949). See also the later David Adams Leeming, *Mythology: The Voyage of the Hero* (New York: Lippincott, 1973), whose book summarizes many of the best-known examples of the hero's quest (including the life journeys of Moses and Christ) and universalizes the monomyth, calling it "a reflection of our own journey from birth to the unknown" (6).

31. For an explication of Saussure's dualistic concept of language: *langue*, or language system, versus *parole*, or the arbitrary nature of individual signs, see Saussure, 65–100. The original words, *langue* and *parole*, from the French edition are employed here simply because they are more concise than the English translation.

32. See the illustrations of the tarot maze in *Castle*, 40 and 98.

33. Teresa De Lauretis presents a thorough discussion of Calvino's subversive, antithetical literary style in "Calvino e la dialettica dei massimi sistemi," *Italica* 53, no. 1 (1976): 57–74.

34. For a history of the ethical, moral, and literary meaning of the *bivium*, or issue of moral choice, see Theodore D. Mommsen, "Petrarch and the Story of the Choice of Hercules," *Journal of the Warbury and Courtauld Institutes* 16, nos. 3–4 (1953): 178–92, and Janet Levarie Smarr, "Boccaccio and the Choice of Hercules," *MLN* 92, no. 1 (1977): 146–52.

35. These are the observations of Guido Almansi in "Il mondo binario di Italo Calvino," *Il paragone* 22 (1971):96.

6. FINAL JOURNEYS

1. See Jacques Derrida's discussion of *spacing, drift,* and the *trace,* terms he uses to describe the subtle shift in meaning that is ongoing in spoken and written discourse, in *Of Grammatology,* trans. Gayatri Chakravorty Spivak (Baltimore: Johns Hopkins University Press, 1977), 65–73, hereafter cited in text as Derrida.

2. Jacques Lacan, *The Language of the Self: The Function of Language in Psychoanalysis,* trans. Anthony Wilden (New York: Dell, 1968), 63. Although a Freudian psychoanalyst by vocation, Lacan has had an impact on literature and on Calvino through his work in linguistics and his study of language at the unconscious level within man.

3. Anika Lemaire, *Jacques Lacan,* trans. David Macey (London: Routledge and Kegan Paul, 1982), 114, citing Lacan's notion of the "crack" in meaning that exists inherently in discourse.

4. Both stories are found in Jorge Luis Borges, *Labyrinths: Selected Stories and Other Writings,* ed. Donald A. Yates and James E. Irby (New York: New Directions, 1964).

5. Kathryn Hume, *Calvino's Fictions: Cogito and Cosmos* (New York: Oxford University Press, 1992), 130, and Markey, "Role," 78, both discuss the role of the traveler or life tourist in Calvino.

6. For other examples of the pleasures of postmodern travel, see Umberto Eco's comforting *The Island of the Day Before,* trans. William Weaver (New York: Harcourt Brace, 1995), or several whimsical postmodern films, including *The Purple Rose of Cairo* (directed by Woody Allen, 1985), and *Joe Versus the Volcano* (directed by John Patrick Shanley, 1990).

7. The Khan's musings are a pointed reference to Sartre's famous words, *"l'enfer, c'est les Autres"* [hell is other people], from the author's famous play *Huis clos [No Exit]* (Paris: Editions Gallimard, 1947), 62.

8. See the foreword by Etienne Gilson to *Saint Augustine: The City of God,* trans. Gerald G. Walsh, S.J., Demetrius B. Zema, S.J., Grace Monahan, O.S.U., and Daniel J. Honan, ed. Vernon J. Bourke (Garden City: Image Books, 1958), 13–35, for a discussion of the allegorical inferences of the city in St. Augustine's masterpiece.

9. From Roberto González Echevarría's review of the Borges biography *The Man in the Mirror of the Book: A Life of Jorge Luis Borges,* by James Woodall, in *New York Times Book Review,* 31 August 1997, 10.

10. Again Calvino refers to the meaningful void left between words in the written text, which is "always the unperceived, the nonpresent, and the nonconscious." See Derrida, *Of Grammatology,* 6–87, specifically, 68.

11. According to Esther Calvino's note to *Under the Jaguar Sun* by Italo Calvino (New York: Harcourt Brace, 1988), 85.

12. Laura Esquivel's novel, *Like Water for Chocolate,* trans. Carol Christensen and Thomas Christensen (New York: Doubleday, 1992), recalls this particular

Calvino tale more than a little in its own use of food as a sexual metaphor.

13. The opera *Un re in ascolto* enjoyed its American premiere at Chicago's Lyric Opera in 1996.

14. See Salman Rushdie, "Calvino," *London Review of Books* 17–30 September 1981, 17, and John Updike, "Italo Calvino," in *Hugging the Shore: Essays and Criticism* (New York: Alfred A. Knopf, 1983), 472–73.

15. See McHale, *Postmodernist Fiction*, 112–30, for a lucid discussion of chinese boxing.

16. Calvino's recursive style in *Winter's night* is elsewhere discussed by McHale, 115, and by JoAnn Cannon, *Postmodern Italian Fiction: The Crisis of Reason in Calvino, Eco, Sciascia, Malerba* (Teaneck, N.J.: Fairleigh Dickinson University Press, 1989), 95–115, hereafter cited in text as Cannon, *Postmodern*.

17. Two particularly celebrated postmodern parodies of the detective genre are the earlier-cited García Márquez's *Chronicle of a Death Foretold* and Thomas Pynchon's *The Crying of Lot 49* (New York: Harper and Row, 1990).

18. See the already-cited volume by Tani, and Cannon, *Postmodern*, 40–59, for lengthier discussion of the role of detective stories in postmodern fiction.

19. In Calvino's already-cited article "La sfida al labirinto" [Challenging the Labyrinth], *Pietra*, 96–7, finding a *"via di uscita,"* or way out of life's quandaries through literature, is one of the author's expressed desires.

20. See Melvin Maddocks's negative review, "Mirror Writing. *If on a winter's night a traveler," Time*, 25 May 1981, K11.

21. In a similar vein, Cannon, *Postmodern*, 96, refers to *Mr.Palomar* as "a parable of the postmodern condition."

BIBLIOGRAPHY

CALVINO'S FICTION (IN CHRONOLOGICAL ORDER)

Il sentiero dei nidi di ragno. Turin: Einaudi, 1947. Published in English as *The Path to the Nest of Spiders.* Trans. Archibald Colquhoun. Boston: Beacon, 1957; New York: Ecco Press, 1976. (Includes Calvino's 1964 preface translated by William Weaver.) Also published as *The Path to the Spiders' Nests.* Trans. Archibald Colquhoun, rev. Martin McLaughlin. New York: Ecco Press, 1998.

Ultimo viene il corvo. [The Crow Comes Last.] Turin: Einaudi, 1949; Milan: Mondadori, 1994. A selection of these stories is found in English in *Adam, One Afternoon and Other Stories.* Trans. Archibald Colquhoun and Peggy Wright. London: Collins, 1957; London: Secker and Warburg, 1983; *Difficult Loves.* Trans. William Weaver, Archibald Colquhoun, and Peggy Wright. New York: Harcourt Brace, 1984.

Il visconte dimezzato. Turin: Einaudi, 1951; New York: Appleton-Century-Crofts, 1968. Published in English as *The Nonexistent Knight and The Cloven*

Viscount. Trans. Archibald Colquhoun. New York: Random House, 1962; New York: Harcourt Brace, 1977.

La formica argentina. In *Botteghe oscure* 10 (1952): 406–411; Turin: Einaudi, 1965. Published in English as *The Argentine Ant.* In *The Watcher and Other Stories.* Trans. William Weaver and Archibald Colquhoun. New York: Harcourt Brace, 1971, 1975.

L'entrata in guerra [Entering the War.] Turin: Einaudi, 1954.

Il barone rampante. Turin: Einaudi, 1957. Published in English as *The Baron in the Trees.* Trans. Archibald Colquhoun. New York: Random House, 1959; Harcourt Brace, 1977.

La speculazione edilizia. In *Botteghe oscure* 20 (1957); Turin: Einaudi, 1958. Published in English as *A Plunge into Real Estate.* In *Difficult Loves.* Trans. D. S. Carne-Ross. Toronto: Lester and Orpen Dennys, 1984.

I giovani del Po [Young People of the Po.] Printed in serial form in *Officina*, nos. 8–12 (1957–1958).

I racconti. [Short Stories.] Turin: Einaudi, 1958. (A collection of short stories with three novellas: *La formica argentina, La speculazione edilizia* and *La nuvola di smog.* Many of these short stories are published in English in *Adam, One Afternoon, and Other Stories* and in *Difficult Loves* (Harcourt Brace, 1984), as cited. *Smog* [*La nuvola di smog*] is found with *The Argentine Ant* [*La formica argentina*] in *The Watcher and Other Stories*, as cited.)

Il cavaliere inesistente. Turin: Einaudi, 1959. Published in English in *The Nonexistent Knight and The Cloven Viscount*, as cited.

I nostri antenati. Turin: Einaudi, 1960; reprint, Milan: Mondadori, 1991. Published in English as *Our Ancestors.* Trans. Archibald Colquhoun. London: Secker and Warburg, 1980. (Both publications include all three novels of the fantasy trilogy: *Il visconte dimezzato* [*The Cloven Viscount*], *Il barone rampante* [*The Baron in the Trees*], and *Il cavaliere inesistente* [*The Nonexistent Knight*].)

La giornata d'uno scrutatore. Turin: Einaudi, 1963. Published in English as *The Watcher.* In *The Watcher and Other Stories*, as cited.

Marcovaldo, ovvero. Le stagioni in città. Turin: Einaudi, 1963, 1966. Published in English as *Marcovaldo, or, The seasons in the city.* Trans. William Weaver. New York: Harcourt Brace, 1983.

Le cosmicomiche. Turin: Einaudi, 1965. Published in English as *Cosmicomics.* Trans. William Weaver. New York: Harcourt Brace, 1968, 1977.

Ti con zero. Turin: Einaudi, 1967. Published in English as *t zero.* Trans. William Weaver. New York: Harcourt Brace, 1969, 1976.

La memoria del mondo e altre storie cosmicomiche. [Memory of the World and Other Cosmicomic Stories.] Milan: Club degli Editori, 1968.

Il castello dei destini incrociati. In *Tarocchi, Il mazzo visconteo di Bergamo e New York.* Parma: Franco Maria Ricci Editore, 1969. Reprint. Turin: Einaudi, 1973. Published in English as *The Castle of Crossed Destinies.* In *Tarots: The Visconti Pack in Bergamo and New York.* Trans. William Weaver. New York:

Franco Maria Ricci Editore, 1976. (This short version of the later novel by the same name was originally written as a companion piece to the elegantly illustrated Ricci volume on tarot cards, as cited.

Gli amori difficili. [Difficult Loves.] Turin: Einaudi, 1970. Some of these stories appear in the already-cited *Difficult Loves* (Harcourt Brace, 1984).

Le città invisibili. Turin: Einaudi, 1972. Published in English as *Invisible Cities.* Trans. William Weaver. New York: Harcourt Brace, 1974, 1978.

Il castello dei destini incrociati. Turin: Einaudi, 1973. Published in English as *The Castle of Crossed Destinies.* Trans. William Weaver. New York: Harcourt Brace, 1976, 1977, 1979. This complete edition of the novel contains eight extra stories grouped under the rubric "The Tavern of Crossed Destinies."

Se una notte d'inverno un viaggiatore. Turin: Einaudi, 1979. Published in English as *If on a winter's night a traveler.* Trans. William Weaver. New York: Harcourt Brace, 1981; Alfred A. Knopf, 1993.

Palomar. Turin: Einaudi, 1983. Published in English as *Mr. Palomar.* Trans. William Weaver. New York: Harcourt Brace, 1985.

Cosmicomiche vecchie e nuove. [Old and New Cosmicomics.] Milan: Garzanti, 1984.

Sotto il sole giaguaro. Milan: Garzanti, 1986. Published in English as *Under the Jaguar Sun.* Trans. William Weaver. New York: Harcourt Brace, 1988.

La strada di San Giovanni. Milan: Mondadori, 1990. Published in English as *The Road to San Giovanni.* Trans. Tim Parks. New York: Pantheon Books, 1993.

Romanzi e racconti. [Novels and Short Stories.] 2 vols. Ed. by Mario Barenghi and Bruno Falcetto, under the auspices of Claudio Milanini. Milan: Mondadori, 1991, 1993. (A two-volume edition of Calvino's complete fiction that includes an important chronology of the author's life.)

Prima che tu dica "Pronto." Milan: Mondadori, 1993. Published in English as *Numbers in the Dark and Other Stories.* Trans. Tim Parks. New York: Pantheon Books, 1995.

OTHER WORKS BY CALVINO (IN ALPHABETICAL ORDER)

Centopagine. [One Hundred Pages.] Ed. Italo Calvino. Turin: Einaudi, 1971. (A collection of readings from some of Calvino's favorite authors, including Stevenson, Stendahl, Hoffmann, and others.)

Collezione di sabbia [Collection of Sand.] Milan: Garzanti, 1984. (A book of travel reminiscences and eclectic observations by the author.)

Eremita a Parigi. Pagine autobiografiche. [A Hermit in Paris: Autobiographical Pages.] Milan: Mondadori, 1994. (A collection of various writings and interviews.)

Fiabe italiane. Turin: Einaudi, 1956. Published as *Italian Fables.* Trans. Louis Brigante. New York: Collier, 1961; also published in English as *Italian Folktales: Selected and Retold by Italo Calvino.* Trans. George Martin. New York: Harcourt Brace, 1980.

Lezioni americane. Sei proposte per il prossimo millennio. Milan: Garzanti,
1988. Published in English as *Six Memos for the Next Millennium.* Charles
Eliot Norton Lectures, 1985–1986. Trans. Patrick Creagh. Cambridge: Harvard
University Press, 1988.

I libri degli altri: Lettere, 1947–1981. [Other Peoples' Books: Letters, 1947–1981.]
Ed. Giovanni Tesio. Turin: Einaudi, 1991. (Business letters to other authors and
to publishers.)

"Main Currents in Italian Fiction Today." *Italian Quarterly* 4, nos. 13–14 (1960):
3–14.

"Nota 1960 to *I nostri antenati.*" Milan: Mondadori, 1991.

"Notes Towards a Definition of the Narrative Form as a Combinative Process."
Trans. Bruce Merry. *Twentieth Century Studies* (May 1970): 93–101.

*Orlando furioso di Ludovico Ariosto raccontato da Italo Calvino, con una scelta
del poema.* [*Orlando Furioso* by Ludovico Ariosto, as recounted by Italo Calvino with a selection from the poem.] Turin: Einaudi, 1970. (Derived from
Calvino's radio presentation of Ariosto's classic.)

Perché leggere i classici [Why Read the Classics.] Milan: Mondadori, 1991.

Preface to *Our Ancestors.* Trans. Isabel Quigley. London: Secker and Warburg,
1980.

Prefazione [Preface] to *La letteratura americana e altri saggi* by Cesare Pavese.
5th ed. Turin: Einaudi, 1962.

Saggi. 1945–1985. [Essays: 1945–1985.] 2 vols. Ed. Mario Barenghi. Milan: Mondadori, 1995. (A collection of the author's critical essays that includes *Una
pietra sopra.*)

Sulla fiaba. [On Fables.] Turin: Einaudi, 1988.

Una pietra sopra. Discorsi di letteratura e società. Turin: Einaudi, 1980. Published in English as *The Uses of Literature: Essays.* Trans. Patrick Creagh. New
York: Harcourt Brace, 1986; also published as *The Literature Machine: Essays.*
London: Secker and Warburg, 1987. Both English translations are incomplete
versions of the original volume.

SECONDARY SOURCES

Addamo, Sebastiano. "Italo Calvino: *Il cavaliere inesistente.*" *Il Ponte*, no. 3
(1960): 416–418.

Almansi, Guido. "Il mondo binario di Italo Calvino." *Il paragone* 22 (1971): 95–
110.

Apter, T. E. *Fantasy Literature: An Approach to Reality.* Bloomington: Indiana
University Press, 1982.

Barenghi, Mario, and Bruno Falcetto. "Cronologia" [Chronology], in *Romanzi e
racconti.* Vol. 1. 2nd ed. Ed. Mario Barenghi and Bruno Falcetto. Milan: Mondadori, 1991, 1993.

Barilli, Renato. "My 'Long Infidelity' towards Calvino." Trans. Franco Ricci In
Calvino Revisited. Ed. Franco Ricci. Toronto: Dovehouse Editions, 1989.

Barth, John. "The Literature of Replenishment: Postmodernist Fiction." *Atlantic*, January 1980, 65–71.

Barthes, Roland. *S/Z: An Essay*. Trans. Richard Miller. New York: Hill and Wang, 1974.

———. *Writing Degree Zero*. Trans. Annette Lavers and Colin Smith. New York: Hill and Wang, 1983.

Beckett, Samuel. *The Unnamable*. New York: Grove, 1958.

———. *Waiting for Godot*. New York: Grove, 1954.

Beckwith, Marc. "Italo Calvino and the Nature of Italian Folktales." *Italica* 64, no. 2 (1987): 244–262.

Benussi, Cristina. *Introduzione a Calvino*. Rome: Laterza, 1989.

Bergson, Henri. "Laughter." In *Comedy:"An Essay on Comedy" by George Meredith, "Laughter" by Henri Bergson*. Ed. Wylie Sypher. Baltimore: Johns Hopkins University Press, 1980.

Bonura, Giuseppe. *Invito alla lettura di Italo Calvino*. Milan: Mursia, 1972.

Borges, Jorge Luis. *Labyrinths: Selected Stories and Other Writings*. Ed. Donald A. Yates and James E. Irby. New York: New Directions, 1964.

Bradbury, Malcolm, and James McFarlane. "The Name and Nature of Modernism." In *Modernism, 1890–1930*. Ed. Malcolm Bradbury and James McFarlane. London: Penguin Books, 1976, 1991, 1992.

Calligaris, Contardo. *Italo Calvino*. Milan: Mursia, 1973.

Calvino, Esther. Note to *Under the Jaguar Sun* by Italo Calvino. Trans. William Weaver. New York: Harcourt Brace, 1988.

Camon, Ferdinando. *Il mestiere di scrittore. Conversazioni critiche*. Milan: Garzanti, 1973.

Campbell, Joseph. *The Hero with a Thousand Faces*. Princeton: Princeton University Press, 1949.

Cannon, JoAnn. *Italo Calvino: Writer and Critic*. Ravenna: Longo Editore, 1981.

———. *Postmodern Italian Fiction: The Crisis of Reason in Calvino, Eco, Sciascia, Malerba*. Teaneck, N.J.: Fairleigh Dickinson University Press, 1989.

Capozzi, Rocco. "*Cosmicomiche vecchie e nuove:* Keeping in Tune with the Times." In *Calvino Revisited*. Ed. Franco Ricci. Toronto: Dovehouse Editions, 1989.

Carter, Albert Howard, III. *Italo Calvino: Metamorphoses of Fantasy*. Ann Arbor: UMI Research Press, 1987.

Cecchi, Emilio. *Di giorno in giorno*. Milan: Garzanti, 1959.

Celati, Gianni. "Il racconto di superficie." *Il Verri* 1 (1973): 93–114.

Collins, James. *The Existentialists: A Critical Study*. Chicago: Henry Regnery, 1968.

Connor, Steven. *Postmodernist Culture: An Introduction to Theories of the Contemporary*. Oxford: Blackwell, 1992.

Corti, Maria. "Intervista. Italo Calvino." *Autografo* 2 (October 1985): 47–53.

Coveney, Peter. Introduction to *The Adventures of Huckleberry Finn* by Mark Twain. New York: Penguin Books, 1985.

De Lauretis, Teresa. "Calvino e la dialettica dei massimi sistemi." *Italica* 53, no. 1 (1976): 57–74.

Derrida, Jacques. *Margins of Philosophy*. Trans. Alan Bass. Chicago: University of Chicago Press, 1982.

———. *Of Grammatology*. Trans. Gayatri Chakravorty Spivak. Baltimore: Johns Hopkins University Press, 1977.

Echevarría, Roberto González. Review of *The Man in the Mirror of the Book: A Life of Jorge Luis Borges* by James Woodall. *New York Times Book Review*, 31 August 1997, 10–12.

Eco, Umberto. *The Island of the Day Before*. Trans. William Weaver. New York: Harcourt Brace, 1995.

———. *The Role of the Reader: Explorations in the Semiotics of Texts*. Bloomington: Indiana University Press, 1984.

Esquivel, Laura. *Like Water for Chocolate*. Trans. Carol Christensen and Thomas Christensen. New York: Doubleday, 1992.

Ferretti, Gian Carlo. *Le capre di Bikini. Calvino giornalista e saggista, 1945–1985*. Rome: Editori Riuniti, 1989.

———. *La letteratura del rifiuto*. Milan: Mursia, 1968.

Fiedler, Leslie. "Faust in the Eden of Childhood." In *Mark Twain's Wound*. Ed. Lewis Leary. New York: Cromwell, 1962.

Forti, Marco. "Temi industriali della narrativa italiana." *Il menabò* 4 (1961): 213–239.

Foucault, Michel. *The Order of Things: An Archeology of the Human Sciences*. New York: Vintage Books, 1973.

Friedman, Maurice. *Problematic Rebel: An Image of Modern Man*. Chicago: University of Chicago Press, 1973.

———. *The Worlds of Existentialism: A Critical Reader*. Ed. Maurice Friedman. Chicago: University of Chicago Press, 1964; reprint, 1973.

Gabriele, Tommasina. *Italo Calvino: Eros and Language*. Teaneck, N.J.: Fairleigh Dickinson University Press, 1994.

García Márquez, Gabriel. *Chronicle of a Death Foretold*. Trans. Gregory Rabassa. New York: Ballantine, 1984.

———. *One Hundred Years of Solitude*. Trans. Gregory Rabassa. New York: Avon Books, 1971.

Gardner, John. *On Moral Fiction*. New York: Basic Books, 1978.

Gatt-Rutter, John. "Calvino Ludens: Literary Play and Its Political Implications." *Journal of European Studies* 5, no. 4 (1975): 319–340.

Gilson, Etienne. Foreword to *Saint Augustine: The City of God*. Trans. Gerald G. Walsh, S.J., Demetrius B. Zema, S.J., Grace Monahan, O.S.U., and Daniele J. Honan. Ed. Vernon J. Bourke. Garden City, N.Y.: Image Books, 1958.

Graff, Gerald. *Literature Against Itself: Literary Ideas in Modern Society*. Chicago: University of Chicago Press, 1979.

Grene, Marjorie. *Introduction to Existentialism*. 11th ed. Chicago: University of Chicago Press, 1970.

Habermas, Jürgen. "Modernity: An Unfinished Project." In *Postmodern Culture.* Ed. Hal Foster. London: Pluto, 1985.

Hale, Jane Alison. *The Literary Encyclopedia of Raymond Queneau.* Ann Arbor: University of Michigan Press, 1989.

Hassan, Ihab. *The Dismemberment of Orpheus: Toward a Postmodern Literature.* 2nd ed. Madison: University of Wisconsin Press, 1982.

Heiney, Donald. *America in Modern Italian Literature.* New Brunswick, N.J.: Rutgers University Press, 1964.

Hume, Kathryn. *Calvino's Fictions: Cogito and Cosmos.* New York: Oxford University Press, 1992.

Hutcheon, Linda. *A Poetics of Postmodernism: History, Theory, Fiction.* London: Routledge, 1991.

———. *The Politics of Postmodernism.* London: Routledge, 1989.

Illiano, Antonio. "Per una definizione della vena cosmogonica di Calvino: Appunti su *Le cosmicomiche e Ti con zero.*" *Italica* 49, no. 3 (1972): 291–301.

Jacobsen, Josephine, and William R. Mueller. *The Testament of Samuel Beckett.* New York: Hill and Wang, 1964.

Johnson, James. L. *Mark Twain and the Limits of Power.* Knoxville: University of Tennessee Press, 1982.

Kearney, Richard. *The Wake of Imagination.* Minneapolis: University of Minnesota Press, 1988.

Kuna, Franz. "The Janus-faced Novel: Conrad, Musil, Kafka, Mann." In *Modernism, 1890–1930.* Ed. Malcolm Bradbury and James McFarlane. London: Penguin Books, 1976, 1991, 1992.

Lacan, Jacques. *The Language of the Self: The Function of Language in Psychoanalysis.* Trans. Anthony Wilden. New York: Dell, 1968.

Leeming, David Adams. *Mythology: The Voyage of the Hero.* New York: Lippincott, 1973.

Lemaire, Anika. *Jacques Lacan.* Trans. David Macey. London: Routledge and Kegan Paul, 1982.

Maddocks, Melvin. "Mirror Writing: *If on a winter's night a traveler.*" *Time,* 25 May 1981, K11–K14.

Markey, Constance. "Calvino and the Existential Dilemma: The Paradox of Choice." *Italica* 60, no. 1 (1983): 55–70.

———. "The Hero's Quest in Calvino." *Quaderni d'italianistica* 4, no. 2 (1983): 154–166.

———. Interview with Italo Calvino (unpublished). Paris, 18 June 1978.

———. "Italo Calvino: The Contemporary Fabulist." *Italian Quarterly* 23, no. 88 (1982): 77–85. (An interview.)

———. "The Role of the Narrator in Italo Calvino's Fiction." Ph.D. diss., University of Illinois at Urbana-Champaign, 1980.

———. "The Tarot Cards as a Subversive Tool in Italo Calvino." In *Aspects of Fantasy.* Ed. William Coyle. Westport, Conn.: Greenwood, 1986.

Marshall, Brenda K. *Teaching the Postmodern: Fiction and Theory*. London: Routledge, 1992.

May, Rollo. "Existential Bases of Psychotherapy." In *Existential Psychology*. 2nd ed. Ed. Rollo May. New York: Random House, 1969.

McFarlane, James. "The Mind of Modernism." In *Modernism, 1890–1930*. Ed. Malcolm Bradbury and James McFarlane. London: Penguin Books, 1976, 1991, 1992.

McHale, Brian. *Postmodernist Fiction*. New York: Methuen, 1987.

McKenna, Andrew. "Postmodernism: Its Future Perfect." In *Post-modernism and Continental Philosophy*. Ed. Hugh J. Silverman and Donn Welton. Albany: State University of New York Press, 1988.

McNeary, Kathleen. *Understanding Gabriel García Márquez*. Columbia: University of South Carolina Press, 1989.

Milanini, Claudio. *L'utopia discontinua. Saggio su Italo Calvino*. Milan: Garzanti, 1990.

Miller, Karl. *Doubles: Studies in Literary History*. Oxford: Oxford University Press, 1987.

Mommsen, Theodore D. "Petrarch and the Story of the Choice of Hercules." *Journal of the Warbury and Courtauld Institutes* 16, nos. 3–4 (1953): 178–192.

Newman, Charles. *The Post-Modern Aura: The Act of Fiction in an Age of Inflation*. Evanston: Northwestern University Press, 1985.

Olken, Ilene. Introduction to *Il visconte dimezzato*. New York: Appleton-Century-Crofts, 1968.

———. *With Pleated Eye and Garnet Wing: Symmetries of Italo Calvino*. Ann Arbor: University of Michigan Press, 1984.

Pacifici, Sergio. *The Modern Italian Novel: From Manzoni to Svevo*. Carbondale: Southern Illinois University Press, 1960.

———, ed. *From Verismo to Experimentalism. Essays on the Modern Italian Novel*. Bloomington: University of Indiana Press, 1969.

Pampaloni, Geno. *Il novecento*. Milan: Garzanti, 1969.

Pavese, Cesare. *La letteratura americana e altri saggi*. 5th ed. Turin: Einaudi, 1962.

Pedullà, Walter. "Calvino alla corte di Lacan." *Il Caffè* 5/6 (1972): 77–85.

Pescio Bottino, Germana. *Calvino*. Florence: La Nuova Italia, 1967.

Piromallo, Agata. "Italo Calvino." *Il Baretti* 42 (1966): 66–76.

Prince, George. *Narratology: The Forms and Functioning of Narrative*. Berlin: Mouton Publishers, 1982.

Propp, V. *Morphology of the Folktale*. Trans. Laurence Scott. 2nd ed. Ed. Louis A. Wagner. Austin: University of Texas, 1979.

Pullini, Giorgio. "*Il barone rampante*." *Comunità* (November 1957): 101–102.

Pynchon, Thomas. *The Crying of Lot 49*. New York: Harper and Row, 1990.

Re, Lucia. *Calvino and the Age of Neorealism: Fables of Estrangement*. Stanford: Stanford University Press, 1990.

Ricci, Franco. *Difficult Games: A Reading of "I racconti" by Italo Calvino*. Waterloo, Ont.: Wilfrid Laurier University Press, 1990.

———. "Introversion and Effacement in *I racconti* of Italo Calvino." *Italica* 63, no. 4 (1986): 331–345.

Robbe-Grillet, Alain. *For a New Novel: Essays on Fiction*. Trans. Richard Howard. New York: Grove, 1965.

———. *Two Novels by Robbe-Grillet: Jealousy and* In the Labyrinth. Trans. Richard Howard. New York: Grove, 1965.

Rosengarten, Frank. "The Italian Resistance Novel (1945–1962)." In *From Verismo to Experimentalism: Essays on the Modern Italian Novel*. Ed. Sergio Pacifici. Bloomington: University of Indiana Press, 1969.

Rushdie, Salman. "Calvino." *London Review of Books*, 17–30 September 1981, 16–17.

Sartre, Jean-Paul. *Being and Nothingness: A Phenomenological Essay on Ontology*. Trans. Hazel E. Barnes. New York: Washington Square, 1977.

———. *Existentialism and Human Emotions*. Trans. Bernard Frechtman. New York: Philosophical Library, 1957.

———. *Huis clos*. Paris: Editions Gallimard, 1947.

Saussure, Ferdinand de. *Course in General Linguistics*. Trans. Wade Baskins. Ed. Charles Bally and Albert Sechehaye. New York: McGraw-Hill, 1966.

Siegel, Kristi. "Italo Calvino's *Cosmicomics:* Qfwfg's [sic] Postmodern Autobiography." *Italica* 68 (Spring 1991): 43–59.

Smarr, Janet Levarie. "Boccaccio and the Choice of Hercules." *MLN* 92, no. 1 (1977): 146–152.

Sontag, Susan. Preface to *Writing Degree Zero* by Roland Barthes. Trans. Annette Lavers and Colin Smith. New York: Hill and Wang, 1983.

Spanos, William V. "The Detective and the Boundary: Some Notes on the Postmodern Literary Imagination." In *Early Postmodernism: Foundational Essays*. Ed. Paul A. Bové. Durham: Duke University Press, 1995.

Stille, Alexander. "An Interview with Italo Calvino." *Saturday Review*, March-April 1985, 36–39.

Stoltzfus, Ben. *Alain Robbe-Grillet: The Body of the Text*. Teaneck, N.J.: Fairleigh Dickinson University Press, 1985.

Tani, Stefano. *The Doomed Detective: The Contribution of the Detective Novel to Postmodern American and Italian Fiction*. Carbondale: Southern Illinois University Press, 1984.

Tillich, Paul. *The Courage to Be*. New Haven: Yale University Press, 1952.

Todorov, Tzvetan. *The Fantastic: A Structural Approach to a Literary Genre*. Trans. Richard Howard. Ithaca, N.Y.: Cornell University Press, 1980.

Twain, Mark. *The Adventures of Huckleberry Finn*. Ed. Peter Coveney. New York: Penguin Books, 1985.

Updike, John. *Hugging the Shore: Essays and Criticism*. New York: Alfred A. Knopf, 1983.

Varese, Claudio. "Italo Calvino. *La giornata d'uno scrutatore.*" *Nuova Antologia* (May 1963): 120–123.

Vattimo, Gianni. *The End of Modernity.* Trans. John R. Snyder. Baltimore: Johns Hopkins University Press, 1991.

Vidal, Gore. "Fabulous Calvino." *New York Review of Books,* 30 May 1974, 13–21.

Virdia, Ferdinando. "Calvino e i paladini." *La Fiera letteraria* 3 (1960): 1–2.

Vittorini, Elio. *Men and Not Men.* Trans. Sara Henry. Marlboro, Vt.: Marlboro Press, 1985.

Vonnegut, Kurt, Jr. *Slaughterhouse-Five.* New York: Dell, 1975.

Weiss, Beno. *Understanding Italo Calvino.* Columbia: University of South Carolina Press, 1993.

Woodhouse, J. R. *Italo Calvino: A Reappraisal and An Appreciation of the Trilogy.* Hull, Yorkshire: Hull University Press, 1968.

Zabel, Morton Dauwen. Introduction to *The Portable Conrad.* Ed. Morton Dauwen Zabel. Rev. Frederick R. Karl. New York: Viking Penguin Books, 1976.

ACKNOWLEDGMENTS

Permission to reprint in this volume excerpts from the followings works by Italo Calvino has been granted by the Wylie Agency: *The Baron in the Trees, The Nonexistent Knight and The Cloven Viscount, The Castle of Crossed Destinies, Cosmicomics, Difficult Loves, If on a winter's night a traveler, Invisible Cities, Marcovaldo, or, The seasons in the city, Mr. Palomar, Numbers in the Dark, The Path to the Spiders' Nests, t zero, Under the Jaguar Sun,* and *The Watcher and Other Stories,* all copyright 1990 by Palomar S.r.l.

Permission to cite from the following Harcourt Brace editions includes:

Excerpts from The *Castle of Crossed Destinies* by Italo Calvino, copyright 1969 by Franco Maria Ricci editore, copyright 1973 by Giulio Einaudi editore, S.p.A. English translation copyright 1977, 1976 by

Harcourt Brace & Company, reprinted by permission of Harcourt Brace & Company.

Excerpts from *Cosmicomics* by Italo Calvino, copyright 1965 by Giulio Einaudi editore S.p.A, Torino. English translation by William Weaver copyright 1968 and renewed 1996 by Harcourt Brace & Company and Jonathan Cape, reprinted by permission of Harcourt Brace & Company.

Excerpts from *Difficult Loves* by Italo Calvino, copyright 1949 by Giulio Einaudi editore, Torino. English translation copyright 1984 by Harcourt Brace & Company, reprinted by permission of Harcourt Brace & Company.

Excerpts from *If on a winter's night a traveler* by Italo Calvino, English translation copyright 1981 by Harcourt Brace & Company, reprinted by permission of the publisher.

Excerpts from *Invisible Cities* by Italo Calvino, copyright 1972 by Giulio Einaudi editore S.p.A. English translation by William Weaver, copyright 1974 by Harcourt Brace & Company, reprinted by permission of Harcourt Brace & Company.

Excerpts from *Marcovaldo, or, The seasons in the city* by Italo Calvino, English translation copyright 1983 by Harcourt Brace & Company and Martin Secker & Warburg Ltd., reprinted by permission of Harcourt Brace & Company.

Excerpts from *Mr. Palomar* by Italo Calvino, copyright 1983 by Giulio Einaudi editore, S.p.A. Torino. English translation by William Weaver copyright 1985 by Harcourt Brace & Company, reprinted by permission of Harcourt Brace & Company.

Excerpts from *t zero* by Italo Calvino, copyright 1965 by Giulio Einaudi editore S.p.A. English translation by William Weaver copyright 1969 by Harcourt Brace & Company and Jonathan Cape Limited, reprinted by permission of Harcourt Brace & Company.

Excerpts from *Under the Jaguar Sun* by Italo Calvino, copyright 1986 by Garzanti Editore. English translation by William Weaver copyright 1988 by Harcourt Brace & Company, reprinted by permission of Harcourt Brace & Company.

Excerpts from *The Watcher and Other Stories* by Italo Calvino, copyright 1963 by Giulio Einaudi editore S.p.A. English translation copyright 1971 by Harcourt Brace.

Also reprinted in this volume are excerpts from:

The Path to the Spiders' Nests by Italo Calvino, translated from Italian by Archibald Colquhoun, revised by Martin McLaughlin. Originally published in Italy as *Il sentiero dei nidi di ragno*, copyright 1947 by Giulio Einaudi, Editore, Torino. Original translation copyright 1956 by William Collins & Sons Co. Ltd., London. Translation of preface and revised translation of text copyright 1998 by Martin McLaughlin. Reprinted by permission of The Ecco Press.

Numbers in the Dark, originally published in Italy as *Prima che tu dica "Pronto"* by Arnoldo Mondadori Editore, Milan, 1993. English translation by Tim Parks. Reprinted by permission of Pantheon Books, Random House, 1995.

"The Tarot Cards as a Subversive Tool in Calvino," from *Aspects of Fantasy: Selected Essays from the Second International Conference on the Fantastic in Literature and Film*, edited by William Coyle. Reprinted by permission of Greenwood Press, 1986, an imprint of Greenwood Publishing Group, Inc.

For permission to use the cover photo of Italo Calvino, thanks to photographer Jerry Bauer.

INDEX

Titles of works by Italo Calvino appear without the author's name in parentheses after the titles.

Ariosto, Ludovico, 127n.15

"Armchair dramas," 48, 49

"Autobiografia di uno spettatore" ["A Cinema-Goer's Autobiography"], 4

Autobiographical works by Calvino: "A Cinema-Goer's Autobiography," 4. *See also Mr. Palomar*

"L'avventura di una bagnante" ["The Adventure of a Bather"], 50–51

"L'avventura di un lettore" ["The Adventure of a Reader"], 57–58

"L'avventura di un soldato" ["The Adventure of a Soldier"], 56–57

Le avventure di Pinocchio. Storia di un burattino [*Pinocchio: The Adventures of a Little Wooden Boy*] (Collodi), 30, 41, 42, 131n.4

Balilla (Fascist Youth), 5

The Baron in the Trees [*Il barone rampante*]: characters in, 75–76; ending in, 80; existentialism in, 15, 75–77; narrator in, 73, 74–75; realism in, 82, 84

Barth, John, 21, 82, 87

Barthes, Roland, 88; influence on Calvino, 18; influence on *If on a winter's night a traveler,* 117; influence on *t zero* stories, 22, 95; on writerly text, 138n.22

Beckett, Samuel, influence on Calvino, 13, 55, 64, 93, 133n.11, 134n.22

Beckwith, Mark, 17

Benussi, Cristina, 97

Bergson, Henri, 50

Berio, Luciano, 115, 129n.33

Il bianco veliero [The White Sailing Ship], 9

The Bicycle Thief [*Ladri di biciclette*] (film), 29

"Big Fish, Little Fish," 31

Bildungsroman, 37, 42, 131n.10, 132n.16

Black comedies, 50. *See also* Fantasy

Bonura, Guiseppe, 40

Borges, Jorge Luis, 88, 97, 107, 110, 113

Bottino, Germana Pescio, 39–40, 128n.27

Bradbury, Malcolm, 49

Bread and Wine [*Pane e vino*] (Silone), 28, 130–31n.2

Buber, Martin, 132n.18

Calvinian witnesses: in "The Albino Gorilla," 123; childlike nature of, 15 (*see also Fanciulli*); in "The Night Driver," 96; in *The Path to the Spiders' Nests,* 8–9, 13. *See also* Narrators

Calvino, Esther Judith Singer, 18, 20

Calvino, Evelina Mameli, 3, 5, 6

Calvino, Floriano, 3, 4

Calvino, Giovanna, 20

Calvino, Italo: American writers as role models, 8, 9, 29; army service of, 6; autobiographical works of, 8–9 (see also *Mr. Palomar*); birth of, 3; Communist Party membership of, 6–7; disillusionment with Communist Party, 10–11; early family life of, 3–4; early writing career of, 7–8; education of, 6; at Einaudi Publishing House, 7–8; fantasy fiction of, 14–17; Fascism and, 4, 5, 6; fifties fiction of, 10–12; good causes and, 62; international literature influences on, 18; literary genres of, 2; marriage of, 18, 20–21; modernism and, 12–14; newspaper works of, 6, 7, 10, 11, 17, 30; Paris years of, 20–23; personality of, 1; politics and, 5, 10, 11, 47–48; posthumous works of, 24, 111, 126n.4; on poststructuralism, 19; prizes won by, 9, 17, 25, 130n.47; radio readings of, 21; religion and, 4; resistance fiction of, 8–10; Resistance involvement of, 6; returned to Italy, 23–24; study of works of, 2; theatrical ventures of, 17; thesis on Conrad, 6; translation work of, 21; travels of, 17–18, 24; in United States, 17–18, 24; unpublished works of, 8; writing habits of, 126n.8

"The Count of Montecristo" ["Il conte di Montecristo"], 22, 96–97

Coveney, Peter, 44

Critics: on Calvino as moralizer, 128n.27; on Calvino fantasy works, 9, 14, 68, 71; on Calvino neorealism, 12; on Calvino speculative literature, 19–20; on *Cosmicomics*, 93; on "I Also Try to Tell My Tale," 101; leftist, 68; on Marcovaldo, 14; on neorealism, 28; on *The Nonexistent Knight*, 135n.3; on *The Path to the Spiders' Nests*, 39–40, 41, 42; on postmodernism, 87–88, 97, 137nn.2,3; on traditional novel, 19

"The Crow Comes Last" ["Ultimo viene il corvo"], 34

The Crying of Lot 49 (Pynchon), 141n.17

De-anthropomorphic narrative, 91

Derrida, Jacques, 19, 88, 89, 107, 140n.1

De Sica, Vittorio, 29, 138n.17

"Desire in November" ["Desiderio in novembre"], 31

Difficult Loves, 8, 48; compared with *Marcovaldo*, 14; English editions of, 128n.23, 134n.16; modernism in stories in, 12, 50–51; neorealism in, 31–36; short stories in ("Adam, One Afternoon," 31; "The Adventure of a Bather," 50–51; "The Adventure of a Reader," 57–58; "The Adventure of a Soldier," 56–57; "Big Fish, Little Fish," 31; "Desire in November," 31; "The Enchanted Garden," 31; "Fear on the Footpath," 32–33; "Going to Headquarters," 34–35; "Hunger at Bévera," 32; "Mine Field," 33; "One of the Three is Still Alive," 33; "A Ship Loaded with Crabs," 31; "Theft in a Pastry Shop," 31); themes in, 13, 33

"The Dinosaurs" ["I Dinosauri"], 94

Doppelganger, concept of: in *The Cloven Viscount*, 72–73, 79; in *If on a winter's

night a traveler*, 119; in *Invisible Cities*, 110

Double coding, 81

"Due storie in cui si cerca e ci si perde" ["Two Tales of Seeking and Losing"], 99, 104

Eco, Umberto, 85

Einaudi, Giulio, 7

Einaudi Publishing House, 7–8, 36

Either/or dialogue, 76–77, 81, 105, 107, 111. *See also* Existentialism

"The Enchanted Garden," 9, 31

L'entrata in guerra [Entering the War], 5

Esquivel, Laura, 140–41n.12

Essays: *Collezione di sabbia*, 24; *Menabò della letteratura*, 17, 129n.32; *Una pietra sopra. Discorsi di letteratura e società*, 20, 24, 129n.32

"Excluded middle," 111

Existentialism: in "The Adventure of a Bather," 50–51; in *The Baron in the Trees*, 15, 75–77; in *The Cloven Viscount*, 72, 73; demise of faith and, 88; demise of religion and, 88–89; freedom of choice as theme in Calvino works, 76–78, 101, 102–3, 106, 121; in "Going to Headquarters," 34–35; in "I Also Try to Tell My Tale," 88, 101–2; "I-Thou" dilemma and, 132n.18; "I-Thou" dilemma in, 132n.18; in *Marcovaldo, or, The seasons in the city*, 52, 54–55, 57; in *Mr. Palomar*, 121; in *The Path to the Spiders' Nests*, 41, 42–43, 45–46; Sartre on freedom of choice and, 76, 133n.9, 136n.12

Eyewitness narrators. *See* Narrators

Fables. *See* Fantasy

Fairy-tales, 41, 45, 98. See also *The Castle of Crossed Destinies; The Cloven Viscount; The Nonexistent Knight*

Fanciulli: in *The Cloven Viscount*, 69–70;

neorealism and, 31, 34, 37, 40; in *The Path to the Spiders' Nests*, 37, 40; in "The Crow Comes Last," 34. *See also* Narrators

Fantasy: critics on Calvino's fondness for, 9; cross-genre play in, 67–68; "I-Thou" dilemma and, 43; life and, 110; literary techniques in, 70; in *The Path to the Spiders' Nests*, 38, 43, 48; postmodernism and, 82; versus realism, 82–83; as response to "I-Thou" dilemma, 43; "Riviera Stones," 31, 38; themes in, 48; traditional, 82. *See also The Baron in the Trees; The Cloven Viscount; The Nonexistent Knight*

Farce, in *If on a winter's night a traveler*, 117–18

Fascism, Calvino and, 4, 5, 6. *See also* Partisans

Fascist Youth (*balilla*), 5

Faulkner, William, 8, 29

"Fear on the Footpath" ["Paura sul sentiero"], 8, 32–33

Ferretti, Gian Carlo, 12, 20, 28, 34, 36, 122

Films, in Calvino's early life, 4. *See also specific films*

I fiori blu [The Blue Flowers] (Queneau), 21

Les Fleurs Bleues [The Blue Flowers] (Queneau), 21

La formica argentina [The Argentine Ant], 14, 50, 64

Foucault, Michel, 89, 137n.11

Freedom of choice. *See* Existentialism

Free will, in "The Waverer's Tale," 104. *See also* Either/or dialogue

Friedman, Maurice, 132n.18

"Funghi in città" ["Mushrooms in the City"], 53

"Furto in una pasticceria" ["Theft in a Pastry Shop"], 31, 131n.7

García Márquez, Gabriel: "magic realism" of, 91, 138n.15; narration style of, 84,

139n.26; parody of detective genre, 141n.17; as postmodernist, 88

"The Garden of Forking Paths" (Borges), 107

Gardner, John, 137n.3

Gatt-Rutter, John, 72

"The Gecko's Belly" ["La pancia del geco"], 122

Gilliam, Terry, 136n.14

Ginzburg, Natalia, 7

La giornata d'uno scrutatore [*The Watcher*], 13, 62–64, 134nn.21,22

I giovani del Po [Young People of the Po], 9

"Going to Headquarters" ["Andato al comando"], 8, 34–35

The Gold of Naples [*L'oro di Napoli*] (film), 138n.17

"Il gorilla albino" ["The Albino Gorilla"], 122–23

Graff, Gerald, 137n.3

"Guarda in basso dove l'ombra s'addensa" ["Looks Down in the Gathering Shadows"], 117–18

Habermas, Jürgen, 137n.3

Hassan, Ihab, 55

Hearing, psychology of, in "A King Listens," 114–15

Hemingway, Ernest: influence on Calvino, 8, 30, 33, 131n.8; influence on neorealism, 29

Heroes: in *The Castle of Crossed Destinies*, 98–99, 100, 105; character regression, 13; either/or dilemma of, 76–77; in "Going to Headquarters," 34–35; Hemingwayesque, 131n.8; in "Hunger at Bévara," 32; in *Marcovaldo, or, The seasons in the city*, 52; models for, 132n.16; in modernism, 77–78; monomyth and, 98, 139n.30; in *The Path to the Spiders' Nests*, 37, 39–40, 42–44; Sartre on, 54–55, 76, 102, 133n.9; traditional quest of, 99; Twain influence

s'addensa"], 118

"Lo Specchio, il bersaglio" ["The Mirror, the Target"], 111, 112–13

Lukács, Georg, 68

"L'ultimo canale" ["The Last Channel"], 111–12

"Magic realism," 91, 138n.15

Manichaean duality, 84

Marco Polo, 107–8, 110

Marcovaldo, name origins of, 133n.6

Marcovaldo, or, The seasons in the city [Marcovaldo, ovvero, Le stagioni in città], 48; endings in, 53, 54; existentialism in, 52, 54–55, 57; humor in, 50, 52, 55–56, 58; short stories in ("City Lost in the Snow," 53; "A Journey with the Cows," 53–54; "Mushrooms in the City," 53; "Park-Bench Vacation," 54); themes in, 51, 52

"Il mare dell'oggettività" [The Sea of Objectivity], 129n.32

Materialism, Calvino on, 10

Mathematics, 90

May, Rollo, 132n.19

McFarlane, James, 48

McHale, Brian, 108, 111, 138n.23

McKenna, Andrew, 89

Melodrama, 33, 39

Melville, Herman, 29

La memoria del mondo e altre storie cosmicomiche [Memory of the World and Other Cosmicomic Stories], 130n.40

Menabò della letteratura (journal), 17, 129n.32

Men and Not Men [Uomini e no] (Vittorini), 28, 131n.2

The Metamorphosis (Kafka), 65–66

Metaphors: in Invisible Cities, 108–9; in "The Night Driver," 96; sexual, 113–14, 141n.12. See also Labyrinth stories

Metaphysics, 49

Il milione (Marco Polo), 107–8

"Mine Field" ["Campo di mine"], 33

"The Mirror, the Target" ["Lo Specchio, il bersaglio"], 111, 112–13

Modernism: Calvino drift toward, 12–14, 34–35, 47–48; definition of, 49; heroes in, 77–78; literary techniques in, 62; metaphysics and, 49; in short stories, 12–13; "small worlds" emphasis in, 55–56, 63–64, 132n.19; stream of conscious in, 13, 49–50; themes in, 48, 51–52, 54, 55, 62, 64–65, 72; women portrayed in, 61, 63. See also Marcovaldo, or, The seasons in the city; The Watcher and Other Stories

Monty Python and the Holy Grail (film), 136n.14

Morality, 36–37, 68, 72, 85

Moravia, Alberto, 7

Morgante (Pulci), 133n.6

Mr. Palomar [Palomar], 111; age in, 123; as autobiography, 25–26, 123–24; ending in, 123–24; existentialism in, 121; postmodernism and, 141n.21; tales in ("The Albino Gorilla," 122–23; "The Gecko's Belly," 122; "Reading a Wave," 122; "The Cheese Museum," 121–22); third-person narration in, 120–21

"Il museo dei formaggi" ["The Cheese Museum"], 121–22

"Mushrooms in the City" ["Funghi in città], 53

Narrators: in "All at One Point," 92–93; in The Baron in the Trees, 73, 74–75; "Chinese boxing" in If on a winter's night a traveler, 116; in The Cloven Viscount, 69–70, 73; in Cosmicomics, 22, 91; in L'entrata in guerra, 5; of García Márquez, 84, 139n.26; in "I Also Try to Tell My Tale," 101–2; in If on a winter's night a traveler, 115; in Mr. Palomar,

Smog [*La nuvola di smog*], 13, 50, 59–61

Sontag, Susan, 95

Sotto il sole giaguaro. See *Under The Jaguar Sun* [*Sotto il sole giaguaro*]

"Sotto il sole giaguaro" ["Under the Jaguar Sun"], 113–14

Spanos, William V., 88

La speculazione edilizia [*A Plunge into Real Estate*], 13, 50, 59, 134n.16

"The Spiral" ["La spirale"], 91

Stevenson, Robert Louis, 30

Stoltzfus, Ben, 95, 97

"Storie dell'indeciso" ["The Waverer's Tale"], 101, 102–4, 121

"Stories of Love and Loneliness," 31, 48

La Strada di San Giovanni. See *The Road to San Giovanni* [*La Strada di San Giovanni*]

Stream of consciousness, in modernism, 13, 49–50

"Tale of Roland Crazed with Love" ["Storia dell'Orlando pazzo per amore"], 99

Tarot cards, in *The Castle of Crossed Destinies*, 99–101, 107

Taylor, Alan, 131n.7

Tel Quel, 18

"Theft in a Pastry Shop" ["Furto in una pasticceria"], 31, 131n.7

"Three Tales of Madness and Destruction" ["Tre storie di follia e distruzione"], 99

Ti con zero. See *t zero*

Tillich, Paul, 43, 132nn.18,19, 133n.12

Todorov, Tzvetan, 68, 83, 91

Tourism, postmodernism and, 108

"Tre storie di follia e distruzione" ["Three Tales of Madness and Destruction"], 99

The Trial (Kafka), 104

"Tutto in un punto" ["All at One Point"], 92–93

Twain, Mark: Calvino on, 127n.14; influence on Calvino, 8, 9, 30, 42, 68, 73; the Other and, 44; traditional fantasy and, 82, 83

"Two Tales of Seeking and Losing" ["Due storie in cui si cerca e ci si perde"], 99, 104

t zero [*Ti con zero*], 22; versus *Cosmicomics*, 94–95; short stories in: "The Count of Montecristo," 22, 96–97; "The Night Driver," 22, 95–96

"Ultimo viene il corvo" ["The Crow Comes Last"], 34

Ultimo viene il corvo [The Crow Comes Last], 8, 30, 128n.23

"Under the Jaguar Sun" ["Sotto il sole giaguaro"], 113–14

Under the Jaguar Sun [*Sotto il sole giaguaro*], 25, 111, 113; "A King Listens," 114–15, 129n.33

L'Unità (newspaper), 6, 10, 11, 30

University of Florence, 6

University of Turin, 6

Unnamable, 63, 64

The Unnamable (Beckett), 134n.22

"Uno dei tre è ancora vivo" ["One of the Three Is Still Alive"], 33

Uomini e no [*Men and Not Men*] (Vittorini), 28, 131n.2

Updike, John, 21, 87, 115, 137n.2

The Uses of Literature: Essays [*Una pietra sopra. Discorsi di letteratura e società*], 20, 24, 129n.32

Varese, Claudio, 129n.38, 137n.3

Vattimo, Gianni, 89

La vera storia [The Real Story], 129n.33

Verismo, 127n.11

"Un viaggio con le mucche" ["A Journey with the Cows"], 53–54

Vidal, Gore, 21, 64, 72